Brief Therapy Client Handouts

Kate Cohen-Posey

John Wiley & Sons, Inc.
New York • Chichester • Weinheim • Brisbane • Singapore • Toronto

This book is printed on acid-free paper. ♾

Published by John Wiley & Sons, Inc.

Published simultaneously in Canada.

Library of Congress Cataloging-in-Publication Data:

Cohen-Posey, Kate.
Brief therapy client handouts / Kate Cohen-Posey.
p. cm.
Includes bibliographical references and index.
ISBN 0-471-32846-4 (paper/disk : alk. paper)
1. Brief psychotherapy Problems, exercises, etc. 2. Mental health education Forms. I. Title.
RC480.55.C64 2000
616.89'14—dc21 99-40382

Printed in the United States of America.

20 19

This book is dedicated to my aunt,
Eleanor Belser, MSW,
who preceded me in the field,
is my link to my past, and
has always inspired me toward forward thinking.

PREFACE

Almost all therapists, regardless of their theoretical orientation, use bibliotherapy. Even purists who believe that change comes from dynamic processes occasionally offer psychoeducational information and recommend helpful literature. Other treatment approaches are more openly instructive with clients and readily rely on the printed word. Regardless of where therapists fall on the dynamic-directive continuum, a little bibliotherapy can go a long way.

PURPOSE

It is the purpose of *Brief Therapy Client Handouts* to help clinicians better utilize the "first aid" of psychotherapy by providing:

- *Condensed information* on life skills, relationships, and disorders with references for additional reading.
- *A user-friendly format* that will encourage nonreaders to acquire knowledge they need.
- *Preliminary assessment tools* to help clients partner with therapists in targeting problems areas and identifying pertinent diagnoses.
- *Literature that explains the "what" and "why"* of problems experienced by clients.
- *Review sheets for behavior strategies* that change problems and help therapists design treatment programs.
- *Exercises for systematic desensitization* that build hierarchies.
- *Lists of negative and positive beliefs* to prepare for restructuring cognitions that contribute to various disorders and relationship problems.
- *Discussion sheets* for spouses, parents, and family members that promote communication.
- *Visual aids* that explain problems at a glance.
- *Materials for workshops* that can support information being presented.

SUGGESTIONS FOR USING THE BOOK

Handouts can reinforce and validate ideas you have presented in sessions through the printed word. In the lonely, anxious moments between sessions, they can serve as transitional objects for clients to keep therapists "with them" by offering adaptive information that can help form new, healthy introjects. You can virtually clone yourself by giving handouts to spouses and parents to read to prepare for conjoint treatment while they are a captive audience in your waiting room. To maximize the full potential of handouts, the following logistics are suggested:

- Become thoroughly familiar with the scope and depth of information offered in handouts.
- Index tab the contents page of each chapter so you can readily access desired handouts.

- Select handouts you are most likely to use and print them from the disks in the back of the book or photocopy them on plain paper.
- Keep quantities of selected handouts in folders so they will be easy to offer clients.
- Use a loose-leaf folder with dividers to hold printouts of selected handouts to make them readily accessible and to reduce storage space.
- Order ready-made booklets in quantity for sections in the book that you are most likely to use. (See coupon in the back of this book.)
- Design your own booklets by combining handouts from various sections of the book and having them photocopied in quantity.
- Use the contents for each section as a cover sheet and mark off multiple handouts you have selected for a client.
- Offer some clients only one handout at a time to discuss at their next session. They may be overwhelmed if given too much information at once.

In some cases the handouts are an expression of my own unique concoction of various treatment styles. In other cases, I have taken information from other authors and therapists and boiled it down to its essence. It is not my intention to replace the presentation of their work, but to offer the reader a thumbnail view of a body of knowledge that they may want to explore further. The advantage of the handouts is that an entire approach can be absorbed in a 5-minute read and reviewed regularly. The advantage of reading original referenced sources is that the repetition of ideas and numerous examples absorbed over a long period of time may help nail down new concepts into the psyche.

In my exploration of various theories and therapies over the last 26 years as a clinician, I have been treated to an array of approaches—Gestalt, Rogerian, Transactional Analysis (TA), Neuro Linguistic Programming (NLP), hypnosis, Reevaluation Counseling (RC), Eye Movement Desensitization and Reprocessing therapy (EMDR), cognitive therapy, behavior therapy, object relations theories, various family therapies, energy therapies, and psychopharmacology. Although I have been eclectic in my treatment approach, I have *consistently* offered clients psychoeducational literature. I now pass these "therapy gifts" on to you so you can give your clients the gems of wisdom from so many theoretical orientations.

ACKNOWLEDGMENTS

Authorship is an illusion. There are many people who bring about the birthing of a book and I would like to express my appreciation to them all:

- Betty Wright and Betsy Lampe at Rainbow Books, Inc. for mentioning my name to Candace Glider.
- Candace Glider for her article about my booklets, "Pamphlets and Self-Help Books as Marketing Tools" in the April 1998 edition of *Psychotherapy Finances.*
- Kelly Franklin, publisher at John Wiley & Sons, for spotting Ms. Glider's article and realizing that we were "on the same page."
- Alex Mummery at Wiley for her constant enthusiasm and support and for giving me a new vision of the printed page.
- John Bennear, my colleague at Horizon Behavioral Services, for his eagle-eye editing of initial drafts and comments on theoretical information.
- Debra Metcalf, also with Horizon, for doing so much of the legwork and always making my life easier.
- Arie Den Breeijen, MD, for reviewing the psychopharmacological information in *Balancing Your Moods.*
- All the original thinkers and authors whose ideas compelled me to put their information into a format that is accessible to clients and easy to digest: Murry Bowen, MD; David Burns, MD; Roger Callahan, PhD; Michele Weiner Davis, MSW; Albert Ellis, PhD; Milton Erickson, MD; Edna Foa, PhD; and Reid Wilson, PhD; Fred Gallo, PhD; John M. Gottman, PhD; John Gray, PhD; Harville Hendrix, PhD; Melvyn Kinder, PhD; Phillip Manfield, PhD; James Masterson, MD; Peggy Papp, ACSW; Ron and Pat Potter-Efron, MSW; Ernest and Sheila Rossi; Martin L. Rossman, MD; Francine Shapiro, PhD; Len Sperry, MD, PhD; Janis Abrahms Spring, PhD; Claire Weekes; and many others whose works are listed as sources in *Therapist's Guides* in the front of each section.
- Gavin Posey for his quick and able response to my need for an illustration of extreme measures for extreme behavior.
- My clients, whose life challenges constantly push me to search for better answers.
- Harry and Lela, whom I woefully neglected at times during this labor of love.

CONTENTS

SECTION I RELATIONSHIPS

SECTION I RELATIONSHIPS

Chapter 1

Waltzing through Emotional Landmines

WALTZING THROUGH EMOTIONAL LANDMINES

OBJECTIVES FOR TREATMENT PLANNING

1. Demonstrate or describe how to use communication tools of active listening, assertive language, and deflecting.
2. Specify how use of communication tools has been helpful.
3. Report that positive cognitions are valid when remembering or hearing upsetting comments.

MINI INDEX TO CHAPTER 1

USING THE HANDOUTS

- Literature on communication: *The Art of Understanding, Effective Expression, The Dance of Deflection.*
- Review sheet for clients to look over before discussion or to "Monday-morning-quarterback" problems: *Listening Pointers, Pointers for Effective Expression, Pointers for Deflecting.*
- Reminder for clinicians to cover important communication points during sessions: *Listening Pointers, Pointers for Effective Expression, Pointers for Deflecting.*
- Preparation for processing incidents that instilled destructive beliefs that interfere with using communication skills: *Beliefs That Aid Communication.*
- Workshops and presentations:
  1. Active Listening Circles are an exercise in which participants role-play comments that bothered them. The next person rephrases, labels, and validates the previous person's feeling. *The Art of Understanding* and *Listening Pointers* can serve as study guides.
  2. Assertive Language Circles are an exercise in which participants make a *you statement* or message to someone they imagine sitting in a chair in the center of the circle: *"You are . . ."; "You make me feel . . ."* Participants then go around the circle three more times, changing

the you statement into (1) an *I Message: "I feel . . . when you . . ."*; (2) a request: *"Would you . . ."*; and (3) an action that sets limits: *"I will (not) . . ." Effective Expression* and *Pointers for Effective Expression* can serve as study guides.

3. Brainstorming Bully Busts in small groups offer participants a chance to take one or several cruel comments and compute 16 responses that would defuse them using *The Dance of Deflection* and *Pointers for Deflecting* as a study guide.

CAUTIONS AND RECOMMENDATIONS

- These handouts can serve as prerequisites to approaching family, relationship, and parenting problems (Chapter 1), difficulties with anger (Chapter 8), and social skills needed by people with ADD and personality disorders (Chapters 9 & 10).
- An overview of all communication skills and handy visual aids can be found in the chart in *Communication That Cures Problems* (3.6).
- *Beliefs That Aid Communication* is best to use with clients who are actively involved in treatment to help them process cognitions that interfere with using communication skills.

SOURCES AND ACKNOWLEDGMENTS

- Carl Rogers originated the active listening skills outlined in *The Art of Understanding* that are now incorporated by many therapeutic orientations.
- Ideas from imago therapy, originated by Harville Hendrix (www.imagotherapy.com), further refines the package of empathy skills explained in *The Art of Understanding.*
- Standard assertiveness skills, as the author first learned them in the book *Between Parent and Child* by Haim Ginott (Avon, 1969) and at Gestalt therapy workshops, are outlined in *Effective Expression.*
- John Gray's approach in *Men Are from Mars, Women Are from Venus* (HarperCollins, 1992) was used to further refine the second step of assertiveness: asking for what you want.
- Hypnosis, neurolinguistic programming, and reevaluation counseling offer a unique combination of communication skills presented in *The Dance of Deflection.*
- Francine Shapiro's formulations for negative and positive cognitions, explained in *Eye Movement Desensitization and Reprocessing* (Guilford Press, 1995), were used in writing *Beliefs That Aid Communication.*

THE ART OF UNDERSTANDING

Active listening, or showing others that you understand them, is the most important step in the dance of communication. Generally, during an emotional moment, two people are desperately trying to get their points across to each other and neither is actually listening. Or one person is going on and the other is tuning him or her out. The way out of this dilemma is the listening paradox:

When you most want someone to hear you, it helps to listen first!

ACTIVE LISTENING TOOLS

True listening is a form of meditation in which you clear your mind of your own thoughts and put your attention entirely on another person. The following steps help build the concentration necessary for active listening:

- Make eye contact, nods of understanding, and listening noises: "Uh huh. . . . hmm. . . ." When you appear disinterested, people talk on and on, desperately trying to gain your attention. Focusing on the speaker shortens monologues by helping the speaker realize you are listening.
- Rephrase: "Are you saying . . . ?" It is better to restate in other words what has been said than to simply repeat. This helps clarify the other person's point. Ask questions if you don't fully understand what has been said: "What do you mean by . . . ?" Your paraphrases don't have to be 100% correct as long as you ask, "What percent of that did I understand?" Keep rephrasing until the other person feels completely understood. This is often signified by a nod.
- Label feelings: "Do you feel . . . ? You seem to feel. . . ." Until emotions are recognized, people tend to hang on to them. Once feelings are identified, people can let them go. Highly accurate responses can draw out tears. Releasing such emotions deepens the connection between two people and takes communication to an intimate level (especially when accompanied by a touch, pat, or hug). When people are mad, identify any hurt their anger may be masking. It is generally better to overstate distress than to minimize it.
- Validate feelings: "It makes sense that you feel . . . because. . . ." Validating the factors that contribute to a feeling requires curiosity. The more irrational an emotion seems, the more fascinating it is to discover the cause. When you understand the "emotional logic" behind a feeling, it starts to make sense: "I can see why you are disappointed in me, since you don't approve of women wearing short skirts." Feelings are not right or wrong, but are the result of helpful or harmful beliefs. Validating shows that you are not making judgments and helps others be less defensive or attacking.

It is far easier to make judgments and sneak in your own viewpoint than to listen. Examine the following comments carefully to find their hidden agenda: "You wanted to run away instead of trying"; "You think I can't ever change even though I'm listening now"; "You shouldn't feel so responsible."

The examples in the following table show that in an emotional moment either person can turn conflict into true communication:

Speaker's Comment	Active Listening Responses: Rephrase	Label Feelings	Validate
1. How can I ever trust you to work out our problems when you left for two days?	You think if things get tense again, I won't be able to handle it and I'll leave.	The idea of trusting me seems to make you feel more worried and anxious.	I can see why you would not trust me until I show you that I can be different.
2. I left because our argument was so bad, I thought it would get physical.	You thought the wisest thing to do was leave and not chance the possibility of a fight.	The idea that we might physically fight must have been really scary for you.	It makes sense that when I pushed you, you were afraid you might strike back.
3. If you think I'm going to do my homework now, you're nuts.	You think that this is a very poor time to do your assignment.	Are you resentful that I'm asking you to do homework when we have company?	I can see why you would feel left out when everyone else is having a good time.
4. You never listen to me—You just try to fix me.	What do you mean when you say I try to "fix" you?	You get frustrated when I think for you and give you solutions.	It makes sense that you want me to hear your ideas instead of giving you mine.
5. I have to do something to help you when you complain so much!	You think that if you don't help me, I'll never feel better.	You must feel a lot of pressure when I get upset.	People have always counted on you, so I can see why you take over.

Although these examples demonstrate the tremendous improvement that can take place in communication with active listening, they may bring up some concerns:

- Active listening sounds so artificial! This is true. Feeding back, labeling feelings, and validating are learned responses. Reassuring, explaining, and insulting come from animal instinct and do not have to be taught. They are generally the worst thing to do during an emotional moment.
- Am I supposed to start repeating everything I hear? You do not have to use active listening every time someone talks to you. Disagreeing and advising can make everyday banter fun and challenging. It is only during emotional moments, when you notice tension, that it is essential to switch gears and become an active listener.
- Will I ever get a chance to speak? When you carefully listen without inserting your views, other people become curious about where you stand. Surprisingly, you will remember your own issues even though you've just put them out of your mind. However, your concerns may diminish when you thoroughly understand others.

Trying to get your point across without thoroughly understanding other people is like venturing into enemy territory without first doing reconnaissance work. Your power comes from understanding others—not from being understood!

EFFECTIVE EXPRESSION

Often, it seems that the harder you try to have your needs met, the less successful you are. Instead of inviting others to listen and cooperate, you may drive them away with complaints, attacks, lectures, or orders. To get what you want, you need to take your attention off others and focus on yourself—your feelings, wants, and limits:

- State your feelings by using the word "I" and naming an emotion: "I feel hopeless when you constantly criticize me." This is a constructive way to express feelings and furnishes others with information about the effects of their behavior. Saying "I think you should . . ." is an opinion that can make others stop listening or strike back. "I feel that you . . ." disguises opinions as feelings. "You make me feel . . ." is blaming.
- Make requests by asking questions: "Would you tell me something I've done well before you criticize me?" Even when people understand how you feel, they still may not know what to do. It is up to you to identify what you would like from them. It helps to list three things others can do to resolve issues. Saying "I would like you to . . ." is a statement and does not require a commitment. "Could you . . . ?" asks if others are able and implies that if they can do something, they should. "Would you . . . ?" gives others the freedom to say "No" while encouraging cooperation.
- Set limits by knowing what you are willing and not willing to do: "I will act hard of hearing when you don't say something kind before you complain." If others do not respond to your requests or offer acceptable solutions of their own, it is time to stop talking and act. Actions can be playful, like the one above, or adamant: "If you continue to yell, I will leave for an hour." Often, it is unnecessary to state your limits out loud. When others can sense that you will take action, they are more responsive.

Complaints, criticisms, and orders focus on others and start with the word "You." Instead, turn useless "you messages" into words that work:

You Message ***You should . . .***	**State Feelings** ***I feel . . . when you . . .***	**Make Requests** ***Would you . . .***	**Set Limits** ***I will (not) . . .***
1. I feel that you have no right to accuse me!	I am sorry you have so much trouble trusting me.	Before making accusations, would you ask me why I'm late?	I will rephrase any accusations for you: "Did you just ask me . . .?"
2. Why don't you just shut up and listen for once!	I feel annoyed when you give me unwanted advice.	Would you ask for my ideas before giving me advice?	I will cut our conversations short when you give me unwanted advice.
3. You make me feel useless.	I feel powerless when you don't consult me about family decisions.	Would you get my input before you make family decisions?	I will not cooperate with decisions when I've had no input.
4. You're not even trying to find a job.	I feel used when you don't tell me what you're doing to find work.	Would you tell me what you've done to find a job?	I'm not willing for you to stay longer than next week.
5. You have no consideration for others.	I feel frustrated when you don't do what I ask you to do.	Would you put away your clothes during the next commercial?	I will turn off the TV until you have done what I've asked.

INTROSPECT TO IDENTIFY YOUR FEELINGS, WANTS, AND LIMITS

The more shades and intensities with which you express your emotions, the better you will be understood. Often, it is important to dig for more painful feelings of fear and hurt that lie beneath surface anger:

Anger:	Irritated —› frustrated —› resentful —› guilty —› envious —› jealous —› furious —› loathing
Fear:	Concerned —› embarrassed —› suspicious —› worried —› tense —› anxious —› terrified
Sadness:	Hurt —› lonely —› helpless —› discouraged —› defeated —› depressed —› despairing

Making requests is especially hard for people who have never given themselves permission to have wants and desires. They may be concerned that their requests will be refused or that others will comply out of obligation instead of desire. If your requests are refused, you are no worse off than if you had not asked at all. It can actually help people further their development when they reluctantly cooperate. It is unfair to require people to *want* to do things they are *willing* to do.

PREPARE PEOPLE TO LISTEN

Before you can even begin to make your point, you may first have to prepare others to listen. This is especially true when others are angry, talkative, or controlling. Often, it is necessary to listen first! Show you understand by rephrasing others' thoughts, recognizing their feelings, and validating factors that contribute to those feelings. Withhold your own ideas until others become curious about where you stand. Then you can help them focus their attention on you:

- Ask suggestive questions before making your point: "Do you want to know my concerns, what I want, if I agree? Are you sure?" This helps others switch gears and put on their listening hats.
- Keep your points brief and frequently ask for a rephrase: "Am I making any sense? What does it sound like I'm saying? You've almost got it. Do you want to know the part that's missing?"
- Help others understand your feelings by asking: "I'm not sure what I'm feeling. Do you know?" "Can you help me understand why I might feel that way?"

Not only will the above questions encourage others to focus on you, they will help you look at yourself. Intently listening to others can clarify any differences between you and make communication more efficient and effective.

THE DANCE OF DEFLECTION

Tension is expected during conflicts of interest. But, when you are caught off guard by a verbal snipe, wounds can cut especially deep. Rude remarks may come from misguided efforts to enhance self-esteem by making others look bad, cries for attention, generalized anger that is spewed at the nearest recipient, or impossible demands for perfection and control. Attempts to understand others and requests for change may do little to squelch a sniper's fire. When dealing with these potshots, it is necessary to take communication to a place where few people have traveled before—to learn a verbal aikido that can neutralize the worst insult. Instead of responding to a verbal attack with an anticipated retaliation, defense, or withdrawal, a technique called bully busting gives you at least 16 ways to turn insults inside out.

TURN KILLER WORDS INTO KINDNESS WITH PUT-UPS

Change put-downs into put-ups and act as if nothing offensive is happening. This is based on the idea that it is worse to take offense than to give offense. Cruelty can be turned into kindness when you:

1. Agree in fact, in theory, or hypothetically to stop power struggles.
2. Give compliments to make it difficult for someone to continue being rude.
3. Act as if you've been complimented: "Thank you. What a sweet thing to say."
4. Find golden nuggets or some actual truth in the worst insult: "Thanks for trying so hard to help me. I know I could (possibly) be more . . ."
5. Dramatize the very insult that has been given: "Am I really a baby (whining)?"
6. Use a mean tone to say something harmless with a tone twister that releases frustration and adds confusion: "Your opinion is none of my business!"
7. Use reverse psychology to encourage people to change their course: "That was quite a put-down. Let's see what you can do with the zit on my nose or the scab on my ankle."

ELICIT THE CAUSES AND EFFECTS OF INTIMIDATION

Intimidators need to be encouraged to focus their attention inward instead of blaming or ridiculing. This is essential when cutting remarks are an expression of anger. You can help people discover the source of their distress when you make statements or ask questions that:

8. Label feelings to recognize troubling emotions and help the other person let them go.
9. Sympathize to kill insults with understanding: "You must have had a hard day to be so upset."
10. Focus on the process (of what someone is doing) and away from the content of the remark: "I wonder why you would want to make me feel bad?" "How disappointed are you in me?"
11. Express your own feelings and limits when a comment hurts too much to deflect: "Now I feel thoroughly rotten. I'll talk to you later when you can be a tad kinder."

GROUND INSULTS WITH LIGHTNING RODS OR "POWER WORDS"

In moments of confusion, people can be redirected to change negative habits. You can apply confusion and subtle suggestion to promote desirable behavior by using hypnotic wording:

12. "Try" blocks people from continuing what they are doing—"You're trying so hard to be upsetting. I hope it isn't too tiring."

13. "Dare" pushes people to do something they are reluctant to do: "I just dare you to say something pleasant!"
14. "But" erases everything that proceeds it. It is especially effective when followed by an unexpected compliment: "Well I may be . . . , but you look great!"
15. Unrelated comments (non sequiturs) help people disconnect from troubling remarks and add confusion: "When the carcass is ripe, you can pick it (crazy tone)."
16. Humor shows that little importance should be placed on cruel comments by using the absurd, silly, and ridiculous.

Examples of the above methods are generic one-liners that can defuse any insult. Memorize them! Specific responses below show how to have fun with the worst remarks:

Remark	Bully Bust Responses	Technique #
• You're such a b_______ !	You say that like it's a bad thing.	(3, 16)
• You're becoming quite the big girl!	Well you're not becoming quite the big boy.	(2, 6)
	You must be one of the new weight monitors we hired.	(16)
• I wouldn't be caught dead with you in a bathing suit like that!	You'll have to look good enough for the both of us.	(2)
	You're right, this suit doesn't quite do my figure justice.	(1, 3)
	I wonder if you really just need time to yourself.	(10)
• I can't believe you missed that parking space!	I know. My tunnel vision never ceases to amaze me.	(1)
	Does that mean I have to do time-out in the parking lot?	(16)
• You can just go to H____ !	You can just go to Disney World!	(6)
	We have been having a bit of a cold spell lately.	(3, 16)
• You're just trying to show off your cleavage.	Oh, heavens no—I charge $2 for cleavage peeks.	(5)
	You sound thoroughly disgusted with me.	(8)
• That therapist isn't helping you a bit!	Could you try just a little harder to discourage me?	(7, 12)
	It must be hard for you to feel so hopeless about me.	(9)

WHY BOTHER?

Defusing abuse exercises your mind and is more fun than simply ignoring nasty comments. Children are often advised to pay no mind to bullies. Such tactics can leaves scars on bitten tongues. Standing up for yourself by making requests of people with whom you are not in a relationship can inspire them to do the opposite. Even family members and your closest buddies may not have the energy to resolve conflicts when they are feeling grumpy. Bully busts add considerable variety to your repertoire of verbal skills. It may be necessary to lighten the mood before you can have your needs met. Any comment that takes tension out of the air is sure to be a bully bust. Blaming, sarcasm, complaining, advice, and orders perpetuate a vicious cycle. With bully busts, you can bring random acts of kindness into the very cradle of cruelty.

LISTENING POINTERS

Listening is not a passive sport. The following pointers show how to focus your attention so you can listen to people in a way that will help them listen to you.

- Make eye contact, nods, and listening noises: "Uh huh."
- Ask questions to clarify anything you do not understand: "What do you mean by . . . ?"
- Show you understand by rephrasing, labeling, and validating feelings:
  "What do you mean by . . . ? Are you saying . . . ?"
  "You must feel . . . You seem . . ."
  "It makes sense that you feel . . . It must be hard when . . ."
- Check your accuracy by asking for a percentage rating of what you understood: "What percentage of your comment did I understand?"
- Rephrase, relabel, or revalidate any points or emotions that you missed.
- Identify any requests that lie behind people's emotions after thoroughly demonstrating that you understand their feelings: "Does it help that I understand? Would you like a hug?"
- Interrupt long monologues with rephrases and validations: This may shorten lectures.
- Use a stopwatch: If one person tries to get too many points across, set a limit on how much time each person has to state his or her case before the other person has a chance to express concerns.
- Welcome tears: They are a sign that you are doing an excellent job of listening by drawing out deep levels of pain. Offer physical support with a pat or a shoulder on which to cry.
- Do not offer solutions, even if the other person asks for them. Find out what the person has thought about doing or what he or she wants to do first.
- Do not disagree without thoroughly understanding how the other person reached his or her conclusions.
- Do not agree just to pacify the person. You do not have to agree to understand!
- When you don't have the attention to listen, ask for time out. Set a specific time to listen later, when you can be more attentive.

RECOMMENDED READING

Between Parent and Child by Haim Ginott (Avon Books, 1969).

Between Parent and Teenager by Haim Ginott (Avon Books, 1971).

Bringing Up Parents by Alex J. Packer (Free Spirit Publishing, 1992).

Getting the Love You Want by Harville Hendrix (Henry Holt, 1988) www.imagotherapy.com

How to Talk So Kids Will Listen and Listen So Kids Will Talk by Adele Faber and Elaine Mazlish (Avon Books, 1980).

The Seven Habits of Highly Effective People by Stephen Covey (Simon & Schuster, 1989).

POINTERS FOR EFFECTIVE EXPRESSION

The following pointers show how to express inner feelings, desires, and limits in ways that get results for times when you need more than idle conversation or fancy repartee.

PREPARE OTHERS TO LISTEN

- Listen first! Feed back, label, and validate others' feelings. Withhold your own ideas until people become curious about where you stand.
- Ask focusing questions: "Do you want to know my concerns?" "There's something I'd like to say. Would you listen and tell me a better way to say it?"
- Keep your points brief and frequently ask for a rephrase: "What does it sound like I'm saying?" "Can you help me understand why I might feel that way?"

STATE YOUR FEELINGS

- Express yourself in one statement that starts with "I": "I feel . . . when you. . . ."
- Avoid (hidden) opinions and blaming: "I feel that you should. . . ." "You make me feel. . . ."
- Appreciate the other person for listening after your first couple of sentences.

MAKE REQUESTS

- Ask questions that begin with the word "Would": "Would you . . . , . . . , or . . . ?"
- Avoid wording that doesn't ask for a commitment: "Could you . . .?" "I'd like you to. . . ."
- Do not threaten, order, convince, justify, or expect mind reading.
- Ask for small achievable steps: "Would you ask about my day, kiss me goodbye, or wash my feet?" Choices and absurd requests help.
- Be specific: "I'd like you to be more loving" is too general.
- When your requests are refused, give only one reason why what you want is important or simplify your request. Then, if it is declined, accept "No" graciously.
- Do not require others to want to do what they are willing to do.
- If others forget to do what they said they would, ask only one more time without making a fuss: "I'm sure you meant to. . . . Would you do it tomorrow?"

SET LIMITS

- Set limits on how much you are willing to do!
- Identify (minimal) actions you can take when others do not meet your needs.
- Avoid thinking in extremes. Do not threaten divorce or punishments for children unless you are ready to follow through.

ADDITIONAL READING

Between Parent and Child by Haim Ginott (Avon, 1969).

Men Are from Mars, Women Are from Venus by John Gray (HarperCollins, 1992).

Bringing Up Parents by Alex J. Packer (Free Spirit Publishing, 1992).

POINTERS FOR DEFLECTING

Most people have someone in their lives who gets on their last nerve. This may be a critical spouse, an adolescent with an attitude, a nosy neighbor, a rude stranger, a tyrannical boss, a perverse coworker, or the resident know-it-all. These people are your teachers. They will give you countless opportunities to practice deflecting. The following pointers will help you make the most of their efforts to educate you.

- Study techniques for turning killer words into kindness, eliciting the causes of intimidation, and "grounding" insults with power words.
- Start with easy responses. Find out what happens when you say "Thank you."
- Make up and review generic one-liners that can defuse any insult. Memorize them! Some require slight alterations, depending on the slur: "Well, I may be . . . (indignant tone), but you're quite . . . (complimentary tone)."
- Rephrase, label, and validate feelings when cutting remarks are an expression of genuine anger.
- Keep a log of insults you've received and think of responses when you're not under pressure. Often, intimidators repeat themselves, so you will have opportunities to use your responses later. This will also give you a handy one-liner: "Oh, that was good. I'll have to add it to my insult collection."
- Brainstorm responses with your children for cruel comments they've received: This can start in preschool: "I'm not your friend." "Well, I'm not your toe."
- Practice on your children when they're having problems with attitudes and anger.
  Child: You must be the stupidest parent I know!
  Parent: Is there an award for that?
  Child: I hate you!
  Parent: It must feel awful to hate your mother. Or, Well you're not the only one (to hate me)!
- Practice making bully busts when you are not a direct target. Focus on helping perpetrators with humor, understanding, and glimpses of their goodness rather than offering sympathy to "victims."
- Brainstorm bully busts in classrooms, at clubs, and at other meetings.
- Be a part of the solution, not the problem! Make sure your bully busts pass the no-retaliation– no-effort-to-control–no-defensiveness test.

Deflecting Techniques			
1. Agree	5. Dramatize	9. Sympathize	13. "Dares"
2. Give compliments	6. Tone twisters	10. Ask questions	14. "But"
3. Take compliments	7. Reverse psychology	11. Express feelings, wants, limits	15. Non sequiturs
4. Golden nuggets	8. Label feelings	12. "Try"	16. Humor

RECOMMENDED READING

How to Handle Bullies, Teasers and Other Meanies by Kate Cohen-Posey (Rainbow Books, 1995).
When I Say No, I Feel Guilty by Manuel J. Smith (Bantam Books, 1980).
The Celestine Prophecy by James Redfield (Warner Books, 1993).

BELIEFS THAT AID COMMUNICATION

The dance of communication has three steps: showing understanding; asserting your feelings, wants, and limits; and defusing abusive remarks.

- Rephrase others' thoughts, empathize with their feelings, and validate the factors that contribute to those feelings.
- State your emotions in a sentence that starts with "I," make requests that start with the word "Would," and take actions that back up your desires and limits.
- Treat cruel comments with kindness, ask questions that identify the distress that contributes to insults, and use "hypnotic" words that subtly suggest desirable behavior.

If the steps of the "communication dance" are difficult for you, it may be because you are hearing the wrong music. Thoughts such as "I have to make others understand," "My feelings aren't important," and "I must never appear weak or lose" are sure to make you trip. To discover any thoughts that are making you stumble, ask yourself:[1]

- What does it mean about me when other people order, yell, complain, or blame?
- What do I think about myself when I express my feelings?
- How do cutting comments make me feel about myself?

Directions: Check off any of the thoughts in the left-hand column that you have in your worse moments. Then, check off the beliefs in the right-hand column that you would like to have when communication is difficult.

Change Thoughts That Hurt into . . .	**Beliefs That Aid Communication**
1. I have trouble listening because I think: __ I have to keep others happy, fix their problems, convince them, etc. __ If I don't retaliate or defend myself, I'm weak, a loser, etc.	1. I can listen when I believe: __ I can understand others without having to fix them. __ My power comes from understanding others, not from being understood.
2. It's difficult to express myself when I think: __ My feelings, wants, and limits aren't important. __ If others get upset, it's my fault. I'm a troublemaker or difficult.	2. I can express myself when I believe: __ My feelings and desires need to be known to reach long-lasting, satisfying solutions. __ I'm responsible for my own reactions and others are responsible for theirs.
3. I have trouble defusing abuse when I think: __ If I make mistakes, break some rules, or change my mind, I'm a failure, defective, or a terrible person. __ I'm trapped, powerless, and helpless.	3. I can defuse abuse when I believe: __ I have the right to make mistakes, be illogical, or have mixed emotions. __ I can learn from mistakes. __ I have choices. __ I can handle this.

Identifying communication-enhancing phrases and affirming them regularly will give you the confidence you need to show understanding, express yourself effectively, and defuse verbal abuse. Surprisingly, you do not have to feel good about yourself to communicate powerfully. But the first time you take the tiniest step toward "power communication," you will feel good about yourself!

[1] See *EMDR: The Breakthrough Therapy* by Francine Shapiro (Basic Books, 1997) or *A Guide to Rational Living* by Ellis (Wilshire Book Co., 1997) for further ideas on how thoughts affect emotions.

Chapter 2

Untangling Family Ties

UNTANGLING FAMILY TIES

OBJECTIVES FOR TREATMENT PLANNING

1. Show understanding of family dynamics through verbal statements about or diagrams of boundaries, alliances, or triangles.
2. Report behavior changes that reflect increased levels of differentiation (greater tolerance of differences, control over emotional reactivity and self-serving goals).
3. Increase scores on the *Level of Differentiation Scales* by 10 points.
4. Verbalize a plan of action to differentiate from family.
5. Describe actions taken to differentiate from family (establishing separate relationships with different family members, taking a stand on issues and having casual comments to counterattacks, remaining neutral, etc.).
6. Describe or demonstrate changes in family interaction that show improvements in tolerance, contact, and leadership and decreases in fusion, domination, and alliances.
7. Improve ratings on the *Observation Sheet for Family Meetings* by 15 points.

MINI INDEX TO CHAPTER 2

USING THE HANDOUTS

- Literature on differentiation: *Understanding Your Family Drama, Differentiating from Your Family of Origin, Differentiating in Marriage and Parenthood.*
- Visual aid to help clients see family patterns and learn to diagram their own: *Diagramming the Drama.*
- Review sheet for clients and clinicians to look over when planning strategies to differentiate: *Pointers for Differentiating.*
- Assessment tools to identify problems clients have differentiating and to suggest goals for change: *Levels of Differentiation, Observation Sheet for Family Meetings.*
- Structured exercise for family therapy sessions: *Observation Sheet for Family Meetings.*

- Workshops and presentations: *Levels of Differentiation* is an interesting way to introduce information on differentiation; *Observation Sheet for Family Meetings* helps people better understand family dynamics. Workshop participants can divide into groups and role-play family discussions. An observer in each group can rate interactions on the observation sheet.

CAUTIONS AND RECOMMENDATIONS

- *Differentiating from Your Family of Origin* and *Pointers for Differentiating* are best used with clients who are actively involved in treatment. Strategies for differentiating can backfire and require careful planning.
- Handouts from *Waltzing through Emotional Landmines* (Chapter 1) should be thoroughly studied to assist efforts to differentiate. They offer more detailed instruction on taking the I position and maintaining contact during expected counterattacks with casual, empathic responses.

SOURCES AND ACKNOWLEDGMENTS

- Family systems therapy, developed by Murray Bowen, as presented in *Family Therapy in Clinical Practice* (Jason Aronson, 1978), is the basis for most of the handouts in this section. Because Bowen's approach is one of coaching people to work through problems with their families, it lends itself well to literature clients can read. Some of Bowen's terms have been changed into more descriptive, everyday language.
- Structural family therapy as developed by Salvador Minuchin also contributed ideas to *Diagramming the Drama* and the *Observation Sheet for Family Meetings.*
- Notation for diagramming family interaction is a combination of various theoretical orientations.

UNDERSTANDING YOUR FAMILY DRAMA

Do you ever feel as if you're trapped in the web of your own personal family soap opera, unable to make a move without inviting disapproval or "wounding" someone? Have you ever thought you escaped your past, only to find yourself caught in dramas with spouses, children, friends, or coworkers? Expressing your individuality or differentiating while remaining close to your family can break this distressing cycle, but this is not easy. Recognizing how expressions of individuality become stalled can help you avoid problems:[1]

- Early in life, you have an outer, false self that keeps you attached and in harmony with those on whom you depend. This false self is capable of acting, pretending, and doing whatever is necessary for the sake of survival.
- Beneath the outer layer is a solid self that strives to be unique and self-governing. When your caretakers are threatened by differences, you may feel unsafe shedding your outer, false self. Your priority becomes maintaining the bonds of survival by fusing or acting as though you are one with others.
- At some point, the desire for independence pushes from within. An emotional cutoff can happen in an impulsive burst. At this stage, you may become rebellious, withdrawn, a relationship nomad, "ruggedly independent," or you may move a great distance from home.
- Surprisingly, attempts to fuse with the first appealing person often follow an emotional cutoff. Initially, the new relationship masquerades as freedom. Eventually, the desire for independence surfaces, causing another emotional cutoff. The more intense the cutoff, the more likely it is that a cycle of fusing and cutting off will repeat itself in other relationships.

DIFFERENTIATION IN MARRIAGE

Courtship is usually the most open period in a relationship, when people express many of their thoughts, feelings, and fantasies. However, after marriage, each spouse becomes sensitive to subjects that upset the other and avoidance of differences begins. When the urge to merge conflicts with the reality of differences, problems develop. Clinging, pleading, helplessness, aloofness, rigidity, arguing, and possessiveness, all indicate anxiety about differences. There are three ways that friction in the struggle for oneness is handled:

1. Dominance/yielding: One spouse becomes dominant and appears rigid, and the other adapts and becomes pliant. Neither person is in touch with his or her true needs. One is constantly giving up self-awareness and the other is overextended. In times of stress, the yielding spouse loses the ability to function and becomes physically sick, depressed, or acts out impulsively. If the dysfunctional spouse dies or takes a healthy stance, the rigid spouse can collapse into the dysfunctional position. In a healthy marriage, the dominant and yielding roles are not fixed. Spouses can alternate roles with ease, and both are comfortable assuming the leadership of the family.
2. Marital conflict: The outer, false selves of both spouses are rigid and resistant to differences. The couple alternates between periods of intense closeness and periods of distance and conflict. During the latter, divorce can occur. Sometimes, conflict evolves from dominant/yielding patterns. The compliant spouse refuses to continue in the role and becomes rigid. The couple may be able to bypass a divorce crisis if one spouse begins to express individuality without being influenced by the other's distress about changes in long-standing patterns.

---

[1] Murray Bowen's ideas on differentiation are summarized in *Family Therapy in Clinical Practice* (Jason Aronson, 1978).

3. Triangulation and projection: Spouses avoid differences and conflict by forming alliances with children or by focusing on "disturbances" in a vulnerable third party. The conflict between the parents is then displaced or projected onto the emotional state of the child, as the following examples show:

   - A mother who does not feel sufficient levels of closeness with her husband tries to meet her emotional needs with her child. The child exhibits the mother's rejection anxiety by being fearful of school.
   - If a father is missing intimacy, he may overfocus on his daughter. The mother supports this bond, as it enables her to avoid anxieties that closeness triggers. At puberty, "Daddy's girl" takes drastic action to break away through an unwanted pregnancy.

Sometimes, all three patterns of domination, conflict, and triangulation can operate to form a very complex system. When tension is great, other people get involved to form interlocking triangles. Social service agencies can even become entangled with a family during crises.

DIFFERENTIATION IN "RECREATED" FAMILIES

Those who cut off from parents and later from spouses often seek intense relationships at work and in social settings. These environments can provide a "safe" means for satisfying emotional needs without the demands of intimacy. Gossiping, alliances, and coalitions in these groups imitate the triangles that occur in families. Expressing opinions by saying "I agree with . . . that . . ." or siding with one of two conflicting parties suggests that triangulation is taking place. You can differentiate in such organizations by having some differing views while remaining involved with the group.

BECOMING YOUR OWN PERSON

Despite an obstacle course of emotional cutoff, conflict, and projection, there are young people who find a way to develop their own views and make independent decisions. In adolescence, some denial of attachment to parents and fusion with peers is necessary, and the more differences a family tolerates, the smoother the journey out of the nest will be. In adulthood, the differentiated individual can have close, intimate relationships while pursuing outside interests. Regardless of the group or relationship you are in, you can avoid alliances and triangles so that you can be tethered to loved ones without being tied.

DIAGRAMMING THE DRAMA

Diagramming the Drama clarifies the design of your "family web" and suggests a starting place for change. Study the symbols and diagrams of typical family patterns below to help you recognize the design in your own family.

------- Clear, fluid boundary between two differentiated individuals or subsystems.
——— Blurred boundary between individuals who are seeking oneness and fusion.
——— Rigid boundary or distant contact that emotionally cuts off people.
═══ An alliance between people who are attempting to fuse and act as one.
Conflict between people due to family triangles or efforts to dominate.
———> Conflict projected by becoming overconcerned with or critical of a third party.

M F c Mother, father, and child with appropriate amounts of family influence.
m f **C** Mother, father, and child with too much or too little family influence.
H W Husband and wife with equal levels of influence.
H w Attempts to become one or fuse through domination and yielding.

Diagram	Family Patterns: Two-Parent Families
H W / **F** **M** / c c c	Healthy Family: Husband and wife have a relationship separate from their role as parents and take turns leading the family. They can express differing viewpoints and can resolve conflicts. Disagreement among family members does not occur in any set pattern.
F M / AC AC / AC	Healthy Family with Adult Children: Adult children are self-supporting and have interests, friends, and/or families of their own. There is toleration of differing viewpoints and lifestyles. Parents do not interfere with decisions adult children make about their own lives.
f m / c c c	Fusion: Family members are overinvolved with each other and pretend that individual differences do not exist. They tend to use the pronoun we ("We think . . .") and assume they know each other's thoughts.
F m / c c c	Dominant/Yielding: The dominant parent leads and the yielding parent functions as a child. Under stress, the adaptive parent may become physically or emotionally dysfunctional and appear incompetent.
F / **M** / c c	Go Between: Father is emotionally cut off from the children. Mother acts as the go-between and relays messages.
F **M** / **C** / c c	Projection: Family problems are centered around concern or exasperation with a child rather than the husband and wife having conflicts over housekeeping, finances, sex, or child rearing. Insignificant behaviors are magnified as objects of concern or criticism. Children who have a preexisting condition (diabetes, hyperactivity, etc.) are often targets for this role.
M **F** / **C C**	Alliances: A child or the children are in an alliance with one parent against the other. Having a buddy relieves stress for one parent. Emotionally cutting off from the family and becoming absorbed in outside interests eases the stress of the other.

<table>
<tr><th>Diagram</th><th>Family Patterns: After a Divorce or Death</th></tr>
<tr><td>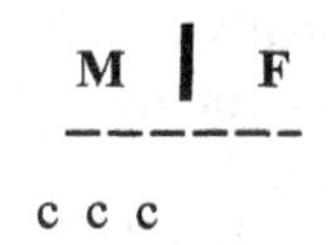</td><td>Healthy Divorce: Adults continue to discuss child-related issues even though they no longer live together. They resolve past conflicts and establish a new life for themselves. Each parent can take the lead when the children are in his or her custody and do not need to assist or interfere when children have visitation. The children maintain a clear connection to each parent.</td></tr>
<tr><td>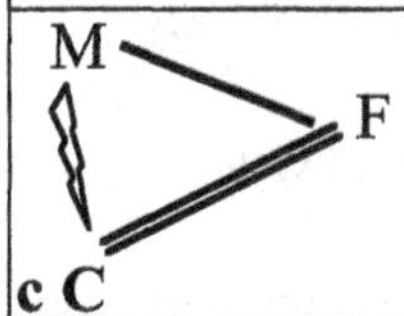</td><td>Family Ghosts: A child is in an alliance with a departed parent against the one with whom he or she is living. There is a role reversal in which the child draws power from the departed parent and belittles the custodial parent.</td></tr>
<tr><td></td><td>Fusion: After a parent dies or divorces, the remaining parent continues an alliance with the children. She is in a sibling position with them and has difficulty assuming leadership. Any unresolved conflicts with the divorced/deceased spouse intensify the problem and cut off the children from him.</td></tr>
<tr><td>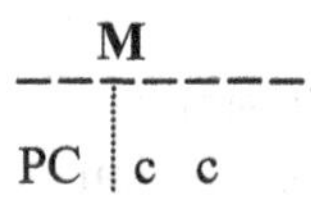</td><td>Healthy Parental Child (PC) System: A single parent may depend on a (significantly) older child to be in charge while she is working. She immediately assumes leadership when she is home. The PC informs the parent of any difficulties that occurred in her absence and she makes independent decisions about consequences.</td></tr>
<tr><td>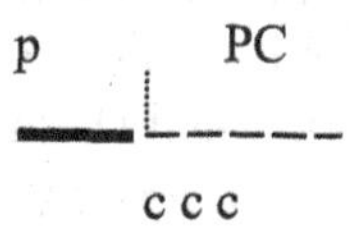</td><td>Disengaged Parent: The PC senses that the parent is not leading and takes over. Or the parent is so preoccupied that the PC performs essential parental tasks. The parent becomes emotionally cut off from the younger children as the PC assumes more responsibility.</td></tr>
<tr><td>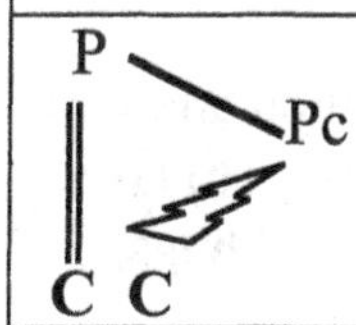</td><td>Triangulation: The above system is very unstable and can develop alliances. The younger children may become further cut off from the parent as the alliance strengthens between the parent and the PC. Or the parent may ally with the younger children against the PC and continually set the PC up for conflicts with the younger children.</td></tr>
<tr><td>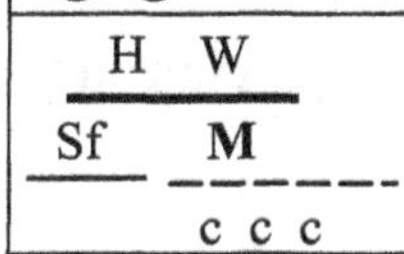</td><td>Healthy Stepfamily: In families with older children, the birth parent is a strong family leader so the stepparent can take time to bond. Once he is well integrated into the family, he can take turns leading, especially when the birth parent is not available.</td></tr>
<tr><td></td><td>Triangulation: If the natural parent is weak and the stepparent takes over the lead, conflict with the children is likely. The natural parent will either ally with her new spouse and emotionally cut off from the children, or she will ally with the children and fuel resentment toward the stepparent.</td></tr>
<tr><td>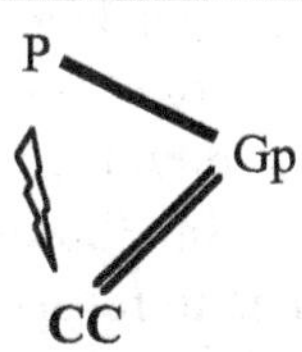</td><td>Three-Generation Families: A health three-generation family functions much like a healthy stepfamily. When the parent has never established her independence, the grandparent may take over, creating a triangle like the one above, or the grandparent may ally with the children, snowballing both emotional cutoff from their mother and parent-child conflicts.</td></tr>
</table>

Draw diagrams that represent how your family operated when you were growing up and how your immediate or extended family functions now. Be aware that patterns in extended families with adult children can be very complex, with many triangles. Make your diagram meaningful to you. Technical accuracy is not important.

DIFFERENTIATING FROM YOUR FAMILY OF ORIGIN

You may handle family pressure by trying to conform or by divorcing yourself emotionally. However, there is an alternative. You can learn how to express your differences or differentiate without getting caught in conflicts or abandoning your significant others. Once you've left home, the best place to reclaim the freedom to be yourself is with the family that raised you because:[1]

- When you are away from home, you will have time to evaluate your interactions with family members, regain a sense of yourself, and plan future strategies.
- Attachments to spouses, bosses, and associates often mimic early entanglements and will automatically change as you develop a new style of being with your parents.
- Your ability to be your own person is determined by how well you have resolved issues with your parents and the degree to which your parents are differentiated.

METHODS FOR DIFFERENTIATING WITHIN YOUR FAMILY

1. Separate, person-to-person relationships: Develop an individual relationship with each parent instead of dealing with them as a unit.
   - Correspond with each parent separately instead of writing Dear-Mom-and-Dad letters.
   - Have individual telephone conversations instead of talking with both parents on extension lines.
   - Balance the time you spend with each parent alone during family visits. Talk about subjects of interest that do not involve others. Stories of past family history, ancestry, philosophies of life, and beliefs are all good topics: "What was it like for you when we were little and Daddy was gone a lot?" "What was your most embarrassing or proudest moment?" "What upset you when you were a child?"
2. The I position: When conflicts emerge in the family, your goal is to state your position and underscore the fact that there are differences in the family. There are few opportunities to take the I position during periods of calm. Deaths, serious illnesses, family gatherings, weddings, divorces, and disclosure of secrets often spawn issues that are fertile opportunities to differentiate. Openly define where you stand on an issue, what you want, and what you intend to do without defending yourself, attacking, or withdrawing:
   - "I won't be getting a prenuptial agreement, even though that may be unwise."
   - "I don't agree with your position on premarital sex, and I'll be glad to keep the details of my weekend plans private if you find them too disturbing."
   - "When you give me unsolicited advice, I feel too resentful to consider it."
3. Neutralizing attacks: After stating your position, it helps to anticipate a series of reactions from your family. This backlash is so important that if it does not happen, you may not have made a successful attempt at differentiation! Initially, family members may be surprised, hurt, or angry and label your ideas crazy, irresponsible, or immoral. Then they will do their best to convince you to change your mind. When this does not work, they may threaten to disown you, but these accusations will probably reach a peak and then subside. Finally, the family will come to respect and appreciate your convictions. "Surviving" expressions of individuality will help all family members differentiate. The hardest part of this task is to maintain contact while under fire.

---

[1] Murray Bowen's ideas on differentiation are summarized in *Family Therapy in Clinical Practice* (Jason Aronson, 1978).

Making a casual, empathic response will empower you and can defuse nonstop tirades. For example, if you are told that you are ungrateful, you can:

- Agree (in theory): "I could be more grateful."
- Act as if you've been complimented: "Is that a bad thing?" or simply say, "Thank you."
- Exaggerate the attack: "I'm very selfish as well."
- Use reverse psychology: "Maybe you should try harder to reform me."
- Label feelings: "You sound very disappointed in me."
- Validate feelings: "It makes sense that you'd think I'm ungrateful because I do not call as much as you'd like."
- Sympathize: "My ways sound difficult for you."

When you truly give up seeking approval, other's judgments will not hurt you. However, if you cannot remain calm, state that you will revisit the discussion later. It is important to resume contact as soon as you are able to show that asserting independence is not the same thing as rejection.

4. The neutral stance: Even when you are not involved in a conflict between two family members, you can use their disagreement as an opportunity to differentiate by simply understanding the difference in each person's position. This takes you out of a judging position, demonstrates tolerance for varying viewpoints, and minimizes the chance for alliances to form. The following situations suggest ways to stay neutral without retreating:
   - Practice the neutral stance in circumstances that are not emotionally charged: Start with conflicts between young children or siblings before the challenge of staying neutral with your parents or when you have strong biases toward one person.
   - If you find yourself reacting negatively to one party, spend time alone with that person until you can understand his or her position.
   - Handle gossip by breaking confidences: Ask the "gossipee," "Why do you allow such stories to be told about you?" This will anger the gossiper, force the family to deal more directly with each other, and give you an opportunity to make a casual comment to any attacks: "With a little bit of practice, I'm sure you could develop as big a mouth as mine."
   - Avoid alliances by exposing them when you sense someone is trying to get you to take sides: "Mom and I have been plotting how to get everyone over this impasse."

Rehearsing possible interactions and writing a script for taking the I position or the neutral stance can help. However, discussing your plans with a family member establishes an alliance and hinders efforts to differentiate.

DIFFERENTIATING IN MARRIAGE AND PARENTHOOD

To become your own independent person it is necessary to define how you are different from the people who raised you while maintaining your connection with them. However, when conflict or dissatisfaction with your marriage is too great, it may be necessary to focus on that problem first. The most common mistake people make in their efforts to improve their relationships is trying to make the other person change. Any real steps toward expressing individuality are replaced by complaining and criticizing one's partner. This is a blatant attempt to fuse and become one person:

- If my husband were more understanding he would [be in my mind and] know what I want.
- My wife should [be like me and] not need so much attention.

THREE STAGES OF DIFFERENTIATION IN MARRIAGE

1. The I-Position and Empathy

Compliant people, who tend to give in, begin to stand up for their requests, make statements that start with the word "I," and express limits. Rigid people, who need to dominate, start to understand how their efforts ultimately hurt themselves. Each spouse becomes more flexible and communication is improved. After years of complaining it requires a conscious effort to turn resentments into requests:

- I've been missing affection from you lately. Would you kiss me good-bye in the morning?
- It seems like I can never give enough. Would you let me have 20 minutes to myself when I get home from work?

At the same time, spouses begin to show understanding for their partners' feelings and wants. It is necessary to stop trying to be one to understand emotions and needs that may be entirely different from your own:

- A little thing like a kiss good-by would go a long way to remind you that I care.
- It makes sense that you would need time alone to unwind when you get home from work.

2. Alternating steps

Through the I-position and the use of empathy, spouses start to learn about themselves and begin to differentiate. This happens in alternating steps. As individuality surfaces in one spouse, the other feels threatened and pleads for oneness. When the individuating spouse stays on track without defending, attacking, or withdrawing, the second spouse discovers the relationship can survive and he or she begins to differentiate. Now the other spouse may plead for togetherness.

3. True closeness

With each gain in individuality, the need for fusion becomes less intense. The couple begins to experience the true closeness of two people making contact instead of acting like one. When problems occur, each person is less reactive and able to own responsibility for his or her part without self-blame. Each person is now free to start differentiating from his or her family of origin. When spouses are able to have close relationships with their extended family on their own terms, the couple is further strengthened.

INDIVIDUATING AS A PARENT

Parenthood will especially challenge any unresolved issues about being unique, independent, and separate. Parents need to be able to lead the family and take a stand on issues. Domineering parents are trying to make their children an extension of themselves. Weak parents may give in due to fears of losing their "oneness" with their children. Even lecturing, nagging, and explaining are attempts to win agreement and avoid any risk of rejection involved in taking action. A parent who is well on his or her way to differentiating is able to:

- Consider differing viewpoints without agreeing or disagreeing.
- Make final decisions (after considering other ideas) on parent-child issues.
- Be comfortable with childrens' anger and listen to attacks without emotionally reacting.
- Back up rules with consequences.
- Remain neutral but involved when children have conflicts.
- Develop one-on-one relationships with each child.
- Take turns functioning as the family leader in two-parent families without feeling intimidated.

Having one-on-one relationships, taking a stand, and remaining neutral but involved in family conflicts helps shed the adhesive skin of the false self that was necessary for your survival when you were young. As more of your self-governing, solid-self becomes exposed, you will be able to walk the tangled web your family weaves without getting caught and discover a lifeline that offers both connection and freedom:

> The common house spider spins a loosely woven tangled web of dry silk. Wherever a spider goes, it is constantly spinning a silk thread called a dragline or a *lifeline* which it uses to escape from and return to its web.

OBSERVATION SHEET
FOR FAMILY MEETINGS

Family meetings kill two birds with one stone: (1) they are a forum in which individuals can resolve problems and conflicts, and (2) they offer an opportunity to practice healthy dynamics. The *Observation Sheet for Family Meetings* provides a vehicle to help all family members become more aware of their interactions. With this awareness comes choice and change.

OBSERVATION SHEET FOR FAMILY MEETINGS

Directions: (1) After a discussion, each person uses suggested point values to rate family interactions. This can be done from memory or by listening to a tape recording. Totaling points and determining a percentage score can offer incentives for improvement. (2) When family members become familiar with ratings, use previous observations to change the way the family interacts in later discussions. The Family Questionnaire that follows the Observation Sheet can be used for initial discussions.

1. Strong Parental Leadership (10 points total) Score: ______
   a. Parents are in charge of the discussion. They decide how to get started, when to do what, and keep the family on task. (2)
   b. Although parents lead the discussion, they encourage input from others. (2)
   c. If children give advise on running the discussion, the parents eventually resume charge. (2)
   d. When there are difficulties reaching agreements, parents can make a final decision. (2)
   e. It does not take excessively long for agreements to be reached. (2)
2. Expression of Differences or Differentiation (10 points total) Score: ______
   a. There are significant variations in individual opinions. (3)
   b. Generally, the family considers several alternatives before making a decision. (3)
   c. Family members disagree with each other as often as they agree with each other. (2)
   d. Disagreements are stated clearly and agreements are finally reached. (Disagreements do not become fuzzy by changing the subject or bringing up unrelated issues.) (2)

Note: There should be more differences of opinion in families with teenagers. Score items more generously in families with younger children.

3. Little Fusion or Attempts to Act as One (10 points total) Score: ______
   a. Family members do not assume they know each other's responses. (3)
   b. Family members do not speak for each other or answer a question for another person. (2)
   c. Generally, family members express their opinions with the pronoun I, rather than saying, "We think . . ." (2)
   d. The discussion is not rushed and sufficient time is used to draw out different ideas. (3)
4. All Participants Have Influence (10 points total) Score: ______
   a. One person does not do most of the talking. (2)
   b. People do not address all statements to one person or talk through a go-between. (2)
   c. Generally, everyone participates and has a voice on issues even though parents may make the final decision. (2)
   d. One person's independent responses do not become the decision for the family. (2)
   e. In two-parent families, both parents are involved in leading the exercise. (2)

5. People Deal Directly, with Few Alliances or Triangles (10 points total) Score: ______
   a. Children tend to agree with children and parents with parents. (3)
   b. Alliances shift: one person agrees with someone at one time and then agrees with another person at another time. (3)
   c. Two people do not present a united front, nor do they ally against the same person. (4)

Note: It is preferable for children to agree with children and parents with parents; however, some shifting in agreements across generations is fine.

6. There Is Good Contact without "Emotionally Cutting Off" from Others (10 points) Score: ______
   a. No one refuses to participate in the discussion. (2)
   b. The family takes time with the discussion, enjoys it, and is able to make the contact with each other that such meetings require. (2)

   The following apply to the Family Questionnaire below:

   c. There is a balance between amount of time and activities the family wants to spend together and time they want apart from each other. (2)
   d. There is not an odd-person-out who is cut off from contact with the family. (2)
   e. There is not an odd-person-out who wants much more time and contact with the family (possibly causing others to cut off from him or her). (2)

Note: Score more leniently in families with teenagers.

TOTAL SCORE: _______ points out of 60 PERCENT: Total divided by 60: ________

FAMILY QUESTIONNAIRE

Directions: (1) Each family member independently fills out the questionnaire. Answers should reflect the way people want the family to be, not the way it currently operates. During the discussion, the family reaches a decision on what would be the best for the *whole* family. Record the final decision on a blank questionnaire. (2) A second discussion can take place using photocopies of the family's previous final decision. Family members now independently rank items in order. Assign numbers 1 and 2 to the two most important items and the numbers 8 or higher to the two least important items. The family then reaches a decision on the order of importance that items have to the family as a *whole.* Use observations from the first discussion to change the way the family interacts.

For me to feel a part of my family, we would:

__ Eat dinner together ___ nights a week.
__ Watch TV, play a game together, etc. ___ times a ________. (week, month)
__ Spend a maximum of ___ hours a day watching TV.
__ Spend ___ evenings at home or together a week.
__ Go to a movie or family outing together ___ times a _________. (week, month, year)
__ Go away for a weekend together (camping, to the beach) ___________ times a year.
__ Go on vacation together for at least a week ___ times a year.
__ Worship together ___ times a __________. (week, month, year)
__ Other: ____

LEVELS OF DIFFERENTIATION

Are you able to express your differences from others while still feeling caring and connected to them? Most people can do this easily when their stress level is low. To gain a better sense of how far you have come in expressing your individuality and differentiating from others, examine the way you operate during crises and conflict.[1]

Directions: Circle a number 1 through 5 to show how similar you are to statements that describe either the undifferentiated or differentiated person. Rate strictly because differentiation is difficult and few people master this task completely.

Undifferentiated Person		**Differentiated Person**
Indifference & Intolerance		Concern & Toleration
• I have few preferences and like others to make decisions.	1 2 3 4 5	I am aware of my preference, even if I choose to go along with others.
• My opinions, beliefs, and principles are almost identical to my family's, friends', or church's.	1 2 3 4 5	I have questioned the beliefs of my family, friends, and religion before reaching my own conclusions.
• I am easily swayed by others' viewpoints.	1 2 3 4 5	I consider others' ideas and choose whether or not to change my own.
• I try to get others to see things my way or I try to defend myself.	1 2 3 4 5	I can state my position without attacking others or defending myself.
• When my preferences differ from others, I either win or lose.	1 2 3 4 5	I can make compromises without fear of giving up parts of myself.
• I express my beliefs with the words "We think . . ., I agree with . . ."	1 2 3 4 5	I express my beliefs with the words "I think . . ."
• I prefer to be with people whose views are similar to my own.	1 2 3 4 5	I enjoy points of view that differ from my own.
Emotions Rule Intellect		Intellect Rules Emotions
• My reactions are usually caused by others.	1 2 3 4 5	I can reason, reflect, and evaluate my reactions to people and events.
• I am rarely emotional, OR I have "knee-jerk" reactions.	1 2 3 4 5	I am able to experience passionate emotions without losing myself.
• When I am emotional, I seem to lose my powers of reason.	1 2 3 4 5	My intellect and logic rule my emotions.
• My decisions are based on instinct and what "feels" right.	1 2 3 4 5	I am able to think through my decisions.
• I often don't know the reasons for my decisions.	1 2 3 4 5	I am aware of the reasons for my decisions.
• When others are in conflict, I am drawn to take sides.	1 2 3 4 5	During conflict, I see both sides of the issue.
Other-Oriented Goals		Self-Serving Goals
• My long-term goals are more for my relationship than for me.	1 2 3 4 5	I have long-term goals that affect only me.
• It is hard for me to act without others' love and approval.	1 2 3 4 5	I can risk losing others' approval when something is important to me.
• I feel angry, hurt, or resentful when others don't approve of me.	1 2 3 4 5	I am temporarily sad or feel calm when others withhold approval.

[1] Murray Bowen's ideas on differentiation are summarized in *Family Therapy in Clinical Practice* (Jason Aronson, 1978).

POINTERS FOR DIFFERENTIATING

Leaving home emotionally can take a lifetime. Doing so is more about carving your own unique identity that simultaneously *differentiates* you from and links you to your family than about how far you live from home. The following pointers can help you begin the journey out of the nest:

- Log incidents in which you try to fuse or become one with others by controlling, yielding, or forming alliances.
- Assess how your family operates by diagramming relationships in your family of origin and your current family and observing interaction during discussions.
- Maintain separate, person-to-person relationships with all family members through discussions about philosophies of life, beliefs, and interests. When unresolved issues interfere with relationships, use empathy skills and express your feelings with statements that start with the word "I" to work through the impasse.
- Take a position on issues that surface during life cycles and crises by making statements that start with the word "I." Express how your stance differs from others while appreciating their views. Make sure you are stating your concerns and intentions without attacking, defending, or trying to ally with others.
- Make casual comments that agree with, exaggerate, or reverse expected counterattacks (for taking a stand). If you have difficulty, role-play scenarios with a friend or therapist who is not involved in your family. Memorize possible responses.
- Dispel misperceptions that independence is the same as rejection: Show that you understand others' points of view to further defuse counterattacks and to maintain contact while the family is absorbing an expression of individuality.
- Take the neutral stance when other family members are in conflict: Empathize with one person's position without attacking or blaming others. State that you intend to understand the other party as well, and that you will not act as a go-between.
- Avoid alliances others try to form with you by exposing them: *". . . and I have been plotting how to help the family through this impasse."*
- Break confidences to disrupt gossip: Ask the third party why he or she is allowing other people to gossip about him or her. You can do this with or without warning the gossiper: *"If you continue to tell me things, I will inform. . . ."*
- Deflect expressions of gratitude for your efforts to differentiate by denying the importance of what you've done. Any endeavors to differentiate must be made for yourself. Attempts to "help" others or gain approval, seek oneness, and promote alliances rather than individuation.
- Assess your level of differentiation by asking for feedback from people you trust on how well you do the above. Work on making needed changes.

EXTRA HELP

The Dance of Anger by Harriet Goldhor Lerner (HarperCollins, 1997).

American Family Therapy Academy, www.afta.org

Chapter 3

Mending Marriages

MENDING MARRIAGES

OBJECTIVES FOR TREATMENT PLANNING

1. Identify factors contributing to relationship problems.
2. Describe three behavior changes that reverse past ineffective attempts to "fix" relationship problems, reduce polarization of roles, integrate masculine/feminine qualities within oneself or improve communication.
3. Report that cognitions necessary to change interaction with partner are valid.
4. Identify any disorders that are preventing relationship healing.
5. Decide whether or not to work on the relationship or separate.

MINI INDEX TO CHAPTER 3

USING THE HANDOUTS

- Understanding sources of relationship problems: *Causes and Cures of Relationship Problems, Communication That Cures Problems.*
- Visual aid to help clients identify destructive and effective communication styles at a glance: *Communication That Cures Problems.*
- Reminders for clinicians and review sheets for clients to look over when planning strategies to change relationship: *The Rules of Change, Training Partners to Be Helpful, Beckoning Instead of Chasing, Defusing Your Partner, Helping Your Partner Defuse You, Turning Control and Jealousy into Passion, Dissolving Sexual Differences, Restoring Romance, Turning "Good Bye" into "Hello."*
- Preparation for processing destructive beliefs that interfere with relationship counseling: *Beliefs That Help Relationships.*
- Assessment tool that can be filled out in the waiting room to identify any problems that could impede couples' counseling: *Disorders That Affect Relationships.*
- Exercise to promote discussion between partners: *Gender Gap Facts, Facts You May Not Know about Sex, Yin/Yang Questionnaire.*

- Workshop discussion sheets to promote understanding between genders and to practice changes that men and women need to make to improve relationships: *Gender Gap Facts* can be used to find out if participants agree or disagree with generalizations; table from *Communication That Cures Problems* can be used as a guide to teach men to listen and women to make requests. (See Active Listening Circles and Assertive Language Circles in *Therapist's Guide to Waltzing through Emotional Landmines,* pp. 1.2–1.3.)

RECOMMENDATIONS

- Handouts from *Waltzing through Emotional Landmines* (Chapter 1) should be thoroughly studied to assist couples in learning communication skills.
- Supplement *Defusing Your Partner* and *Helping Your Partner Defuse You* with handouts in *From Mad to Mellow* (Chapter 8).
- *ADD at Home and in the Workplace* (Chapter 9) and handouts from *In Search of Self* (Chapter 10) can further help identify disorders that affect relationships.
- *Dissolving Sexual Differences* and *Facts You May Not Know about Sex* can be used together to help couples with sexual difficulties.

SOURCES AND ACKNOWLEDGMENTS

- Theories of reciprocity in relationships, as presented by Peggy Papp, in *The Process of Change* (Guilford Press, 1983), contributed to *Causes and Cures of Relationship Problems.*
- Imago therapy, developed by Harville Hendrix and explained in *Getting the Love You Want* (Henry Holt, 1988), contributed to *Causes and Cures of Relationship Problems* and *Restoring Romance.*
- Short-term behavior therapy, found in *Divorce Busting* (Simon & Schuster, 1992) by Michele Weiner Davis, forms the basis of *The Rules of Change.*
- The work of John Gray presented in *Men Are from Mars, Women Are from Venus* (HarperCollins, 1992) and *Mars and Venus in the Bedroom* (HarperPerennial, 1997) contributed to *Training Partners to Be Helpful, Beckoning instead of Chasing, Helping Your Partner Defuse You, Dissolving Sexual Differences, Gender Gap Facts,* and *Facts You May Not Know about Sex.*
- *After the Affair* (HarperPerennial, 1997) by Janis Abrahms Spring formed the basis for handling infidelity in *Turning Control and Jealousy into Passion.*
- *Women's Reality* (Minnesota: Winston Press, 1981) by Anne Schaef was used to develop the *Yin/Yang Questionnaire.* Although Ms. Schaef's intentions may have been to offer support for the feminist position, her idea of the "white male system" and the "female system" are used in this handout to integrate masculine and feminine qualities as suggested by Jungian psychology.
- EMDR formulations for negative and positive cognitions explained in *Eye Movement Desensitization and Reprocessing* by Francine Shapiro (Guilford Press, 1995) were used in *Beliefs That Help Relationships.*

CAUSES AND CURES OF RELATIONSHIP PROBLEMS

If your car was stuck in sand, would you continue to press on the gas pedal or would you get out and figure out a new line of action? Most people would do the latter. Yet, when it comes to relationships, people often keep their foot on the gas and dig themselves deeper. A man may continue to provoke his spouse to be "rebellious" by attempting to control her. A woman may drive her partner further away by chasing him when he distances. How do these vicious cycles get started? The answer lies in the mystery of romance. High levels of attraction actually produce a chemical change. A person's system becomes flooded with endorphins, nature's painkiller, and while on this "high" it is easy to be blinded to signs of trouble. This type of attraction is often created because:

- Your partner has characteristics similar to early caretakers and you unknowingly think he or she will fulfill unmet childhood needs. If you had a controlling parent, you may strive to win freedom from a rigid spouse.
- Your partner has positive qualities you believe you are lacking: Someone who is insecure may be attracted by confidence. A person who is cool and nonchalant can become captivated by another's warmth.

Often, the seeds of trouble are sown when the relationship becomes "official" and partners make a commitment. Each person begins to focus on being taken care of and is less inclined to accommodate the other's needs. As a result, full-fledged conflict may emerge or resentments may slowly build over the years. For example, a woman may wake up and realize that her efforts to be docile and compliant are never going to win her the approval she seeks; or a wife's warmth and attentiveness may suddenly seem like a demand for smothering closeness.[1]

FROM DESIRABLE DIFFERENCES TO INCOMPATIBLE POLARITIES

When unresolved resentments build, the differences that were once a source of attraction become sore spots. Instead of complementing each other, differences begin producing conflict. The ways couples can "polarize" their differences are endless:

Differences	Polarities
Creative/Organized	Sloppy/"Neat freak"
Free spirit/Self-disciplined	Irresponsible/Responsible Impulsive/Rigid Emotional/Reserved
Independent/Relationship-oriented	Distancing/Pursuing Detached/Dependent Underinvolved/Overinvolved Uncommitted/Committed
Receiving/Nurturing	Sick/Healthy Helpless/Competent Master/Servant
Leading/Following	Dominant/Yielding Parent/Child

[1] Ideas on infatuation come from *Getting the Love You Want* by Harville Hendrix. (Henry Holt, 1988).

In healthy relationships, differences are interchangeable and a source of learning. Partners can take turns giving and receiving or being spontaneous and setting limits. The relationship achieves a balance of closeness and freedom so that neither suffocation nor detachment results. Unfortunately, when both people in the relationship resist fulfilling their potentials, they become stuck playing certain roles and cease growing. A couple may be satisfied acting out this polarization for years until a crisis occurs. For example, a woman who stubbornly holds onto her role as nurturer (out of a fear of her own "selfishness") may find this too taxing when she starts working. To make the relationship more open and flexible, one person must change and *allow the other to be upset.* If this is done with firmness and sympathy, even rigid "tyrants" can realize their partners can act independently and remain committed to the relationship.

GENDER DIFFERENCES

Recent research on the brain and nervous system explains how common male-female patterns can become stuck in gender polarities:

- The corpus callosum is 40% larger in women than in men:[2] This explains why some women readily access emotions and share feelings that are housed in the right side of the brain, whereas men may find it easier to focus on goals and solutions due to reduced "right-brain interference."
- Men are more rapidly aroused than women during conflict by the part of their nervous system that controls automatic body functions such as heart rate, blood pressure, and digestion. This explains why some men retreat from contact after periods of intensity and desire freedom from emotional encumbrances.

Although male distancing/detachment and female closeness/caretaking patterns can be common, a free-spirited, self-absorbed woman can trigger a man to be dependent and doting. Likewise, a talkative man may prod a woman to be the guardian of space and distance in the relationship. Furthermore, polarities are not stable and can flip-flop wildly over time. When a woman who has fought for closeness for years gives up and decides to exit the relationship, a man who was previously distant may pursue ardently. To discover the polarities in your relationship, create a metaphor:[3]

Exercise: Relationship Metaphors

1. Choose an image or symbol of how your partner would appear to you in a dream, fairy tale, or cartoon—A playful satyr dancing through the woods.
2. What form would you take in relationship to your partner's—The moon above.
3. What interaction or dance happens between the two forms—I watch him frolic in my light.
4. What is the worst nightmare that could happen between the two forms—He goes off on his escapades, never noticing that I light his way.
5. What would be the best outcome—He would wait for me and play with the shadows I make.

[2] The corpus callosum is the mass of fibers connecting the right and left sides of the brain. Information on physical gender differences was taken from *Divorce Busting* by Michele Weiner-David (Simon & Schuster, 1992), pp. 50–51.

[3] Exercise from *The Process of Change* by Peggy Papp (Guilford Press, 1983), p. 142.

COMMUNICATION THAT CURES PROBLEMS

Opposites attract and likes repel. When a couple cannot accommodate their "attractive differences" and tries to act as one person, the second half of magnetic law is set into action. A widening gulf develops as partners start to repel each other and differences become extreme. The first step to bridging this chasm is to become aware of the communication patterns that feed it. You can start by identifying what your partner does that bothers you. However, immediately examine how you react. For example, if your partner is sloppy, have you become the critic? If your partner is critical, do you find yourself on the defensive or withdrawing? Whenever a problem occurs, the variety of responses to it is endless. Yet, most people get stuck in "fight" or "flight" reactions.

Directions: Do you use automatic defend-withdraw-attack communication patterns that are oriented toward winning and losing, or learned responses that offer a way to resolve problems by which both parties win? Mark habit reactions on the left or thoughtful responses on the right that are typical for you.

Change Habit Reactions . . .	**into Thoughtful Responses**
Instead of defending or withdrawing:	**Use active listening:**[1]
__ Apologizing: "I'm sorry I . . ." __ Reassuring: "I really do . . ." __ Explaining: "The reason is . . ." __ Justifying: "I was just . . ." __ Tuning out	__ Clarify/rephrase: "What do you mean by . . . ?" "Are you saying . . . ?" __ Label feelings: "You must feel . . ." "You seem . . ." __ Validate feelings: "It makes sense that . . ." "It must be hard when . . ."
Instead of controlling:	**Use effective expression:**[2]
__ Convincing: "You have to understand . . ." __ Disagreeing: "You're wrong about . . ." __ Advising/lecturing: "Why don't you . . . ?" __ Ordering: "You have to . . ." __ Threatening: " . . . or else"	__ State your feelings: "I feel . . . when you . . ." __ Make requests: "Would you . . . ?" __ Set limits: "I'm willing/not willing to . . ."
Instead of condemning:	**Use deflecting and defusing:**[3]
__ Complaining: "You don't . . ." "Nothing ever . . ." __ Blaming: "You never . . ." __ Criticizing: "You should/shouldn't . . ." __ Comparing: "Why can't you be more like . . ." __ Predicting the worst: "You'll never . . ." __ Accusing: "I know you're . . ." __ Insulting, name-calling, making slurs __ Taunting, teasing, rejecting __ Using sarcastic, mocking, patronizing tones	__ Turn killer words into kindness: Agree in fact or theory, take or give compliments; find golden nuggets, dramatize, twist the tone; use reverse psychology. __ Understand causes and effects of intimidation; label feelings, sympathize, ask questions; express feelings, wants, and limits. __ Use "power words": try, dare, but; unrelated comments and general humor.

[1] See *Getting the Love You Want* by Harville Hendrex (Henry Holt, 1988).
[2] See *Men Are from Mars, Women Are from Venus* by John Gray (HarperCollins, 1992).
[3] See *How to Handle Bullies, Teasers and Other Meanies* by Kate Cohen-Posey (Rainbow Books, 1995).

The most important learned communication response to use when either you or your partner is upset is to *show* understanding. The word "show" is emphasized because it does not help to understand unless you demonstrate your understanding by rephrasing thoughts, labeling feelings, and validating factors that contribute to emotions. Using all three active listening responses can produce powerful results.

ADVANTAGES OF FIRST SHOWING UNDERSTANDING

Many people have fears that they will never be understood, resolve their feelings, and have their needs met unless they talk. When the art of listening is understood, it makes sense why the opposite is true:

- You can reduce the intensity of your own reactions by understanding the hurt that underlies your partner's undesirable behavior. Always assume that when your partner does not treat you well, there is an old resentment or fear behind that behavior.
- Your partner will have less need to defend, withdraw, attack, or give long-winded speeches: It may take several statements of understanding before your partner realizes that you simply want to understand without trying to force changes.
- The best way to obtain understanding is by giving it: As your partner's defenses come down, he or she will want to understand how things have been for you. Your persistent efforts to show understanding will serve as a model that can teach your partner to rephrase, identify feelings, validate, and sympathize. You can aid the process (after you thoroughly understand your partner's feelings) by asking, "Would you like to understand why I acted the way I did?"
- Long-lasting solutions come from understanding: They are never reached by convincing, ordering, threatening, and nagging. Over time, deep levels of understanding will develop and conflicts will begin to resolve themselves.
- You and your partner will begin to encourage the best in each other by appreciating good intentions in difficult behavior: "I imagine you think I get the credit I deserve when I'm all fixed up and you must be puzzled when I don't mind not being noticed."

Showing approval and appreciation of the little things your partner does to meet your needs goes one step beyond understanding and promotes continued success. When you find things to criticize, you ensure disaster. You can even appreciate things that have not happened as though they have, and start a desired change: "I've noticed how you've begun to pick things up around the house more. That really helps me relax."

Understanding the pain that underlies troublesome behavior and noticing the little things a person does to change is simple, but it's not easy. It can be extremely difficult to put your own need for understanding aside to focus on your partner. However, once you are freed of the need to attack, defend, and withdraw, the rigid divisions in the relationship will begin to fall apart. Your mind will open to a vast array of tactics that can change the way you and your partner deal with problems.[4]

[4] See *The Seven Principles for Making Marriage Work* by John M. Gottman (Crown Publishers, 1999) for more information on the dangers of attacking, defending, and withdrawing.

THE RULES OF CHANGE

It is very easy to believe that change can't happen or that it's too late to make adjustments. Actually, the duration of a problem has nothing to do with your ability to change it. You can start making a difference all by yourself by following the rules of change:[1]

1. Do more of what works: When things are going well, don't just take it for granted. Examine what you are doing that is helpful and do more of that! Focus on what you can do rather than on what you cannot do. Instead of saying, "If we succeed once, we can again," couples say, "If we have any failures, we'll never make it." People have many labels for destructive conduct (such as being insensitive, controlling, or selfish). They are less likely to have names for desirable behaviors and, therefore, overlook them. If you can't see any positive efforts, look at what you are doing when the problem is less intense. Do what used to work to fix a problem (you probably stopped doing it). Do what works, even if you shouldn't have to. Ask yourself:
   - What do we do when we get along well that we haven't been doing lately?
   - What finally puts an end to our conflicts? Do it sooner.
   - What is different about times when something constructive comes out of a fight or when a problem happens but doesn't bother me?
   - What did we do in the beginning of our relationship that made it more satisfying?
2. Do the opposite of what doesn't work: Look at what you have been doing that is not working (nagging, withdrawing) and do the opposite! Changing attack reactions to approval and appreciation, and defensiveness into sympathy and agreement are obvious 180 degree changes. However, sometimes making a total change takes a lot of faith. You may feel you are "joining the enemy." But you can do anything on an experimental basis. Make the change with complete sincerity because if you seem disingenuous, your plan won't work. Notice how the following 180 degree changes brought about desirable results:
   - A woman who had been begging her husband to spend more time at home began encouraging him to stay away and he started showing interest in the family.
   - A man was upset by how much his wife always criticized their daughter and he always intervened. One time, as an experiment, when his wife was critical he agreed with her. His wife was so surprised that she stopped her lecture all together.

   When you see any progress, stick with the plan. Going back to your old behavior will cause you to lose what little ground you've gained. Continue to do what you are doing until you are convinced that your partner's improvements have become habits.
3. Change anything: If you can't make a 180 degree change, change anything. What would your spouse say you need to change for your marriage to work? What would you have to do for your partner to see a difference in you? The idea is not to just give in and please your spouse, but to shake up your mind and start thinking about changes you can make in yourself. When either spouse does something different, it interrupts the negative sequence of events and prevents a vicious cycle from continuing. A small change can lead to bigger changes:
   - Change where you fight: You can make a rule to fight only in the bathroom or to argue in writing or by phone.

---

[1] Ideas about change were taken from *Divorce Busting* by Michele Weiner-Davis (Simon & Schuster, 1992).

- Change when you fight: Postpone fights until after dinner. Pick specific weekly times when a hurt spouse can ask any questions about an infidelity. The guilty spouse can answer questions more compassionately when he or she knows there is a limit to constant rumination.
- Change how you fight: Wear Groucho Marx glasses or hold your nose when you argue. Stick out your tongue when things get intense.[2] Time "rounds" of fights so that each person has just three minutes to state the case. Require the other person to paraphrase before making his or her own point.
- Change who is in charge: Flip a coin to determine who handles specific discipline issues. Decide who makes the rules for different children. Let one person make decisions on odd days and the other make decisions on even days.

4. Act as if the change you want has already happened: Seeing or speaking things as you want them to be is a powerful way to induce change. Good can be found in almost any negative behavior and used as a wedge to start things moving. A partner's withdrawal can be taken as thoughtful silence. Notice how even criticism can be responded to as though it was caring and concern:

   A woman got home at 1:00 A.M. after a night out with her friends and found her husband glaring at her. She thanked him for waiting up for her and told him it was very sweet of him to be concerned. An argument was avoided and they went to bed with a hug.

5. Don't talk, act: Talking too much can block solutions. Lecturing, pleading, complaining, explaining, and threatening are usually signs that you're trying so hard to change another person that you are overlooking actions you can take. Even if you are not lecturing but simply expressing your feelings, wants, and limits, your partner may have stopped listening to you. Most people have some "wild" idea about what could be done to change their problem but are afraid to try it. One "daring" action will speak a thousand words:

   After years of complaining that his wife always made them late, a man simply left when it was time to go. Of course, she was furious about the incident but was on time after that.

6. Give change a chance: You may need to consistently practice a new behavior for two to three weeks before you start to notice any progress. Don't expect too much too soon, but when it is clear that an approach is not working, try something else. Have realistic goals. Expect neither failure nor perfection. When you do see some progress, don't assume your partner is now a changed person. You will need to keep up your efforts for improvements to last. Make sure you aren't "backsliding." Review what you've been doing:

   - Is the strategy you're using different enough?
   - Is it too soon to tell if your approach is having an effect?
   - Are you overlooking small changes?
   - Are you making half-hearted efforts or reverting back to your old ways?
   - When you run out of ideas, seek help. You can discover the strategy that is just right for you.

[2] See *The Seven Principles of Making Marriage Work* by John M. Gottman (Crown Publishers, 1999) for "repair attempts."

TRAINING PARTNERS TO BE HELPFUL

Some relationships feel like all give and no get. The flexible nurturing and receiving that flows back and forth in a healthy relationship becomes stuck in master/slave or thankless/martyred roles. Often, "givers" think that if *they* just give enough, others will follow their example. Because they anticipate others' needs, they think people should be equally capable of foreseeing theirs. When givers finally do ask for help, often it is done with so much complaining that others don't feel like responding. They know that after all the nagging, givers will end up taking care of things themselves. The truth is that giving is *not* a sign of love and caring—it is a sign of *good training*! There is much that givers can do to teach people around them to be more thoughtful:[1]

1. Set limits on how much you give: This is the first step to getting more help! Simply stop doing some things and find out how long it takes others to pick up the ball.
2. Be specific: Do not say "I'd like you to care more." Say "Would you ask about my day, give me a hug, or wash my feet?" Choices and absurd requests help.
3. Break the problem into small, achievable steps: What is the first thing your partner could do to help you to trust him or her more?
4. Make direct requests: Say, "Would you . . .?" This helps others make a commitment to do something.
5. Do not make statements or orders: ". . . needs to be done" and "I would like you to . . ." are statements. "Get me the . . ." is an order and causes resentment.
6. Give your partner the choice to refuse: The more freedom people have to say "No," the more likely they will say "Yes." Asking, "Would you . . .?" suggests that freedom. "Could you . . . ?" asks if they are able and implies that if they can do something, they should.
7. Ask with one short question without giving a list of reasons to justify requests. The latter sounds demanding or manipulative.
8. Practice accepting "No" graciously by making some unreasonable requests so you can simply say, "That's OK. No problem."
9. Practice asking properly for things others are likely to do before asking for things that will stretch them.
10. When others do what you ask, show appreciation! You can even appreciate things they haven't done as though they have. Saying, "You've really been putting away your dishes more lately" is a wonderful reminder.
11. Ask in a trusting manner, as if you believe your partner will really do it.
12. When your partner forgets to do something, just ask again without making a fuss—"I'm sure you meant to. Would you do it tomorrow?"
13. Don't require other to want to do things to be helpful. When their initial response is to grumble, remember that they're in the first stage of considering your request. Listen quietly and trust them to work through their struggle.
14. When other refuse to do something, ask once more, with only one reason why your desire is important or simplify your request. Then, if they decline, accept graciously.

---

[1] Some strategies for partner training are adapted from *Men Are from Mars, Women Are from Venus* by John Gray (HarperCollins, 1992).

BECKONING INSTEAD OF CHASING

Many relationships have a pattern in which one person is distant or detached and the other person wants closeness and pursues. The more the pursuer seeks closeness, the more the distancer pulls away. The distancer may avoid (nonsexual) intimate contact for fear of being suffocated, controlled, or robbed of independence. The pursuer may find that spending time alone feels like abandonment or that independent action is uncomfortable. Often, the pursuer will be the person to become dissatisfied with the situation and need to start making a difference. Change can begin with the following steps:[1]

1. Leave others alone when they pull away. Don't follow, worry about, or punish them when they are in their own world.
2. Ignore your partner's distress if he or she doesn't want to talk: If your partner looks upset but says "I'm OK," he or she may mean, "Support my by not worrying" or "Let me handle it by myself." You can ask, "Would you tell me what is bothering you when you're ready?"
3. Develop your own pursuits and support system for times when your partner withdraws: Many people lose themselves (their interests, desires) in relationships. If you are upset or depressed when your partner is withdrawn, find other people to talk to.
4. When your partner shows interest in making contact, welcome him or her warmly: This is not the time to be punishing or to retaliate. Take advantage of these times for discussions and intimacy. Healthy relationships have a natural flow of distance and closeness.
5. At opportune times, initiate conversations by sharing your own ideas on a subject and then pause to hear your partner's. Tell your partner how much you've been enjoying yourself and wait to hear what he or she has done or thought. Do not interrogate!
6. Identify any underlying disorder that may be contributing to the problem: If your partner is unwilling or unable to get help, make a decision about whether or not the relationship has enough benefits to make it worth continuing.
   a. Depression is a mood disorder that is usually very responsive to medication and/or therapy. Signs of mild depression that may go untreated are withdrawal, disinterest in sexual contact, inability to experience pleasure, few interests, little energy, difficulty organizing thoughts, and indecisiveness.
   b. Personality disorders are long-standing patterns of behavior that significantly impair relationships. Loyalty, dependability, and a strong work ethic may be enough to sustain some relationships, but the following characteristics suggest a person who has little potential for intimacy and change:
      - Lack of interest in or enjoyment of close relationships.
      - Preference for solitary activities.
      - Rarely experiences or admits to strong emotions, even anger.
      - Unaffected by praise or criticism.
      - Almost no close friends other than first-degree relatives.
      - Avoids eye contact; unresponsive to facial expressions such as nods or smiles.

[1] Strategies for beckoning are adapted from *Men Are from Mars, Women Are from Venus* by John Gray (HarperCollins, 1992).

DEFUSING YOUR PARTNER

If your partner is constantly pouring out emotions, you may have become tired of listening. When one person is stoic, the other may carry all the worry, anger, or grief for the relationship. When reserved people shut others out, their partners feel compelled to try to get through to them. If the less emotional person learns to show understanding, there can be an infusion of love, romance, and even sexuality into a relationship. The following steps can begin to reverse this painful pattern:

1. You only need to understand your partner: When he or she is upset, take a deep breath and remember: you don't have to take the blame for problems or "fix" them.
2. Show your interest by asking questions and making listening noises: "Uh huh."
3. Show you understand by rephrasing, labeling feelings, and validating factors that contribute to emotions: "Are you saying . . . ?" "It sounds like you're feeling . . ." "It makes sense you would feel . . . because . . ."
4. Welcome tears: They can help the healing process. Offering your hand or arm can help release painful feelings. Do not discourage people from crying.
5. Do not invalidate feelings by saying, "You shouldn't feel that way," "Don't worry about it," or "I understand." (Show you understand, as in number 3 above.)
6. Do not express your viewpoint until you feedback your partner's ideas.
7. Do not offer solutions: Even if your partner asks you what to do, find out his or her ideas first. Pretend you are not sure what to do until your partner comes up with a plan.
8. When you disagree with your partner's views, ask how he or she reached that conclusion before you say anything. Point out what is good about such thinking even when it differs from your own. Do not agree just to pacify your partner. You do not have to agree to understand.
9. When you don't have the attention to listen, ask for a time-out. Assure your partner that he or she will have your full attention later and be sure to follow through.

DISTRESS BETWEEN PARTNERS

When your partner is upset with you, it can be especially difficult to follow the above strategies. In many relationships, people become stuck in parent/child roles, in which one person is critical and the other defensive. Be your own judge and strive to meet your own standards. This will free you to be more understanding and even playful in the face of your partner's disapproval. If you have been so beaten down that you've lost self-confidence, get help, because you must learn to feel good about yourself or you will always be at the mercy of critics. At times, both partners can be emotional and attacking. Each one is trying so hard to get his or her point across that neither is listening and the situation escalates. Generally, the person experiencing the lesser amount of distress will find it easier to break this cycle. After using the above strategies, you can fine-tune them with the following:

10. Label any disappointment your partner may be feeling: "You are disappointed with me because. . . ." This will greatly reduce the intensity of the attack.
11. Give yourself the right to make mistakes so that you can take an honest look at yourself. Understand your shortcomings rather than condemn yourself.
12. Agree with any part of a criticism that is true, even if it is too harsh. Or admit to how you may have contributed to a problem. Agreeing with possible truths will take the wind out of a critic's sails.

13. If you have done something wrong, express your remorse and concentrate on sympathizing with your partner's distress rather than apologizing for your behavior.
14. Come up with a plan for specific changes that you are willing to make: Express your desire to change rather than make false promises.
15. If you are "in the doghouse" for something you did wrong, acknowledge what you did and give a little extra.
16. Decide whether your partner's standards are right for you after carefully considering his or her complaint. Be willing to change some things about yourself but not everything.
17. If you decide not to comply with your partner's requests, be sincerely sympathetic: "It must be hard for you when I don't act the way you want."
18. Help your partner become aware of his or her behavior in a lighthearted way: "You're trying so hard to improve me"; "I hope you're not charging too much for this educational moment"; "It really helps me sharpen my viewpoint when we disagree."
19. If your partner tends to be too much of a caretaker, take responsibility for giving more. Look for little things you can do, rather than think that your paycheck or buying expensive items are enough. Ask, "Is there anything I can do?"
20. If your partner is passive and quietly resentful, find out what his or her preferences are before making any decisions about what to do or how to spend money. Reach compromises or take turns. Don't always give in or try to get your way.
21. If your partner brings up "old" issues, empathize and investigate what is triggering it this time. This will relieve some of the frustration of having to go over it again. Often, people have to release their feelings with a compassionate listener several times before they can let go of a concern or get to the underlying problem.

EXPLOSIONS

When your partner's distress is approaching an explosion, it is easy to feel helpless. The first step to regaining your power is to understand that people usually feel powerless when they are yelling. They think the only way they will ever be heard is by raising their voice. When others withdraw or argue back, shouting becomes louder. Several strategies can change this pattern. Practice different approaches and use the one that works best for you:

22. If you can, tell your partner that you will talk when he or she is calmer, and leave the room or house. Do something to soothe yourself and be sure to follow up later![1]
23. Focus on your partner and make listening noises if you cannot leave or if you do have the strength to withstand the storm. Do not try to talk yourself. While you're looking at your partner, keep asking yourself, "What is really hurting him or her?"
24. Show that you understand your partner's point when you see an opening (see number 3).
25. Do not try to reason or disagree with people who are fuming, because in that frame of mind they are unable to consider others' ideas. After your partner has felt completely understood, he or she may be more capable of understanding you.
26. Do not tolerate physical abuse: You may need to separate from your partner until he or she is involved in therapy and demonstrates a commitment to making changes. Do not count on promises.

---

[1] See *The Seven Principles for Making Marriage Work* by John M. Gottman (Crown Publishers, 1999) for more information on resolving relationship conflict.

HELPING YOUR PARTNER DEFUSE YOU

When you want to let off steam, it can be frustrating if you are open and your partner is closed. Some people have a hard time listening because they fear they will be criticized or they think they have to solve others' problems. However, there are things you can do to help such partners be more attentive:

1. Let your partner know that he or she is being helpful within two sentences of starting to talk: "You don't know how much relief I feel already!"
2. Assure your partner that you are not upset with him or her, but rather with yourself, your day, or someone else. Use the golden words, "It's not your fault."
3. Find a good time to talk: Don't insist on talking immediately.
4. If your partner gives you a solution (and that's not what you want), say "That's a good idea, but I'm not sure what I'm feeling. What does it sound like I'm saying?"
5. Appreciate any understanding your partner shows: "That's right. That's just what I'm feeling!" or, "That's almost it."
6. Remember that listening has more to do with skill than with love: If your partner seems insincere, it may be because he or she is just learning how to show understanding.

DISTRESS BETWEEN PARTNERS

When you are upset with your partner, it may be even more difficult to gain the understanding you want. This is especially true if you have become stuck in the role of the critic and question whether your partner can do anything right. The more you disapprove, the less likely he or she is to cooperate and the more upset you feel. Although your disapproval may feel completely justified, strong opinions suggest that you are seeing a situation only from your point of view. There are steps you can take to feel better about your partner and to help him or her be more cooperative:

7. Make every effort to thoroughly understand behavior before you criticize it: Let your partner know you believe there is a good reason for what he or she did. Once you understand what happened, you may not object to it.
8. Appreciate the good intentions behind your partner's behavior: "I know you were trying to. . . ."
9. Point out good things about a mistake your partner made. Do not say, "I told you so." Remember to notice things your partner does that please you.
10. Encourage your partner to pay attention by saying, "There's something I'd like to say. Would you listen and tell me a better way to say it?"
11. Express your frustration in one brief statement that starts with "I": "I felt . . . when you. . . ." Do not blame, complain, or tell others what they should and shouldn't do.
12. Express the want behind your hurt with requests: "Would you . . . , . . . , or . . . ?" It helps to give choices. Do not threaten, order, or try to convince.
13. Identify (minimal) actions you can take when others do not meet your needs: Avoid extreme ideas such as divorce unless you are willing to act.
14. If your partner gets upset, say, "What you do is up to you. I only want you to consider my idea."
15. If it's a touchy subject, talk about it later, not while it's happening: "Remember when you . . . ?" "Would you . . . instead?"
16. Overlook unimportant mistakes: "Allow" people to do things their own way and trust them to eventually get it right. Give as little unsolicited advice as possible.

17. Act as if the change you want has already happened: "I've noticed that you listen to me more." "I appreciate the way you are starting to trust me."

EXPLOSIONS

Frustrated efforts to talk or general dissatisfaction can cause an explosion. Even nonemotional people can hold in feelings for so long that they become enraged and make statements that can do irreparable harm. You may think you are simply expressing your feelings, but explosions always come out as an attack full of blame, accusations, and threats, and they rarely express the underlying hurt or frustration causing the problem. Even if you think you have to get your feelings out, you can take steps to do this in constructive ways:[1]

18. Sort out your feelings before you go to your partner in anger: Write down how a situation makes you feel or talk to an objective friend. Writing or talking identifies and releases feelings, whereas thinking about a situation over and over simply intensifies emotion.
19. When you write, cover all four negative emotions: anger, sadness, fear/worry, regret/guilt. If you do not cover all these feelings, you may be avoiding dealing with some of your pain or unresolved hurt. Do not worry about how you sound in this part of your "letter." You can rewrite it later or not show it to anyone. It's just important to release what you are feeling.
20. Write down any caring, hope, appreciation, and understanding that you have for your partner after expressing negative emotions. After all, if you did not care for your partner, you would not feel so hurt.
21. Close your letter by describing the response you would like to hear: This can make you more open to receiving support and helps teach your partner how to be helpful.
22. Rewrite the first part of your letter (number 19) if it's full of blame, criticism, accusations, or threats. Express the hurt and fears that underlie your anger and make simple requests that would help resolve the problem.
23. Ask your partner if he or she is willing to listen to what you have written. Pick a time when there are no distractions.
24. To avoid defensive reactions, first show your partner the part of the letter that expresses your caring (number 20) or describes the type of response you want (number 21).
25. If your partner is too upset to listen, take the time to understand how the situation is difficult for him or her: Show you understand by rephrasing, labeling feelings, and validating factors that contribute to your partner's distress.
26. Write first! Later, bring up the issue with your partner when you can do so constructively.

---

[1] Strategies for letters to partners and other ideas in this handout are adapted from *Men Are from Mars, Women Are from Venus* by John Gray (HarperCollins, 1992).

TURNING CONTROL AND JEALOUSY INTO PASSION

When your partner tells you what you can and cannot do, it is easy to feel powerless and victimized. When adults take orders from their partners, they are reenacting childhood obedience and contributing to their own domination. Although partners may try to punish "defiance," they are not likely to do anything other than get angry or withdraw. The best way to break a vicious cycle of domination and submission is for compliant people to start doing what they need to do and allow their partners to be upset. The following steps show how to start taking charge of your life:

1. Show you understand your partner's objections to what you want to do by restating his or her point: "You don't want me to . . . because. . . ."
2. If you decide what you want to do is reasonable after making sure you understand your partner's objections, do it!
3. Do not argue with your partner and try to convince him or her that you have the right to do what you want to do.
4. Sympathize when your partner attempts to control you with moodiness or threats and realize that your attempts to change may be threatening. Your compassion will ease the relationship through the transition much better than endless reassurances or arguing.
5. Offer extra affection (without changing your plans) to help compensate your partner for his or her "loss of power."
6. Separate if your partner attempts to control you with physical violence.

UNFOUNDED JEALOUSY

Jealousy is often the cause of attempts to control. Women may become jealous when their partner notices other females. They need to understand that men are visually oriented and "cruise" women in the same way that they enjoy noticing flashy cars. Expecting a man to be blind to beauty in other women places a devastating demand on a relationship. Some men get jealous when their partner is not under their direct protection and they may project their own lustful urges onto their partner. However, men need to understand that women are capable of handling everyday encounters without falling prey to men or sexual urges. In actuality, the real cause of jealousy is always insecurity about attractiveness or control. When it is expressed in the form of accusations and orders, it can destroy a relationship. However, there are ways to turn jealousy into passion and tenderness:

7. Admit you are jealous before you even have a chance to conjure up accusations.
8. Express your jealousy with a statement that starts with "I": "I felt so insecure (worried, lost) when you. . . ." Do not interrogate or assume.
9. Make simple requests that will help relieve your feelings: "Would you give me a hug, call me when you're late, or include me in the conversation . . . ?"
10. Treat jealous accusations as though they were expressions of affection: "You really do love me, care about me. . . ."
11. Ask questions directed at insecurities causing jealousy: "What is it like for you when I . . . ?" Remember, unfounded jealousy has nothing to do with your faithfulness.
12. When you notice the opposite sex, do so appropriately, without gaping, and then give your partner a little extra attention.
13. When your partner says you cannot do something because of his or her unfounded jealousy, follow steps 1–6 for dealing with another person's attempts to control.

JUSTIFIED JEALOUSY

Justified jealousy is inevitable after learning that your partner has been unfaithful. You may think you cannot continue a relationship once trust has been violated. Actually, losing the illusion of complete trust is realistic. Taking some of the following steps can rebuild the openness, companionship, and confidence necessary to restore a relationship:[1]

14. Hurt partners can decide if the relationship is worth saving on the basis of having shared good times in the past and on the unfaithful partner's willingness to commit. Remember that people who are dishonest, unlawful, irresponsible, impulsive, reckless, aggressive, and violent often cannot remain faithful even with therapy!
15. Hurt partners need to set and stand by conditions for continuing the relationship suggested in points 16–23.
16. Unfaithful partners should admit to and start treatment for any sexual addiction that contributes to the problem. People who need sex to relax or feel loved, push their partners into unwanted sexual activity, or have sexual interests that become a substitute for contact with spouses may have sexual addictions.
17. Unfaithful partners should admit to and get help for any substance abuse that contributes to problems with commitment.
18. Unfaithful partners should agree to stop all contact with previous lovers: It may help to formally end any current affairs in the presence of one's partner.
19. Unfaithful partners should agree to or take initiative for getting an AIDS test.
20. Both partners should agree to set realistic boundaries for the relationship. For example, no contact with "friends" of the opposite sex outside of work without the other partner present.
21. Unfaithful partners should agree to have bank statements, phone bills, or email monitored for an indefinite period of time.
22. Unfaithful partners should agree to thoroughly discuss factors that contributed to infidelity and to participate in therapy to ensure that important issues are covered.
23. Unfaithful partners need to learn and demonstrate the use of active listening skills to help hurt partners express unresolved issues constructively.
24. Hurt partners need to keep communication lines open by focusing on current needs. Interrogations often have hidden agendas in which hurt partners make themselves feel more inadequate, insecure, or unsupported.
25. Hurt partners need to be responsible for healing their wounded egos by changing beliefs that they are inadequate or stupid for not having "prevented" the infidelity.
26. Hurt partners need to clearly identify caring behaviors their partners can do that would help them heal, and then should show appreciation for demonstrations of caring.
27. Hurt partners need to be willing to show caring behaviors to unfaithful partners that will help them recommit to the relationship. This may involve acting in caring ways even when feeling very resentful.
28. Both partners need to examine unrealistic beliefs about love, sex, and forgiveness.

---

[1] See *After the Affair* by Janis Abrahms Spring (Harper Perennial, 1997) for further elaboration of these ideas.

TURNING "GOOD-BYE" INTO "HELLO"

When people who have been frustrated for years announce that they are ending a relationship, it can prompt their partner to act in desperate ways. Partners may promise to change, beg for another chance, and try to convince spouses to stay. Although it may look as though people who are ardently pursuing have changed, they may actually be continuing a pattern of trying to control by discounting their spouse's desire to separate. It would be far more out of character, and therefore more meaningful, if they were to:[1]

- Show understanding of their partner's reasons for wanting to leave.
- Encourage their partner to take all the time needed to make a decision.
- Seek help to make needed changes in themselves, regardless of their partner's plans.

Relationship crises can become opportunities to change destructive interaction patterns by taking some of the following steps:

1. Give your partner enough distance to experience some feelings of loss and think about the real consequences of leaving. Attempts to convince him or her to stay will put the focus on the struggle with you rather than on what it means to be without you.
2. Surprise your partner by agreeing that a decision to separate may be a good thing. It may take some time or even remarriage after a divorce for each person to make needed changes. The less pressure your partner feels, the better your chances.
3. Spend time together on dates if your partner is willing: Use dates for enjoyable activities, not to discuss your relationship or to talk him or her into taking you back.
4. Learn to enjoy yourself without your partner: Do things with people who can give you support or find fulfilling activities. In healthy relationships, people do not count on their partner to make them happy. Instead, they find happiness on their own and share it with their partner as a gift.
5. Do not use your children as an excuse to be with your partner or to spy. Remember, this is time that should be devoted to building your relationship with them.
6. Make casual conversation: Tell your partner what is new in your life, and find out what is going well with him or her.
7. Do not ask your partner what he or she is feeling: Your partner may be genuinely confused and not be able to give an answer. If he or she is starting to enjoy being with you, you will know without asking.
8. Do not repeatedly tell your partner how much you love him or her: This may only add pressure to have emotions he or she does not feel yet. Likewise, do not be overly romantic or giving. Allow your partner room to take the initiative.
9. Do not talk to your partner if you are depressed or argumentative: This will greatly lessen any chances you have of reuniting.
10. Do not bargain: "I'll change if you do too." If you decide to make changes, do it for yourself! Later, you can address what you want from your partner as a separate issue.
11. Take a good look at yourself before discussing your relationship: In what way did your partner find you difficult? If you don't know, it may be because you disputed past comments. If your partner's objections don't make sense, talk to people who can help you understand. Be careful not to blame jobs, family, or friends for your problems.

---

[1] See *Divorce Busting* by Michele Weiner-Davis (Simon & Schuster, 1992) for additional ideas.

12. Admit any mistakes you made or problems you have: Let your partner know your plan for getting help and express gratitude for being pushed to take a long overdue look at yourself.
13. Do not promise to be different: First, see if you really can be different or if you like the changes your partner wants you to make. Being separated is a perfect opportunity to practice being less critical, angry, controlling, and demanding. Eventually, your partner will see changes even if you aren't living together.
14. Starting over means starting over: Take time to build your relationship slowly, without pushing.
15. You may have irreconcilable differences and be better off apart: If, after careful consideration, you do not agree with the changes your partner wants you to make and he or she is still dissatisfied, it is time to end the relationship.
16. If the end is final, go on with your life: Relationships are not about whom you love, but about loving someone well. You can learn from past mistakes.

WHEN YOU ARE THINKING OF LEAVING

Deciding whether or not to end a relationship is just as hard as being left. Although you may be very dissatisfied or wonder if you have any love left, you may be reluctant to really make a break. Tormenting yourself over whether or not to continue the relationship may interfere with looking at the changes you need to make in yourself. Don't count on a new partner to take away any underlying insecurity you might have. Before making the final decision to stay or leave, consider the following:

1. Do not expect yourself to feel love for your partner when you are feeling resentful. These two emotions are almost incompatible.
2. Imagine yourself living with your partner on even days and living apart on odd days: Do not let anyone pressure you into a decision.
3. Discover how you allow yourself to be a victim by talking to friends or a therapist. You will not stop feeling resentful until you stop giving up your power.
4. Identify one change you are going to make in yourself: Make this change consistently until you sense that you are no longer acting like a victim.
5. Make a final decision after making changes in yourself: This will give you a much better sense of what you need to do.
6. If there are problems with physical or substance abuse, a separation may be needed to save the marriage. Often, people stay in such relationships until they have no love left. It is better to recognize problems early and insist on living separately until the other person has sought help. Promises to get help should be ignored until the person takes action and makes significant changes.

DISSOLVING SEXUAL DIFFERENCES

One of the most common conflicts in relationships is over sex. The more demanding one person becomes, the less the other wants to give. Often, if the sexually inhibited partner switches roles, the other person backs off. When children enter a relationship, the energy one or both partners have for sex can also be dramatically reduced. Gender differences in sexual needs and arousal patterns almost seem to be nature's recipe for disaster. However, these differences can become assets that actually create a more passionate, fulfilling sex life.[1]

TO HELP THE WOMAN BE MORE SEXUALLY RECEPTIVE

1. "Foreplay" starts hours before sex. Go on a walk, go out to dinner, take her shopping, help her with domestic chores, and listen to her feelings and thoughts.
2. Go to bed 20 minutes before the woman is at the point of exhaustion. You can turn the TV or computer back on after lovemaking if you're not ready to fall asleep.
3. Do not expect a woman to want sex. She may not be aware of any sexual needs until she is excited through stimulation. Because she does not have to perform, she does not even need to be aroused to enjoy the benefits of sex (good bedtime exercise, a better night's sleep, increased estrogen levels, and possibly a longer life).
4. Do not ask a woman if she wants sex. Help her get in the mood by building a fire, lighting candles, bringing chocolate to bed, talking, cuddling, or massaging. If she doesn't respond, leave her alone!
5. Do not exceed your partner's limits for the amount of sex she can handle. Discuss the days and frequency that are best for her (at other times than during lovemaking).
6. Focus on what you have in your sex life, not on what is missing. Pressuring your partner to do things that make her uncomfortable can kill all interest. It is fine to occasionally ask if she has changed her mind, as long as she has absolute freedom to reject your idea.
7. Masturbation can help even out sex drives. When done while being held by one's partner, it adds intimacy to a relationship. When done in privacy, it may create compulsions and erode relationships.

TO REKINDLE A MAN'S SEXUAL DESIRES

1. Use indirect "mating signals" to reduce performance pressure or feelings of rejection—wear perfume, lingerie, jewelry, get into bed naked, light a candle.
2. Assure your partner that he does not have to perform when you need a sexual release. Ask if he is willing to hold you while you masturbate. He may get turned on by the time you are ready to climax and join in, or he can enjoy your pleasure vicariously.
3. Do not berate a man for being aroused by sexual stimuli in his environment. Encourage him to direct that arousal toward you by making sexual touches when he is turned on by his surroundings.
4. If your partner wants something "distasteful," keep an open mind. Say, "That's too big a stretch for me now, but I'll consider it." Meet him halfway on sexy lingerie and so on.
5. Reassure your partner that you love sex with him and that you will want it later if you are too exhausted for any contact at that time. When possible, ask for a quickie or offer to help your partner masturbate rather than making a total rejection.

---

[1] Strategies in this handout are adapted from *Mars and Venus in the Bedroom* by John Gray (Harper Perennial, 1997).

TO ENHANCE SEXUAL AROUSAL AND SATISFACTION FOR BOTH PARTNERS

1. Take turns! The first few moments of lovemaking can be spent stimulating a man's penis to heighten his sexual energies. He can then focus on pleasuring his partner for the next 20 or more minutes.
2. Use foreplay to give a woman the opportunity to have her orgasm first. Use a teasing approach—start with her least erogenous zone. However, there may be times of the month when a woman is not capable of having an orgasm due to hormone ratios.
3. A man can penetrate when a woman signals she is about to climax or even afterwards. This reduces pressure on a man to maintain his erection without depriving his partner of any pleasure. Although many women enjoy the sensations of penetration, most need other stimulation to have an orgasm.
4. A man can build control by focusing on pleasuring his partner. He may even tell her she doesn't have to do anything. During intercourse, he can focus on stimulating her, lie quietly inside her, or briefly withdraw. If he comes too soon, he can help his partner or hold her while she masturbates.
5. If a man's erection goes away, it will usually come back if he pretends things are fine and focuses on his partner's pleasure. This reduces dependency on his erection. The worst mistake is to focus on getting the man's erection back.
6. A man or woman may increase the intensity of an orgasm by backing off when close to a climax and building up again. Women who are multiorgasmic may find that one big orgasm is more satisfying than several.
7. Both men and women need a balanced diet of quickies and longer sexual delights. Negotiate quickies for cuddles, romantic evenings, or back rubs. Intercourse that regularly lasts longer than 30 minutes can make one or both partners sore and gives some women infections and leg cramps. After the initial endorphin high of courtship has worn off, use hour-long lovemaking sessions sparingly.
8. Faking sexual responses can help a woman focus on her arousal and give her partner nonverbal feedback about what is turning her on. However, a woman should not fake orgasms and can tell her partner when it is not a good time for her to have one (see number 2).
9. Discuss turn-ons when sex is not an option to decrease the chance of feeling criticized during lovemaking. Read sex manuals together and discuss interesting ideas. Focus on turn-ons rather than turn-offs: "I really like it when you . . ."
10. When more variety is desired, develop several different routines. This eventually helps build spontaneity during lovemaking.
11. Do not try to coordinate simultaneous orgasms. This can interfere with enjoyment and prevents you from giving your partner support during his or her orgasm.
12. Do not use sex to reassure yourself that your partner loves you! That can upset delicate patterns of sexual desire and lead to compulsions. Ask for hugs and cuddles instead. However, at times "sexual healing" can help a man overlook petty annoyances, melt his anger, and may be worth the improvement in his mood.
13. Use your sexual longings to arouse your partner by writing what you are feeling, buying a card, or quoting from the *Songs of Songs*. Share your "sex note" hours before any relations so arousal can build in a nonpressured way. Long-distance sexual phone calls can keep romantic energy in the relationship when partners are apart.

RESTORING ROMANCE

In the beginning of a relationship, both partners are leading separate lives and have much to share with each other. Over time, couples often give up independent activities. They may let go of friends and interests and start "living for" the other. When people don't have some time apart, a marriage loses its mystery. The opposite can also occur: both people may go separate ways, and when things are bad, their differences become glaring. In addition to the natural forces that can dull relationships, resentments will choke the very life out of anything that is left. But love does not have to die. There are many things couples can do to rekindle fading embers:[1]

1. Heal the resentments that are choking your relationship. Take action to reclaim your power and repeatedly sympathize with any distress your partner feels as a result. When you can't resolve conflicts on your own, find help!
2. Get a life. Be sure to have interests or hobbies separate from your partner. Make yourself happy and share what you've been doing. Ask yourself, "What would I do if I didn't spend so much time worrying about my partner?"
3. Make separate lists of fun and exciting activities each person would like to do with the other. This can include simple activities such as showering together, massage, walks, or dancing. Do one activity a week, even if you are feeling "lazy."
4. Make separate "caring lists" of things your partner does or used to do that make you feel loved. Add any behaviors that you've always wanted but have never had, such as cards, flowers, little presents, hugs, opening car doors, compliments, holding hands, nonsexual touches, and good-bye kisses. Romantic gestures are particularly important for helping caregivers find relief from constantly attending to others. The resulting improvement in mood will make romance well worth the effort.
5. Perform caring behaviors regularly. They are gifts. Give them in spite of how you feel about your partner and regardless of the caring that is being shown to you.
6. Train your partner to be romantic by showing appreciation of caring and by giving gentle reminders: "Don't forget my kiss good-bye." "You don't know what a relief it was going out tonight." Even if you have to ask for it, a caring behavior counts. The best way to love someone is to help him or her to be successful in loving you.
7. Go on weekend getaways to make romantic connections without distractions. Just planning and looking forward to an event can reenergize relationships.
8. Make changes that will give your union the balance it needs. Decide if you need more separation (number 2) or more togetherness (numbers 3–7).
9. Find a cause that interests you separately or as a couple. Extending the energy in your relationship beyond yourselves creates "soul mates." Political groups, charities, and religious organizations offer "transcendent" opportunities.
10. Don't compare your relationship to movies and dime store romances. Mature love is more about being comfortable with and enjoying someone than about an all-consuming obsession. Relationships need some common ground, but not a lot. You may have more to share than you realize.

---

[1] Several of these strategies are adapted from *Getting the Love You Want* by Harville Hendrix (Henry Holt, 1988).

BELIEFS THAT HELP RELATIONSHIPS

Often, problems that surface in relationships are indications of underlying self-destructive beliefs. If you have difficulty making changes that could help your marriage, it may be because of such ideas. These thoughts are not actually caused by your partner, but were instilled in you from early life experiences. To discover thoughts you have that cause relationship glitches, ask yourself:[1]

- When my partner's behavior disturbs me, what does that mean about me?
- How do my partner's upsetting actions make me feel about myself?
- When did I first have this disturbing thought(s) about myself?

Directions: Mark any of the thoughts in the table below that come to you during relationship problems. Then, mark any of the beliefs you would like to have when your partner upsets you.

Change Thoughts That Hurt into ...	**Beliefs That Help Relationships**
1. I have trouble asking my partner for help or expressing myself because I think: ___ I have to fix everything and keep others happy, or I'm a failure. ___ I'm not important. ___ I cannot get my needs met. ___ I can't show emotions or express feelings.	I can ask for help or express myself when I believe: ___ I can understand others without having to fix them or keep them happy. ___ I am important. ___ I can get my needs met. ___ I can show emotions, express my feelings, etc.
2. I have trouble handling my partner when he or she is upset because I think: ___ I'm trapped, helpless, or powerless. ___ I have to get my way or I lose. ___ I'm responsible for others' distress.	I can handle my partner's distress when I think: ___ I have options and choices; I can do something. ___ I can do things to reach a satisfying solution. ___ I decide when I contribute to others' distress.
3. I have trouble when my partner wants distance or a separation because I think: ___ I'm alone or empty. No one is there for me. ___ I can't survive if I'm "abandoned." ___ There is only one right person for me.	I can handle my partner's desire for distance or a separation when I believe: ___ I can find many sources of support. ___ I can enjoy myself without my partner. ___ I can love more than one person in a lifetime.
4. I have trouble with jealousy and control because I think: ___ I'm stupid or foolish if I'm deceived. ___ I can't trust anyone. ___ Other:	I do not have difficulty with jealousy when I believe: ___ Deception is caused by my partner's dishonesty. ___ I can take appropriate action when I'm deceived. ___ I can find people to trust.

When your relationship is going well, the above desired beliefs may seem completely true. It will be harder to maintain them during conflicts of interest or when your needs are not being met. Affirming new thought patterns regularly will help you adopt positive beliefs that can overcome your resistance to change and put you and your partner on the fast track to relationship success.

---

[1] See *EMDR: The Breakthrough Therapy* by Francine Shapiro (Basic Books, 1997) and *A Guide to Rational Living* by Ellis (Wilshire Books, 1997) for further ideas on how thoughts affect emotions.

DISORDERS THAT AFFECT RELATIONSHIPS

Not all relationship problems result from unhealthy patterns of interaction. Sometimes, one person has a disorder that has a direct impact on his or her partner. The better a spouse is able to recognize such disorders, the less chance there is of intensifying them. Mark any of the problems described below that may be affecting your relationship.

DISORDERS

__ **Chemical dependency** is one of the most common problems affecting relationships. It often goes unrecognized because the substance abuser is still able to work and is competent in many ways. Spouses who have been accused of being too tense or unreasonable often think they are overreacting. The truth is that whenever someone else's use of drugs or alcohol is a problem for you, it is time to get help! Self-help groups such as AL-ANON and NAR-ANON address many of the problems non-using spouses face. Telephone listings for these organizations are found in most community phone books.

__ **Sexual compulsions** are another kind of addiction that have a tremendous impact on relationships. Normal differences in sex drive and interest can usually be worked out through empathy and good communication; but, when one person has a sexual compulsion, he or she can make demands or show interests outside the home that have a devastating impact on the relationship. Learn to recognize the signs of sexual addiction:

- A person feels compelled to have sex repeatedly within a short time period.
- Sexual activity becomes the only or main way a person has to relax or feel loved.
- Sexual interests cause a person to feel empty or remorseful afterward.
- Pursuit of sex interferes with family life, friendships, work, or school.
- Partners are pushed to engage in unwanted sexual activity.
- Contact with one's spouse is replaced by such sexual activities as masturbation, pornography, chat rooms, massage parlors, telephone sex, or affairs.

Realizing that your partner's sexual preoccupations have little to do with how much he or she loves you can free you from feeling unloved or inadequate. Take a firm but sympathetic approach by standing up for what is right for you sexually and setting limits on what you will not tolerate.

__ **Sexual dysfunctions** such as premature ejaculation, impotence, sexual aversion, underactive interest, underarousal, and inhibited orgasm can also cause relationship problems. Usually, these conditions are more easily recognized than sexual compulsions and there is less confusion about who needs help. If your partner has such a problem, it is important to realize that it is not a reflection of your attractiveness and that you cannot solve it by badgering him or her to be more sexual. If you are unable to resolve sexual differences on your own, persistently request that you and your partner seek help.

__ **Obsessions and compulsions** that are nonsexual also affect relationships. When a person is overconcerned with safety, tidiness, germs, and order, the whole household can be affected. Feeling as though you can never meet your partner's standards may be an indicator that an obsession is operating. Seek help to distinguish between obsessions and standards that fall within the normal range. Let your partner know that compulsions can be treated with medication and therapy. Even if your partner won't get help, recognizing obsessions for what they are will relieve you of the pressure of trying to satisfy them.

__ **Depression and moodiness** may go undetected in their milder forms. Your partner may be tired, withdrawn, unmotivated, and have little sexual desire. You may feel rejected or frustrated with this lack of initiative. At other times, your partner may show increased interest in sex, spending money, traveling, business ventures, new projects, religion, or talking, and cause you real concerns about his or her poor judgment. It is important to know that mood disorders are biochemical in nature and are very treatable. Assure your partner that feelings of hopelessness or (unrealistic) fears of losing "high energy" are part of the disorder and encourage him or her to seek help. Recognizing mood disorders for what they are will help you have more realistic expectations and develop your own sources of support for periods when your partner has little to offer.

__ **Attention deficit (ADD) and hyperactive disorders (ADHD)** are often missed in adults. One partner's forgetfulness, disorganization, distractibility, impulsiveness, moodiness, restlessness, and temper may cause the other to become increasingly critical. The person with ADD withdraws, criticism mounts, and the added stress increases symptoms. Often, spontaneous ADD people and organized perfectionists are drawn to each other because they seek what they lack in themselves. This can greatly compound problems.

__ **Personality disorders** can significantly impair relationships and employment. People with this problem have a self-image that is dependent on the actions of others. They scrutinize their partner to find out if they are loveable, good enough, or safe. Their ability to look inside themselves for the cause of distress is limited, and they avoid painful emotions with anger, blame, distancing, fantasy, or addictions. In a no-win fashion, they vacillate between feeling abandoned or suffocated, thinking they're superior or worthless, and fearing intimacy or isolation. Two personality disorders are especially toxic to relationships:

1. **Erratic personalities** seem to have stormy relationships with everyone. They may be unpredictable, engage in self-destructive behavior, act impulsively, avoid being alone, change moods wildly in just a few hours, and think in extremes (good/bad, black/white). At the same time, their passion and intensity can (initially) make them enticing. If your spouse has such a problem, it helps to avoid the extremes of withdrawing from or trying to control him or her. Over time, he or she may become more moderate. Long-term therapy and medication can help these people achieve more stability.
2. **Defiant personalities** have so little empathy for others and knowledge of right and wrong that fulfilling relationships (and therapy) are impossible. They may relate to others only to get sex, money, or power and be irresponsible, unlawful, violent, aggressive, impulsive, dishonest, reckless, or unfaithful. The more pronounced these traits are, the less hope there is of change. Because they know how to charm and con people, it may be difficult to face how destructive a relationship with them can be. The spouses of such people need to face their own addiction to control or "save" their partner.

GENDER GAP FACTS

Gender Gap Facts Checklist
Directions: Discuss each of the following generalizations about men and women with your partner to find out if any apply to your relationship:
• Men are goal-oriented and depend on achievements for self-esteem. ° Women are relationship oriented and can overcome fears of being unlovable by doing for others. Self-esteem often depends on being involved with someone.
• Men value success, autonomy, independence, efficiency, and competence. ° Women value sharing, nurturing, supporting others, and being considerate.
• Men need acceptance, admiration, appreciation, encouragement, and faith in their ability. ° Women need understanding, interest, concern, reassurance, devotion, loyalty, commitment, and respect for their ideas and feeling.
• Men want the right to be free and often withdraw after periods of closeness to meet needs for autonomy. They may fear becoming dependent or need time alone to take a break from feeling responsible. Even irresponsible men rebel against an inner pull to take care of everything. Irritability or withdrawal is a sign that a man needs his "space." ° Women want the right to be upset and need to release emotions to be loving. They get depleted from giving, "hit bottom", and go all the way into the depths of their feelings before they can "come up." A women may reexperience hopelessness, insecurity, and resentment over and over until she gets the understanding she needs. Talking in absolutes ("We never . . ." "You always . . .") is a sign that a woman has hit bottom.
• Men release tension through activity: watching TV, driving, sports, or exercise. They become "entranced" with activity and use it to cleanse their minds of troubling thoughts. ° Women release tension through talking and crying. They talk to understand what upsets them and then they let it go. They cleanse their minds through releasing emotion.
• Men need to withdraw to think about what is bothering them, or they put their difficulties aside with activity (see above). Feelings are not part of a man's problem-solving style so he is likely to tell a woman, "You shouldn't feel that way." ° Women seek a sounding board to process feelings that are flooding them. Solutions can interfere with emotional discharge but come automatically after releasing feelings.
• Men favor getting help as a last resort and talk about problems to find solutions or to place blame. Their pet peeve is being offered unsolicited advice. ° Women seek help at the first sign of or before a problem occurs to make sure they are on the right track. Their pet peeve is being given solutions instead of understanding.
• Men often ignore others' problems unless they have been asked for help. In their world, it's rude to offer help without being asked because that would imply the other person was incompetent. When a woman talks to a man about her problems, he assumes he is being asked for advice or that he is being blamed, so he will offer solutions or defend himself. ° Women monitor others' problems to see if they are okay, offer help without being asked, and worry about how others are doing.

Gender Gap Facts

• Men give what they think is fair and assume women will do the same. They give only when asked and focus on big things such as paying rent or buying a car rather than little things like compliments or hugs. Even if a man is aware that a woman is in need, he may not know what to do unless he is told and avoid giving because it might not be "good enough." Men need women to train them how to give and to appreciate any evidence of change.

° Women give freely without being asked and assume that men will do the same.

• Men are comfortable saying "No" because they give only what they think is fair. The more freedom a man has to say "No," the more likely he is to say "Yes." Men assume that when a woman says "Yes" or agrees to do something, she wants to do it.

° Women can have difficulty saying "No." They may say "Yes" even when something is difficult and give up their preferences to accommodate others. When women do say "No," they may feel inclined to justify themselves with long lists of reasons.

• Men can ask for what they want and have many models of being served. Because some men feel entitled, they tend to give orders instead of asking. Men assume a woman's needs are being met unless she asks for what she wants.

° Women can have difficulty asking for what they want because of their training as caregivers. They may justify their needs and ask for things in indirect ways—"This needs to be done . . ." "Could you . . .?" Women often assume that if a man loves her, he will know what she wants without being told.

• Men can be resistant to therapy or making changes in themselves when they think they aren't being accepted as they are. Their motto is: If it's not broken, don't fix it!

° Women frequently look for ways to improve themselves and enjoy having "makeovers." Their motto is: Even if something works well, it can always be improved.

• Men are inspired to be loving when they feel needed. To be loving, men must overcome their desire for self-gratification.

° Women are motivated to be loving when they feel nurtured. To feel cared about, they must overcome their "need" to take care of others. Women are afraid to stop giving because they might not "have enough to offer."

• Men flee (withdraw) or fight (blame, criticize, yell). They typically start fights by invalidating a woman's feelings—"It's not important . . . Don't worry." When hurt, a man may hold things against a woman, give her "penalty points," punish her, or get even.

° Women fold (give in) or fake it (pretend they're not upset until they're overwhelmed). They start fights with questions—"How could you . . . ? Why do you always . . . ? "They interrogate with a negative tone of voice although they're actually trying to teach.

• Men can be more comfortable with aggression than with sadness, hurt, fear, or guilt.

° Women can get stuck feeling hurt to avoid being mad. Resentments build up from suppressing anger.

These "facts" are adapted from *Men Are from Mars, Women Are from Venus* by John Gray (HarperCollins, 1992).

FACTS YOU MAY NOT KNOW ABOUT SEX

Sex Facts Checklist
Directions: Discuss each of the following generalizations about male/female sexuality with your partner to find out if any are accurate to your relationship:
Sexual Drives, Desires, and Rejection
• Men need sex to feel connected. ° Women need to feel connected (through talking, romance, or affection) to want sex.
• Men are usually aware of sexual urges prior to sexual contact. ° Women often are not aware of feeling aroused until they are sexually stimulated.
• Tension and stress can trigger a man's arousal system and aid performance. ° Women need to relax and open up to enjoy sex. Stress and constantly caring for others can inhibit sexual responsiveness.
• Unusual ideas or waking a man up to have sex can excite him because of the above. ° Pressuring a woman to try "unusual" activities or waking her up to have sex can kill her desire.
• Sexual rejection will feel doubly painful when a man is aroused. After too much rejection, a man may lose his sexual desires. ° A woman needs to feel safe to say "No" to sex, or she may lose her desire to say "Yes."
• When women initiate sex regularly, men can feel worse about themselves (due to performance pressure) and eventually lose all interest. A man needs clear messages that his partner loves sex with him (without feeling pressure to perform) to maintain interest. ° Women may appreciate a man regularly initiating sex as long as he can read her "signals" when she is too exhausted or tense and be willing to settle for hugs and cuddles.
• Expressing confidence in a man's sexual expertise can arouse him. ° When a man appears confident in his sexual expertise, a woman may feel aroused.
• Sexual discussions can turn a man off if he isn't in the mood. ° Talking about a woman's feelings without pressure to have sex can help her mood.
Arousals and Orgasms
• A man first needs direct stimulation of his penis to "wake up" other erogenous zones (testicles, perineum, or other areas.) ° A woman may first need her least erogenous zones (feet, thighs, etc.) caressed for her to be comfortable having her breasts, nipples, or clitoris stimulated.
• Men need a direct approach for an orgasm, which can take five minutes or less. ° Women need an indirect, teasing approach (moving toward and away from erogenous zones), which can take 20 minutes or more.
• Men are usually consistently capable of orgasms due to steady levels of testosterone. ° Women are not always capable of having orgasms or enjoying certain types of touch due to constantly changing ratios of estrogen, progesterone, and testosterone.

Facts You May Not Know about Sex

• Men may be more likely to have one routine sexual approach due to consistent hormonal levels. o Women may need different types or amounts of stimulation because of varying hormone levels.
• Men need orgasms to be satisfied because sexual pleasure comes from releasing tension. o Women can be satisfied with closeness without having an orgasm because they enjoy the building of tension and like the intimacy that comes with penetration.
• Men need occasional quickies to maintain sexual interest and have the patience to regularly focus on their partner's needs. o Women need quickies for times when they are not capable of having orgasms or when they are too exhausted for longer lovemaking.
• Arousal enhances a man's visual appreciation of his partner's body. o Insecurities about appearance unnecessarily inhibit a woman's sexual desires.
• When a women responds with sexual sounds, men feel validated and aroused. o When a man makes love verbally ("I love your . . ." "You're so . . .") women are often aroused because they feel a sense of connection and are reassured about their bodies.
• A man can be pushed out of control or turned off if a woman takes charge and tries too hard. A woman's sexual responses will arouse a man and help him last longer. o A woman's orgasms will be inhibited either by pressuring her to or by not giving her opportunities to have a climax. If sex regularly lasts too long, passion can die for both sexes.
• After his orgasm a man's desire disappears. o After her orgasm, a woman can enjoy penetration. It will not matter to her how long her partner's erection lasts if he gives her the opportunity to have an orgasm first.

These "facts" are adapted from *Men Are from Mars, Women Are from Venus* by John Gray (HarperCollins, 1992)

YIN/YANG QUESTIONNAIRE

Oriental wisdom suggests that all matter is made of yang (masculine) and yin (feminine) qualities. People need to learn to balance their masculine and feminine characteristics because when these two opposing forces are not in harmony, discord results. In some circles, the *vital* yang approach has become politically incorrect and individuals may try to deny it within themselves. However, awareness of and ability to use both yin and yang qualities must be fostered to achieve full maturity.

Yin	Yang
Feminine Energy	Masculine Energy
Passive, responds	Active, initiates
Diffuse awareness	Focused concentration
Dark, wet, mysterious	Bright, dry, warm
Desire to merge, unite	Desire to penetrate and explore
Forms selective attachments	Incapable of commitment
Protects, nourishes, breeds	Fertilizes, creates
Restrains as it embraces	Explosive, daring, independent
Preserves beauty and integrity of others	Delighted with its own power, and is unaware of limitations
Pure form: nothing moves, lacks all initiative	Pure form: rapes and plunders everything in its path

Directions: To discover if your approach is primarily yin, yang, or both, mark the side of the chart that best describes the way you operate or view life. Mark both sides of the chart for any items in which either approach is comfortable for you. Total the number of items you mark in each column. Discuss ratings with your partner to enhance the validity of the scores and to increase awareness of changes you could make to better balance yin and yang qualities in yourself.

Yin Approach	Yang Approach
__ Accepts differences.	__ Judges superior and inferior, right and wrong
__ Looks at all the angles.	__ Focuses on relevant data
__ Uses creative and diffuse thinking style.	__ Uses direct and logical thinking style.
__ Finds that logic balances and connects ideas.	__ Uses logic as a tool to explain and convince.
__ Relies on intuition.	__ Relies on senses.
__ Waits for decisions to come.	__ Makes decisions and is decisive.
__ Learns through observation and experience.	__ Learns through exploration & taking things apart.
__ Values process over product.	__ Values success and production
__ Seeks meaning.	__ Seeks accomplishments.
__ Values unseen accomplishments like touching a life.	__ Values tangible accomplishments like production and promotions.
__ Sees death as a part of life.	__ Believes accomplishments survive one's death.
__ Is people-oriented.	__ Is task-oriented
__ Puts others' needs first.	__ Puts own needs first.
__ Places relationships before goals.	__ Places goals before relationships.
__ Believes relationships bring new opportunities.	__ Believes relationships require sacrifice.
__ Experiences love as an energy flow.	__ Experiences love as an exchange of gifts.
__ Communicates to connect.	__ Communicates to exchange ideas.
__ Connects through sharing thoughts and feelings.	__ Connects through sharing activities.

Yin Approach (continued)	Yang Approach
__ Negotiates to appease.	__ Negotiates to win.
__ Seeks consensus in groups.	__ Seeks majority rule.
__ Sees power as strength, flexibility, and self-control	__ Sees power as command, control, and influence.
__ Strives to change self.	__ Tries to change others.
__ Finds rank, order, and position unimportant.	__ Respects rank, order and position.
__ Sees responsibility as the ability to respond.	__ Sees responsibility as accountability.
Believes:	**Believes**:
__ Good leaders delegate power & facilitate others.	__ Good leaders are a source of strength & authority.
__ Healers facilitate the natural healing process.	__ Healers identify problems & prescribe remedies.
__ Rules serve the needs of the individual and can be interpreted on a case-by-case basis.	__ Rules serve the needs of society and should be followed to the letter of the law.
__ Each person must discover what is right or moral for him or herself.	__ There are fixed standards of right and wrong towards which everyone should strive.
__ Time is "organic" and adjusts to individual needs and schedules.	__ Time is "fixed" and personal schedules should be adjusted for punctuality.
__ Natural resources, plants and animals require attention and protection.	__ Natural resources, plants and animals exist to serve human needs.
__ Science promotes understanding of and living in harmony with the universe.	__ Science enables better control of the Universe.
__ Maturity is achieved by integrating Yin/yang energies.	__ Maturity is measured by successes, accomplishments and respect from others.
__ **Total Yin Score**	__ **Total Yang Score**

The "White Male System" and the "Female System" described in *Woman's Reality* by Anne Schaef (Minnesota: Winston Press, 1981) were used in creating this chart.

RELATIONSHIP WORKSHEET

1. What qualities first drew me to my partner?

2. What troubling qualities does my partner have that are similar to my early caretakers?

3. What qualities does my partner have that I think I lack?

4. What needs am I (unsuccessfully) trying to meet through my relationship:

   ____ Understanding
   ____ Appreciation
   ____ Approval
   ____ Freedom
   ____ Other:

5. Which of the above needs did my early caretakers have difficulty meeting?

6. What opposite roles do my partner and I currently take (teacher/student, rigid/impulsive…)?

7. What action would I need to take to change conflicting roles in my relationship?

8. What facts about gender differences help me better understand my partner?

9. What changes would I need to make to better balance Yin/Yang qualities in myself?

10. What defend-withdraw-attack reactions do I use when communicating with my partner?

11. Which understand-express-defuse responses am I willing to start using regularly?

12. What am I currently doing to "fix" or tolerate relationship problems that is no longer working:

    ____ Nagging
    ____ Begging
    ____ Pleasing
    ____ Criticizing
    ____ Ignoring
    ____ Disagreeing
    ____ Other:

13. What could I do that would be the opposite or different from the above?

14. What things do (did) I do when my relationship is (was) going well that I no longer do?

15. What would my partner say I need to change for my relationship to improve?

16. What could I do to change *how, where*, and *when* a problem happens or *who* handles it?

17. What *action* could I take when attempts to solve a problem through talking are not working?

18. For which problems do I need strategies?

    ____ Selfishness
    ____ Distancing
    ____ Jealousy and control
    ____ Lack of romance
    ____ Sexual problems and differences
    ____ Handling my partner's upsets
    ____ Helping my partner handle my upsets
    ____ Preventing or making the best out of separations

19. What strategies am I willing to start using today?

    a.

    b.

    c.

20. What strategies would my partner most like me to use?

    a.

    b.

    c.

21. Does my relationship need more/less distance to add passion and romance?

22. If we have too much togetherness, what can I do to meet my own needs?

23. If there is too much distance, what fun, exciting, meaningful activities would I be willing to ask or arrange for my partner and I to do?

24. What caring behaviors would I be willing to ask for from my partner:

    ____ Hugs
    ____ Messages
    ____ Flowers
    ____ Cards
    ____ Other:

25. What things am I willing to do that would pleasantly surprise my partner?

26. What negative beliefs do I get about myself when my partner's behavior disturbs me? What early life experiences first gave me those beliefs?

27. What positive beliefs would I like to adopt about myself instead?

28. What disorders do my partner or I have that could make progress difficult without help?

Chapter 4

Powerful Parenting

POWERFUL PARENTING

OBJECTIVES FOR TREATMENT PLANNING

1. Describe actions that have increased cooperation, obedience, or responsibility.
2. Describe responses that have reduced anger, bad attitudes, and resistance.
3. Demonstrate skills during sessions that increase compliance and reduce anger.
4. Improve scores on the *Child-Rearing Skills* inventory by 10 points.
5. Report that beliefs necessary to improve parenting skills are valid.
6. Reach agreement on *Child-Rearing Beliefs* with fellow caretakers.

MINI INDEX TO CHAPTER 4

USING THE HANDOUTS

- Assessment tools: *Child-Rearing Skills, Child-Rearing Beliefs.*
- Literature on parenting methods: *Incentives That Require Cooperation, Actions That Encourage Obedience, Responses That Reduce Anger,* and *Limiting Power.*
- Review sheets of behavior strategies: *Attitudes and Back-Talk, Daily Routines and Habits, School-Related Problems, Extreme Measures for Extreme Behavior, Moral Matters, Dependent Adult Children, Disagreeable Distant Adult Children.*
- Visual aid that helps parents understand skills at a glance: *Behavior Contract, Be-Nice-to-Others Worksheet.*

- Preparation for processing destructive beliefs: *Beliefs That Empower Parents.*
- Exercises to promote discussion: *Limiting Power, Child-Rearing Beliefs.*
- Workshops and presentations: *Child-Rearing Beliefs* can be used to introduce and discuss powerful parenting strategies. *Limiting Power—Seven Value-Clarifying Processes* can be used to practice clarifying children's values in role plays. *Directives That Defy Resistance* can be used in small groups to brainstorm 12 ways to "hypnotically" suggest desirable behavior.

CAUTIONS AND RECOMMENDATIONS

- *Extreme Measures for Extreme Behavior* is *only* for parents who are committed to remaining in treatment and are not at risk for abusing children.
- Supplement *Responses That Reduce Anger* with *The Art of Understanding* (3.1), and *The Dance of Deflection* (3.7).
- Use the *Behavior Contract* to support parental authority for situations in which clients fear recrimination from family members or authorities for being firm.
- Attach a copy of *Extreme Measures for Extreme Behaviors* when restraining methods have been recommended.

SOURCES AND ACKNOWLEDGMENTS

- Behavioral approaches are found in *Incentives That Require Cooperation, Actions That Encourage Obedience, Daily Routines and Habits, School-Related Problems,* and *Moral Matters.* These handouts contain ideas similar to those in *Children: The Challenge* by Roudolf Dreikurs (NAL Dutton, 1993) and *Back in Control* by Gregory Bodenhamer (Simon & Schuster, 1984).
- Communication approaches are found in *Responses That Reduce Anger* and *Attitudes and Back-Talk.* They contain ideas similar to *Between Parent and Child* and *Between Parent and Teenager* by Haim Ginott (Avon 1969, 1971), and *How to Talk So Kids Will Listen and Listen So Kids Will Talk* by Faber and Mazlish (Avon, 1980).
- Milton Erickson's approach in *Advanced Techniques of Hypnosis and Therapy* (Grune & Stratton, 1967), pp. 436–442, is found in *Extreme Measures for Extreme Behavior.* The focus is on establishing a family hierarchy rather than on rage reduction or holding therapies that provoke catharsis to reach core issues.
- Erickson's hypnotic use of language as studied by Ernest and Sheila Rossi in *Hypnotic Realities* (Irvington Publishers, 1976) was adapted for parents in *Directives That Defy Resistance.*
- Dr. Charney Herst's work in *For Mothers of Difficult Daughters* (Random House, 1998) forms the basis for *Dependent Adult Children* and *Disagreeable Distant Adult Children.*
- Formulations for distinguishing negotiable, nonnegotiable, and noncritical issues found in *Limiting Power* can be explored further in *Parent Effectiveness Training* by Thomas Gorden (Penguin, 1989).
- A theory of values as presented in the book *Values and Teaching* by Louis Raths, Merrill Marmin, and Sidney Simon (Merrill, 1966) was used to develop the value-clarifying questions in *Limiting Power.*
- EMDR formulations for negative and positive cognitions as explained in *Eye Movement Desensitization and Reprocessing* by Francine Shapiro (Guilford Press, 1995) were used in *Beliefs That Empower Parents.*

INCENTIVES THAT REQUIRE COOPERATION

The most common problem parents have with children occurs when the child does not perform a required task. Not doing chores, taking medicine, getting ready for bed, feeding pets, wearing seat belts, and doing homework are prime examples of these "acts of omission." Surprisingly, punishments have very little power to motivate children to cooperate, but fortunately, uncooperative, irresponsible behavior can easily be corrected by making children an irresistible offer. Which of the following statements is a punishment?

1. "You can't watch TV tonight because you didn't put your clothes away."
2. "You can't go skating next Friday because you did not put your clothes away."
3. "You can watch TV as soon as your clothes are put away."

Statements 1 and 2 are punishments. Technically, a punishment is an unpleasant consequence that cannot be avoided. The child has no control over the outcome of the situation and the parent has to do all the enforcing. Statement 3 is an irresistible incentive. The child can escape or avoid the unpleasant consequence by performing the desired behavior. Privileges are not taken away, they are only withheld until the task is performed. Because the child has the option to avoid a nasty outcome, parents can throw tremendous weight into the incentive:

> You can watch TV (talk on the phone, eat snacks, go outside, finish playing that game, have your prize collection of baseball cards back, listen to the stereo, play video games, cuddle your "blankee," go to bed, or continue whatever else you are doing) after you have put away your clothes.

IRRESISTIBLE INCENTIVES

Irresistible incentives are guaranteed to work as long as parents withhold privileges and immediately reward children as soon as they have cooperated. If children vegetate to avoid doing a task, that is their choice. Parents are wise to watch for potent moments in the day when an irresistible incentive will have a speedy impact. The following pointers will help parents set the most direct course for success:

- Establish deadlines for starting chores before favorite TV shows, other desired activity, or snacks. Arrange fixed deadlines for starting routine chores.
- Use everyday events for deadlines. Don't threaten to take away a special event next week.
- Pick deadlines that your can enforce. Don't expect chores to be done before you get home from work, but offer rewards (see next page) when tasks are done on time.
- Give children time to mentally prepare themselves. For example, ask children to complete an unscheduled task during the next TV advertisement rather than telling them to do it right now.
- Don't nag! When the deadline starts, enforce the consequence until the child cooperates.
- Use a timer to "announce" the deadline. This will ensure that you follow through.
- Use nonverbal communication as reminders. For example, hang a bag of things that need to be put away in front of the TV or stick a note on the TV screen explaining that the video control box will be returned once rooms have been cleaned.
- When a deadline isn't available, be your child's shadow, sing opera, hold his or her earlobe, or hug him or her until the task is started.
- Move the arms and legs of very young children like a puppet when they have not cooperated with a request by the count of 3.

- Ignore pouting and complaining as long as the child is performing the task. If you find it hard to do this, remove yourself from the scene. Discussions about the "unfairness" of a chore should take place after it is completed to avoid manipulation.
- In some cases, it is fine to delay the return of privileges until children are ready to perform the desired task. Save power struggles for essential issues.
- When children are upset about something other than their chores, they may be given the option of talking about what is bothering them before starting their work.

When a child's responsibilities seem to unduly frustrate him or her, even with the above approaches, it is important to investigate what might be causing the difficulty: Is the child depressed and not motivated to do much of anything? Does the child have an attention deficit disorder that makes it difficult to complete a task without constant supervision? Does the child know that he or she can "get away with things" because one or both parents wish to avoid conflict? Is the chore unreasonable? Professional assistance may be needed to identify these and other underlying problems.

NATURAL AND LOGICAL CONSEQUENCES

Whenever possible, use natural and logical consequences instead of irresistible incentives. Older children who are supposed to do their own laundry can run out of clean clothes until they are ready to put through a wash. A child who doesn't want his food can simply wait for the next scheduled meal to eat and, perhaps, experience a little hunger. This is much healthier than creating power struggles over food.[1]

REWARDS

Rewards can give an extra boost to irresistible incentives and are helpful for times of the day when powerful deadlines are not available. For example:

- A 5-year-old can be given a sticker for cleaning her room before the timer rings.
- "Purchase points" can be earned for being ready for school on time, to be used later to buy desired items.
- When chores are done before the parents get home, a child can expect a special treat.
- Children can report when they have hung up their towel or returned their glass to the sink for a prize.

Even when children earn rewards for being responsible without reminders, it is still important to enforce deadlines with irresistible incentives for the tasks they will inevitably forget. Use verbal rewards liberally. Describe what you see and feel—"It's such a relief to have the dishes done early!" Let your children overhear you say positive things about them to other people—"The kids surprised me and had everything put away before I got home."

---

[1] See *Logical Consequences: A New Approach to Discipline* by Roudolf Dreikurs (NAL Dutton, 1993).

ACTIONS THAT ENCOURAGE OBEDIENCE

When children do not do what they have been asked to do, privileges can be withdrawn until they cooperate. Because they are in control of the length of the consequence, desired results usually happen quickly. When children do things they have been told not to do, privileges can be taken away for a specific period of time. Such punishments do not guarantee that children will act appropriately. They only ensure that parents have done their part to help young people follow rules.[1] However, children will learn from their mistakes when punishments are designed to:

- Teach good conduct rather than cause distress or prevent mistakes from ever happening.
- Be severe enough to produce tension, but not so severe as to cause undo frustration.
- Start as soon as possible after misbehavior.
- Provide opportunities for children to stop consequences by performing the desired action—A child can go to bed a half hour early until she gets up on time two mornings in a row.
- Directly relate the consequence to the behavior—A child who leaves the door open may have to close it behind him twice before he goes about his business.

TYPES OF PUNISHMENTS

The greater the variety of punishments parents use, the more effective they will be. The following are reminders on the do's and don'ts of common punishments:

√ Hands-on action allows parents to take advantage of their size and strength. When you use your voice, you are on the same level as your children. They can scream as loudly as you can. When children do not respond to one verbal request, take prompt action. In many cases, you can interrupt disobedience and then provide an immediate chance to perform the desired behavior:

- Put your hand on a child's shoulder to help him or her move along when it is time to go.
- When the stereo is too loud, the plug can be pulled for five minutes.
- Toys that are used destructively can be taken away briefly.
- When a young child won't give up a fragile object after three counts, simply take it away.

√ Time-out is a consequence that interrupts undesirable behavior, focuses attention, and creates the earliest possible opportunity for correct conduct. One minute per every year of age is a standard guideline for the length of time-out. A baby who eats dirt can be put in the crib for one minute. A preschooler who leaves the house or yard unattended can be placed in a corner for four minutes. The following increase the effectiveness of a time-out:

- Place children where they can be observed. They often enjoy "time-out" in their rooms or act destructively.
- Walk children to time-out and hold them until they are capable of complying.
- Ignore fretting or fussing as long as children stay in the time-out spot or position. Distress shows that the punishment is having impact.
- Increase concentration by having children watch a timer or hold a glitter wand.
- Give one warning and then act—"If you touch that again, you need to take a time-out."
- Be consistent when children repeatedly break the same rule. It is better to give a 6-year-old four time-outs for pushing the baby than one 24-minute-long time-out.
- In public places, immediately take children to the car, a bathroom stall, or an outside back wall for time-out. This is amazingly effective!
- Briefly pull to the side of the road if children are disruptive while you are driving.

---

[1] More ideas on firm parenting can be found in *Back in Control* by Gregory Bodenhamer (Simon & Schuster, 1984).

- Use a "moving time-out" with hyperactive children who make up for time they sit still by being overly active later. For example, they can walk back and forth on a line 10 times.
- Children can shorten time-out by stating the behaviors they need to change.

√ Essays are an excellent way to logically relate a consequence to a "crime." They require children to concentrate, think about their behavior, empathize with others, and comply with parents. Very young children can make "pictorial essays" or copy a simple sentence. Depending on the child's age, an essay, sentence, or picture can cover the following points:

a. Why do my parents think this rule is important, and how do they feel when it is broken?
b. What was on my mind when I broke the rule?
c. What disagreements do I have with the rule, if any?
d. What do I plan to do to keep myself from breaking this rule in the future?

Even resistant children will write an essay when they are told they will have no privileges until it is correctly completed. Children may need to interview their parents or even do research to complete (a). If children are given only one sentence to write, it is much better for them to cover (a) than to make promises they may not keep. Do not correct children's reasoning on (b) and (c), even if you disagree. Children can write the essay more than once, depending on the seriousness of the rule broken. For example, a 13-year-old who has been sneaking out at night might be required to rewrite the essay every night for a week.

√ Restrictions are a form of time-out for older children. Privileges such as using the phone, visiting friends, using the car, or having time alone can be taken away. Be specific about the length of restrictions, but do not make decisions in the heat of anger. Lengthy restrictions often punish parents and do not give children the opportunity to demonstrate that they can change their behavior. Restrict or supervise contact with friends with whom your child tends to break rules, but never criticize a child's choice of friends. Explain restrictions in terms of misbehavior, not character. When possible, allow children to reduce the length of restrictions by writing an essay or correcting misbehavior. For example, allow your children to go out with friends if they succeed in coming home on time five days in a row.

X Spankings are not recommended in this action-oriented approach for the following reasons: (1) Often, parents are not comfortable giving spankings. They may threaten children many times before taking action. (2) When spankings are used, the parent is active and the child is passive. Time-out, essays, and restrictions, on the other hand, require the child to comply with the parent. (3) Spankings can encourage young children to hit. If you don't spank, you can tell the children "We don't hit in this house." (4) Spanking older children can create anger and resentment that lead to further defiance.

RESPONSES THAT REDUCE ANGER

Anger understandably occurs when a person of any age is overpowered. Because young people have so many rules to learn, they are likely to be overpowered many times a day. Thinking that children should accept your decisions without comment will only make you frustrated and do little to resolve the situation. Although it is natural for children to get angry with parents, they do need to express their feelings in a productive way. Understand that refusing to allow children to express any anger at all is just as destructive as allowing them to vent it how ever they please.

UNDERSTAND AND FEED BACK FEELINGS

Labeling and feeding back feelings are the first steps in teaching children how to express distress without acting out inappropriately.[1] Making at least three statements that rephrase, understand, validate, or encourage children to express feelings can reduce anger. For example:

- You don't like it when I correct you. I see you are really mad. You can stomp your foot (scream in this pillow, smash this can, draw a picture, give me a mean look) to show me how mad you are. I know it's hard to have to learn so many rules.
- I know you don't like being on this restriction until your grades improve. It must tear your heart out not to get to talk to your friends every night. For a while, you may be very upset with me because I am holding firm.

Postpone talking to children if you are too angry to listen and feedback feelings. Tell them, "I'm too upset for talking right now. We'll discuss this as soon as we've both cooled down." Anger can take many forms. You can use other responses in addition to the above, depending on the way hostility is being expressed:

1. Arguments: When children are angry, you may be tempted to explain why their feelings are unjustified or to defend your actions. This is generally an undesirable course of action because it provokes arguments and creates power struggles. Even if children don't get their way, they have reduced you to their level. Remember that children often have difficulty understanding consequences and rules. Therefore, the best thing to do is to remain firm and avoid arguing by:
    - Repeating your decision like a broken record when feeding back feelings does not end arguments—"Nevertheless . . .", "Regardless . . ." and walk away.
    - Not expressing your point unless your child truly wants to understand it. State the feeling behind your reason. It is difficult to argue with emotions—"I worry when you go that far from the house." Your child can disagree with you if you say "You're too young to go that far."
2. Temper tantrums and explosions: Even when you feed back children's feelings and refuse to argue, anger can escalate into a full-blown tantrum. Several strategies can be used when this happens. Find the one that works best for your child:
    - Ignore the tantrum as though it is not happening or calmly watch without talking.
    - Place the child in another room or leave the room yourself until the child can talk calmly.
    - Join the tantrum. Lie down next to the child and mirror the outburst.

---

[1] Several books elaborate on skills that improve communication with children: *How to Talk So Kids Will Listen* and *Listen So Kids Will Talk* by Adele Faber and Elaine Mazlish (Avon, 1980). *The Explosive Child* by Ross Green (HarperCollins, 1998) is especially important reading for parents whose children have anger problems.

- Physically restrain a child who is hurting self or others or is being destructive. It helps to hold a small child's hands or feet in such a way that he or she can push without hurting you.
- Call the authorities if older children hit. When children go to this extreme, they are asking for outside intervention.
- If children destroy anything, they can replace it or give up something of their own.
- Withhold privileges until the issue causing the tantrum has been calmly discussed.

3. Hitting or biting: When people are mad, their natural inclination is to strike out. Very young children have not yet learned to contain this energy. Toddlers who hit or bite can have their hands or mouths firmly held while being told "Hitting (biting) hurts people." Maintain this position until the toddler clearly is upset and then let go to see if he or she can handle the frustration without striking out. If not, repeat the procedure. Older children who hit can be made to copy statutes on domestic violence.

4. Fighting: Anger often results from conflicts of interest with siblings. As soon as your children's bickering becomes annoying, separate them until they are calm enough to follow the three steps for conflict resolution:

   - Each child makes three statements beginning with, "I want . . ." "I feel . . ." "I want/feel because . . ."
   - Each child reverses roles and accurately repeats or paraphrases what the other has said.
   - Together, the children generate three possible solutions to the conflict and choose the best idea.

   Initially, children may need guidance, but eventually, they should be able to follow the steps independently. Keep a set of *Conflict Resolutions Steps* posted and simply tell them to go to the "conflict board" until they can reach an agreement. Reward both children when they reach an agreement.

5. Name-calling is often the forerunner of fights. Using reverse psychology can markedly reduce this. Make a rule that anyone who gets called a name or is hit without striking back receives a "victim's compensation point" or reward. These points can add up to earn snacks or prize money. This creates an incentive for children to adopt a totally different viewpoint about being called names. They can thank their adversaries for saying or doing mean things that help them earn points. If the parent doesn't hear or see the conflict, a child can still earn points by telling the parent something that he said to "thank" the one who tried to start the fight. To avoid tattling, the child needs to report what he or she did to help, not what the other person did to cause hurt.[2]

[2] Ideas in *How to Handle Bullies, Teasers and Other Meanies* by Kate Cohen-Posey (Rainbow Books, 1995) help children deal with name-calling and reduce fighting.

DIRECTIVES THAT DEFY RESISTANCE

Parents are in the unpleasant position of telling children to cooperate and follow rules over and over. Asking children to perform tasks gives them the option to say no. They will test the limits of this "freedom" by refusing. True requests are phrased, "Would you . . . ?" These should be reserved for relationships with spouses and friends with whom parents are not in a position of authority. Outright demands and orders can also provoke resistance. You can lighten your load as taskmaster by using the following "indirect directives" that speak to the part of every child that wants to cooperate and succeed:

Truth or Choice

1. A truism is a statement of fact that cannot be denied—"You can tell people how you feel without saying that they are stupid."
2. A bind restricts children to a narrow range of responses, allows them to make an acceptable choice and provides an image of success—"Would you rather say, 'I don't understand you' or, 'I don't agree with you?'"
3. A double bind asks a question in a way that makes children agree regardless of how they answer—"Do you know how you are going to say that differently?"
4. A false choice is a double bind worded as an option—"If you're not going to do it right, just do it!"

Suggestions and Implication

5. An underlying assumption uses a pause to insert an indirect suggestion—"I'm not sure when . . . you will find a polite way to say that."
6. Questions are an easy way to embed suggestions and double binds simultaneously—"Just how will you . . . say that differently?"
7. An implied directive assumes something will happen and suggests a way to signal when it is done—"As soon as you . . . think of a nicer way to say that . . . you can just walk away."
8. Serial suggestions use the momentum of linking a difficult task or a response children are not likely to make with expected behaviors—"Don't change your tone of voice until you've finished rolling your eyes at me."

Confuse to Create Change

9. The word "try" blocks the action following it—"You can try to keep saying nasty things to people."
10. Dares push children to do something they are reluctant to do—"You couldn't say that politely even if you wanted to."
11. Reverse psychology encourages children to do what they are doing to help them do the opposite—"Someone your age couldn't think of a nice way of saying that so you might as well keep dishing out insults until it isn't worth the effort."
12. Pairing opposite words adds confusion—"Sometimes the harder you try to insult people, the easier it is to be kind."

Indirect directives are equally powerful when used in a negative way—"Please try to do the dishes" blocks cooperation. "Will you ever learn to do anything right?" implies failure. With this kind of talk parents can literally hypnotize children to do the very behaviors they least want them to do. It is fine for parents to be direct and say, "I would like you to . . ." However, the more ways parents have to make daily demands, the less children will be able to resist them.

The following chart shows how the 12 types of indirect directives can address a variety of behaviors by approaching children through the "back door" of their minds. Notice embedded suggestions to be spoken with special emphasis. Pregnant pauses (. . .) and words like "surprising" help children focus their attention:

Behavior	Indirect Directive	Type
Attitude	Surely you could try to complain a little more	9, 11
	Before you even . . . think of agreeing, let me hear your argument.	8, 11
	You wouldn't dare to . . . talk this out . . . when you are so angry.	5, 10
	I don't think you could even . . . begin to look at me . . . right now.	5, 10
Compliance	How long will it take you to . . . get ready for your bath?	6
	Should we get pizza after you mow the lawn or when you're done?	4
	Do you know exactly when . . . you will start washing the dishes?	3
	Don't . . . start the dishes . . . until you've had a moment to relax.	7, 11
	On your way out the door, you can put your clothes in the closet.	1, 8
Cooperation	Can you tell me what is good about the agreement we reached?	3
	I don't know how . . . you will solve this problem.	5
Honesty	It might take you 2 hours or 2 days to . . . decide to tell me the truth.	2, 5
	You can take time to . . . reach your decision.	1, 5
	Your can forget to lie or . . . remember to tell the truth.	4, 12
Hyperactivity	You can't even stand still without wiggling and wanting to sit down.	5, 8, 10
	I'm not sure how . . . you will learn to focus and concentrate.	5
	It's surprising . . . how politely you could get out all that extra energy by wiggling your toes or doodling on a scrap of paper.	2, 5
Manners	When you know that . . . you will not play with your food, you can pick up your fork and start eating.	7
	It can be fun to . . . remember to thank people for having you over.	1, 5
Tantrums	This is the best of your worst tantrums.	12
	Pretty soon you will . . . get so weak from screaming that you'll find out you can't even . . . be calm.	5, 7, 8
	The harder shake your fist at me, the better you'll start to feel.	8,10,11
Violence	While I'm sitting on you, you'll have plenty of time to figure out how you are going to . . . stop giving everyone a bloody nose.	5, 8
	If any part of you wants to . . . stop all this fighting . . . it could make your eyes blink . . . Otherwise, it would just have you stare.	3, 4

Indirect directives will not eliminate the need to withhold privileges or take action; but they can implant subliminal suggestions before children have a chance to resist. However, even the best hypnotist can only implant acceptable suggestions. Therefore, do not use this approach to attempt to alter beliefs and interests that children hold dear. Harness the power of positive speaking to help children accept reasonable requests.

LIMITING POWER

Trying to control every aspect of a child's life provokes rebellion and loss of power. When to act or not to act is the question, it helps to divide problems into three areas:[1]

- The issue is not negotiable and parents are directive and take action to ensure that children follow through when their behavior affects others— "I would like you to. . . ." "Will you do . . . now or in five minutes?"
- The issue is not critical and parents act as a sounding board to help children express feelings and solve their problem when their behavior affects only themselves. Parents can openly disagree with their children's choices but state that the decision is up to them. Losing some battles makes children more willing to let parents win others.
- The issue is negotiable and conflict resolution steps are taken to resolve disagreements and reach long-lasting, satisfying solutions.

CONFLICT RESOLUTION STEPS

1. Set a time to discuss the problem when neither parents nor children are pressured.
2. Both parties express their point with the statements—"I want . . . I feel . . . I want/feel because. . . ."
3. Both parties reverse roles and accurately paraphrase what the other has said.
4. Generate possible solutions. Have children give ideas before parents offer theirs.
5. Evaluate all alternatives and pick the one that is most satisfactory to all.
6. When solutions cannot be found, review step 2 and set another time for discussion.
7. When agreements are broken, reevaluate to find out if the original agreement was unrealistic.

TO ACT OR NOT TO ACT

Approaches to Problems

Directions: To practice deciding how to approach parent-child problems, cover the column on the right and then find out if you (and fellow caretakers) agree with suggested approaches.

Situation	Problem Approach
• The parents think their daughter wears too much makeup to school.	Not critical
• The parents do not like the way their son dresses on family outings.	Negotiate
• The child does not let his parents know where he is going.	Not negotiable
• The child thinks parents are overprotective about where he can go.	Negotiate
• The child avoids doing his chores.	Not negotiable
• The child thinks he has too many chores to do.	Negotiate
• The child is upset because friends never call her.	Not critical
• The parents are upset because too many boys call their daughter.	Negotiate
• The child thinks his bedtime is too early.	Negotiate
• The child keeps putting off bedtime.	Not negotiable

VALUE CLARIFYING

When an issue is not critical, parents do not have to stand idly by. In addition to feeling back thoughts and labeling feelings, parents can ask value-clarifying questions that help children examine their alternatives, choose carefully, and act on choices. Values can be seen in the judgments people make, in the rules by which they live, and in their attitudes, desires and goals.

Children's values are changing constantly: at various times, it may be important to have lots of friends, make good grades, make the football team, wear the right clothes, be different from everyone else, have a pet, stand up for yourself, or get along with others.

SEVEN VALUE-CLARIFYING PROCESSES

To form values, children need to go through seven stages. Parents can ask questions based on each stage to help young people develop their own personal guidelines:[2]

1. Being aware of alternatives:
   - Did you think of anything else before you made this choice?
   - What makes this choice better than . . .?
   - What else have you thought about doing?
2. Choosing freely:
   - Where do you suppose you first got this idea?
   - For whom are you doing this? What pressure are you feeling about this?
   - Is there anything you are avoiding?
3. Choosing carefully:
   - How is this bad for you? How is it good for you?
   - What is your objection to doing . . .? How did you make this decision?
   - What are your priorities? What do you most want to happen?
4. Prizing and cherishing:
   - Are you glad you feel this way?
   - How is this important to you?
   - Could you manage without this?
5. Affirming:
   - Are you willing to tell others how you feel?
   - Does anyone else know you want this?
   - Are you willing to stand up for that?
6. Acting on choices:
   - What will you have to do?
   - What is your first step?
   - What kind of changes will you have to make in your life?
7. Repeating:
   - Would you want to do this again?
   - Have you done this before?
   - Is this worth the energy you've put into it?

Persuading, judging, suggesting, interrogating, and repeating your own credo is not value clarifying. Nor is it helpful to ask why questions that put children on the defensive and prod them into making excuses or even lying. However, when children are facing a problem and have no guideline to deal with it or when a value that used to work is no longer paying off, they may welcome the above what and how questions to help them discover their own inner truths.

---

[1] See *Parent Effectiveness Training* by Thomas Gorden (Penquin, 1989) for further information.

[2] Adapted from *Values and Teaching* by Raths, Harmin, and Simon (Merrill, 1966), pp. 63–65.

ATTITUDES AND BACK TALK

Back talk, smarting off, and being fresh are disrespectful because they do not recognize the power structure of the family. The child is either treating parents as subordinates by giving orders or as peers by criticizing, using sarcasm, swearing, name calling, or not complying. Although it is important to consider children's ideas, when parents do not "carry the weight in the family," it is like sailing a boat with no ballast—the boat will capsize!

WHY CHILDREN TALK BACK

Understanding the following sources of disrespect can help parents take it less personally and free their minds to have a quick-witted response:

- Young children talk back to test the limits of their power by ordering and verbally refusing to comply. High-energy children are especially prone to back talk because their exuberance gives them a confusing sense of strength.
- Adolescents talk back as a part of their struggle to establish their own identity and independence. They are critical of parents about almost everything—being too strict, too overprotective, old fashioned, or "clueless."
- Children of all ages will talk back when parents engage in power struggles with them.
- Comments that parents make out of hurt and anger can provoke disrespectful retorts from children.
- Children who are being empowered by another adult who is undermining the parent's authority will talk back.
- Children who feel too powerful because parents don't take action to establish their authority or too powerless because parents are overbearing will talk back.
- Children who have not learned respectful ways to disagree or express anger will talk back. This includes almost all children.

HOW TO RESPOND TO BACK TALK

Telling a child not to talk back or to be more respectful will inspire the opposite. Psychologists usually advise parents to be consistent. In the case of back talk, it is important for parents to use a variety of responses. Surprisingly, the gentlest responses often produce better results than intense ones. Consequences will be more powerful when they are not overused. The following suggest levels of responding to back talk:

1. Label what the child is feeling without making any judgment. Fight back talk with feedback. This increases children's awareness of what they are doing without triggering a power struggle—"You really like to give me orders" (use with 6 below). "You seem quite disappointed in me." "You're frustrated with the way I worry."[1]
2. Sympathize to defuse anger—"It's really hard being 3 years old and having to learn so many rules." "It's very frustrating to lose that taste of freedom."
3. Being playful can increase awareness and break tension. Excuse yourself to get your broomstick if your child is treating you like the Wicked Witch of the West. Ask "Do I get demerits for that?" "How many IQ points do you think I've lost?" "Am I a completely hopeless worrywart or am I trainable?"
4. Match the child's attitude and back talk for him or her in your sassiest voice.

---

[1] Several books elaborate on skills that improve communication with children: *Between Parent and Child* and *Between Parent and Teenager* by Haim Ginott (Avon 1969, 1971) and *How to Talk So Kids Will Listen and Listen So Kids Will Talk* by Adele Faber and Elaine Mazlish (Avon, 1980).

5. Model appropriate ways to disagree or express anger. Talking as though you are the child, say "Mom, I disagree with your decision. Are you willing to hear my idea?"
6. Never take orders. Let children know that you cannot help them when they talk disrespectfully. Do not argue with verbal noncompliance. Simply withhold privileges until a task is complete.
7. Postpone discussions until you are calm enough to listen and until your child has more composure. Encourage your child (and yourself) to talk to a friend, write, or engage in some activity that will help you each be more objective.
8. Swearing can be handled like back talk and other disrespectful language. Focus on acceptable expression of feelings instead of punishment. If you are comfortable with it, allow children to use the "rhyming method" of creating swearing substitutes to use during emotional moments—"Oh sam-it! I had a mitty day."
9. Withhold privileges until children can restate their previous comments with desirable words and tone of voice, demonstrate understanding of your point of view, or talk about what is really bothering them.

Technically, back talk is an act of omission because children are failing to talk in a desirable manner. They can easily be motivated to communicate more effectively if you give them time to collect themselves and withhold key privileges until they can perform the task in number 9 above. Putting a child on restriction for back talk is like trying to kill a mosquito with a machete and does little to teach desirable expression.

THE SILENT TREATMENT

Some children prefer pouting, withdrawing, or "the silent treatment" to back talk. Simply require such children to tell you or write you a letter about what is bothering them before they can use the phone, eat snacks, or have other privileges. If you do this, you must be willing to feedback their feelings and sympathize with their viewpoint (although you may not change your position). If you attempt to dispute feelings, the approach will not work and the negative attitude will continue!

DAILY ROUTINES AND HABITS

Children are creatures of habit. Undesirable behavior patterns will develop a life of their own if they are unchecked. The following suggestions can help ease children through transitional times with a minimum amount of frustration.

BEDTIME

Use the following actions to help children settle down at night and get needed rest:

- Make sure children are completely ready for bed in advance by withholding favorite activities until baths are taken, pajamas are on, and teeth are brushed.
- Establish a routine of reading or talking with children while they are lying in bed.
- Allow children to keep a light or music on if this helps them stay in bed.
- Children may need to cry it out until they learn to fall asleep in their own beds. Prepare yourself for one to four nights of screaming. You can go to the room every 10 minutes to reassure children that they are not abandoned and calmly say, "Time for sleep."
- If children leave the room, physically take or return them to bed without any discussion and hold the door closed until they demonstrate that they can stay in bed.
- Do not allow children who stay up late to oversleep. This creates vicious cycles.
- Use rewards in the morning (points, stars, TV with breakfast, bacon for breakfast, or special cereal) to reinforce desirable bedtime behavior until it becomes a habit.
- When the above do not help, therapy may be needed for trauma or obsessive concerns.
  Note: When children prolong their bedtime but can get up when they are supposed to and are not tired during the day, their bedtime may be too early.

BED-WETTING

If children had good bladder control and have regressed, they may be reacting to trauma and need therapy. However, a small, immature, bladder often causes bed-wetting. Many children do not grow out of this condition until they are 10 or older. Often, a parent had the same problem as a child. Medication and "bladder training" can help:

- Withhold liquids two to three hours before bed.
- Have children drink lots of liquid during the day to stretch the bladder and then gradually increase the length of time they must wait until they are allowed to urinate.
- Teach children how to stop and start their stream while urinating to build muscle control.
- Give children a choice of wearing padded pants at night or washing their own sheets until they learn control.

BEDROOM STANDARDS

Should children be required to keep their room clean, or can they be allowed to set their own standards? There is no right or wrong answer, but teenagers who have had their rooms kept clean for them when they were young will not automatically take over the responsibility just because they are older: Most children need training!

- Supervise and help toddlers—"I'll pick this up and you pick up that."
- Withhold privileges until school-age children clean their rooms. Do the same for at least a month with teens who have never been taught to keep their rooms neat.

- When teens who have had some training in keeping their rooms clean become resistant, allow them leeway on how they "define" their territory. This will give them an option for "healthy rebellion."

CURFEW

Although parents can become panic-stricken when a child does not come home on time, it is natural for children to be late now and then. Make sure you have considered the child's viewpoint before establishing curfews and seek input from other parents or professionals. If problems persist, several courses of action can be taken:

- Assign the writing of essays that show understanding of the need for curfews and plans for keeping them.
- Withhold important privileges (telephone or TV) until curfews are kept.
- Put children on restriction from going out—a day for every 20 minutes late.
- Go after children who violate curfews if you know their whereabouts.
- As a brief punishment, insist on accompanying children when they go out.

HYGIENE

Children vary greatly in the ages at which they become interested in good grooming. Simply train children who have other priorities by withholding privileges until they have taken baths, and brushed hair and teeth. Reassure children that they will not always need reminders. Make sure you are not overly concerned. Remember that some children do not need daily baths.

SNEAKING OUT

Many young teens engage in this behavior. Assess if young people are sneaking out due to an adventurous spirit or if it is a symptom of a more serious problem. The severity of the consequences will depend on the underlying causes.

- Assign essays on the dangers of sneaking out, its effect on others, and plans to change.
- Withhold privileges until there is no evidence of sneaking out for a couple of weeks or until essays are written.
- In extreme cases, use locks or alarms on doors, bar windows, or sleep in front of the child's door.

SOILING

When children over 4 are under stress or are chronically angry, they can tense their anal sphincter and not eliminate feces properly. Eventually, their bowels may stop sending messages to the brain when elimination is needed and some feces may leak out. A doctor should be consulted to rule out any medical condition. Stool softeners can be prescribed to relieve impacting, and the child can be rewarded for relaxing on the toilet and having clean pants. Relaxation training and helping children express feelings may be needed.

WAKING UP AND GETTING READY FOR SCHOOL

When an alarm clock or one reminder does not help a child get out of bed, find an action that does: use a fine water mist spray, hold a piece of vinegar-soaked cotton under the nose, or send rowdy pets into the room. A special breakfast treat, watching TV with breakfast, or another reward can be used as an incentive if the child is completely ready for school at a specified time. Always eat breakfast after a child is dressed and ready. When they are running late, children can be put into cars in their pajamas, provided you have a change of clothes and an instant breakfast.

SCHOOL-RELATED PROBLEMS

If the school's consequences for problems are effective, there is no need to further punish children at home. That would be "double jeopardy." However, there are times when parents need to take action.

BEHAVIOR PROBLEMS

When students have persistent difficulties, they may have attention-deficit hyperactivity disorder, or they may have lost or never had a bond with a significant caretaker. Older children who show sudden changes in behavior may have been traumatized or become involved in substance abuse. In addition to seeking evaluations for such problems, parents can:

- Require daily school reports to stay in close contact with teachers.
- Offer rewards on days when students bring home a good report.
- Withhold privileges (TV, video games, etc.) until an acceptable report is brought home.
- Take away important privileges while students are serving out-of-school suspensions.
- Write essays about what can be done to prevent further suspensions.
- Investigate medication or herbs for children who may be hyperactive.[1]

HOMEWORK AND POOR GRADES

Ask the school to have children tested for learning disabilities or attention disorders if academic problems have been present since the third grade or earlier. You may need to be persistent. Employ any of the strategies below that are helpful:

- After eating a snack, children should finish homework before watching TV or playing.
- Require a study hour until grades improve. If children deny having homework, supply your own. Although you can make children sit with books, you cannot make them study.
- Require children to bring home a satisfactory daily or weekly school report to have evening or weekend privileges. Parents can consider shortening restrictions if children are responsible enough to bring home a report.
- Arrange rewards for good school reports if this motivates students.
- When parents are engaged in many other power struggles with children, it may be best for young people to experience the natural consequences of failure until other issues improve.

SKIPPING CLASSES AND TRUANCY

Teens who miss school may be experiencing peer pressure or developing serious conduct problems. However, anxiety due to panic or fears of looking foolish can require therapy. It is common for children to have "school phobia" in fifth through seventh grades due to the transition to larger schools. Allowing children to avoid school can aggravate problems, so take immediate action to get them back on track:

- Verify attendance and withhold privileges unless children have been in school all day.
- In serious cases, accompany students to school and escort them between classes.
- If children refuse to go to school, physically carry them and enlist the aid of other adults if needed.
- Do not allow children to stay or come home early unless they have a temperature.

---

[1] *Miracle Cures* by Jean Carper (HarperCollins, 1997), pp. 233–234, suggests that oligomeric procyanidins (OPCs) in the herbs pycnogenol and grape seeds may regulate enzymes that control dopamine and norepinephrine.

SCHOOL REPORTS

Many schools have their own form to communicate with parents when students are having academic or behavioral problems. If none are available, parents can use the generic forms below. Minimum standards can be set for students to gain rewards or to have evening and weekend privileges:

- Rewards: Stickers, special snack, prize from a grab bag, purchase points,[2] money.
- Privileges: Television, video games, telephone use, visiting with friends, leaving the house, stereo, CD or cassettes, computer use, snacks.

SELF-CONTAINED CLASSROOM

Home ◄—► School Communication			
Student:		**Date:**	
Points: 2 (mostly) **1** (sometimes) **0** (rarely)	**Self-Rating before Lunch**	**After Lunch**	**Teacher's Rating and Initials**
Followed classroom rules			
Stayed on task			
Finished and turned in assignments			
Turned in homework: __ Yes __ No			
Test/quiz grades:			
Major projects due:			

___ Points = ___ minutes __ playing video games, __ watching TV, __ using the telephone.

CHANGING CLASSROOMS

Home ◄—► School Communication					
Student:				**Date:**	
G = Good S = Satisfactory NI = Needs Improvement	Behavior: **G S NI**	Complete Assignments	Missing Homework	Test/Quiz Grades	Teacher's Initials
1st Period:					
2nd Period:					
3rd Period:					
4th Period:					
5th Period:					
6th Period:					
7th Period:					
Next quiz/test dates:					
Major projects due:					

[2] Students can earn points toward purchasing desired objects.

EXTREME MEASURES FOR EXTREME BEHAVIOR

In extreme cases, children lose all sense of boundaries and wantonly destroy property, defy teachers, assault peers, and even physically attack their parents. They are testing the ability of adults in their lives to provide external controls until they can internalize the ability to govern themselves. Monstrous behavior can happen when children are:[1]

- Not bonded with or have lost a bond with an important caretaker.
- In an alliance with another adult against a parent.
- Acting out rage against a parent who has violated or abandoned them.
- Acting out rage against a caretaker with whom they feel safe.

It can be necessary to restrain these children until struggling gives way to crying and deep relaxation. Positions that can be used for physical restraint are shown below.[2] The basic strategy is to create a "strait jacket" for children by crossing their arms and holding their hands from behind. Parents can straddle children without using their full weight or can wrap their legs around children to prevent them from kicking. The relative proportions of parent-child strengths and body builds make some positions more practical than others. If parents have any doubts about their ability to assume or maintain a position, they should wait until another adult is available to assist. When done properly, the parent appears calm, confident, and unemotional.

[1] *High Risk: Children without a Conscience* by Ken Magid and Carole A. McKelvey (Bantam Books, 1987) gives further information about causes and treatment of children with attachment disorders.

[2] Drawing by Gavin Posey.

Extreme Measures for Extreme Behavior

Although children can be restrained when they are in the throes of destructive behavior, often it is better to plan a full-fledged, surprise session for a later time:[3]

- Prepare by making arrangements for other children to be out of the home. Gather supplies for a prolonged session: towels, diapers, mats, snacks, telephone, and reading materials. Explain what you will be doing ahead of time to neighbors or family who might walk in and give them copies of this handout to read so they can understand and even assist you.
- Schedule the session when you will have plenty of time so the child can exhaust himself and realize that it is useless to struggle. This could take one to eight hours.
- Set the tone by explaining to the child that you have arranged an interesting experience so he or she can talk to the angry part that has been tricking him into so much trouble lately.
- Assume control: Grab the child by both hands, turn him inward so arms are crossed, use your leg to unbalance him, and bring him to the floor or sofa.
- Make casual, confusing comments to demands, orders, and pleas to be released—"I haven't finished thinking about ways to change your behavior, but since I don't know any, it will all be up to you."
- Disregard or subtly encourage yelling, crying, and sobbing. This will release deep levels of hurt and promote the exhaustion necessary for capitulation. Remember that hunger and weakness will also aid in causing submission.
- Handle pleas to use the bathroom by offering to place a diaper under the child or use a towel to mop up. When the child's demeanor suggests he is starting to recognize the parent's authority, he can be allowed to use the bathroom with the understanding that the session will resume when he is finished.
- Handle complaints of being hurt or hungry by saying "I hope your hunger (pain) doesn't make it too hard to think of a plan to change your behavior."
- Do not push the child to realize that he is not all-powerful. The longer the time spent in the initial session, the less likely a repeat performance will be needed.
- Terminate the session only when the child's manner suggests he can accept this extreme demonstration of parental authority. This might include polite language and quietly waiting while the parent reads or talks on the phone with friends.
- Read *The Taming of the Shrew* to the child for an interesting touch.[4] Use of Shakespearean text will test the child's tolerance of an adult whim and make it difficult for him to consciously resist the message of the plot. If the child complains that he doesn't understand, say you don't either and that you hope someday he'll explain it to you.
- Give the child immediate opportunities to demonstrate compliance following the session by suggesting that it might be a good idea for him or her to rest in bed for a couple of hours before eating or playing.

Restraining should only be used when all other techniques to reduce anger and encourage obedience have been ineffective! Bones that are not mending properly must be broken and reset. Likewise, a spirit that has gone awry may also need to be broken to redirect it on a fulfilling course. Seek professional consultation to make sure your child's behavior warrants such intervention. Even when conducted by professionals, restraining may not be appropriate for children 14 or older.

---

[3] This approach to restraining was developed by Milton Erickson and is described in *Advanced Techniques of Hypnosis and Therapy* (Grune & Stratton, 1967), pp. 436–442.

[4] *Tales from Shakespeare* by Charles and Mary Lamb (Dilithiu Press, 1986) contains a shortened version with enough Shakespearean language to defy the child's conscious mind.

MORAL MATTERS

The best insurance against children acting in immoral ways is building a strong bond. But, even in the best parent-child relationships, young people can be led astray. This handout offers parents guides on what they can and cannot do to help children develop moral principles.

Alcohol and Drug Problems. Consult alcohol and drug treatment services when you first become concerned that this may be a problem. They have information on the warning signs of substance abuse and how and when to implement drug screens.

Dishonesty. Children lie to avoid punishments, rules, disappointing parents, admitting mistakes, or to look good and get attention. Understanding the pressures that make dishonesty a common problem can help parents take it less personally and help children understand why they lie. If you find that you continue to be upset by lying, examine yourself—What does it mean about me if my child lies or "betrays" me? If you have thoughts such as, "I'm stupid or a fool," you may have unresolved issues. It is important to realize that you are still perceptive even when children are deceptive. Then you can calmly execute several courses of action:

- Focus on misbehavior rather than the issue of lying. Confront children with the facts of what they did. Asking questions to which you know the answers may encourage lying.
- Concentrate on the rule that was broken when it is not possible to uncover what happened. Find out if children understand the reason for the rule and feedback their feelings about it—"It looks like someone was in my closet. I know you get bored and like to explore forbidden territory. Do you know how I feel when people go through my things?"
- Help children understand why they lie—"I wonder if it's hard to admit . . . because. . . ."
- Assign essays or discuss the good and bad points of admitting mistakes.
- Use rewards when children are truthful even if consequences are needed for wrongdoing.
- Express the belief that your child will eventually grow out of lying.

Sexual Misconduct. When young children are involved in sex play, they should be told it is natural to have such interests but that it is not allowed because private parts are special. Restrict unsupervised play. Return privileges gradually and monitor play intermittently until it appears that the preoccupation is broken. If you suspect abuse, consult authorities on how to approach the child. Encourage casual discussions of older children's beliefs about sexual behavior and birth control. Refrain from stating your own views until you understand your children's or you will never hear theirs. Have consequences for broken curfews and dishonesty regarding whereabouts rather than attempt to control what teens are actually doing. If children are blatantly promiscuous, they may have a sexual compulsion and need therapy.

Smoking. Require children to write an essay and do research on the costs and hazards of smoking. This report can be rewritten as needed. If you are engaged in many power struggles with children, trying to prevent smoking can actually increase it. Parents who can accept smoking can use cigarettes as reinforcement for desired behavior. However, do not buy children cigarettes.

Stealing. Place children on "probation" in which "found" or "borrowed" items cannot be kept. They must go for one to two months with no evidence of stealing to get off probation. Require them to interview police officers or inmates. Never allow a child to avoid legal consequences.

DEPENDENT ADULT CHILDREN

One of the hardest tasks for parents is to set limits with adult children who have become dependent. Rescuing your children from their problems suggests that they are not competent to make their own way (eventually). Although it may initially feel good to be needed, this can quickly become exhausting. The best way to know if you are fostering dependency is by paying attention to your own internal barometer:

- Does the closeness you once enjoyed now feel suffocating?
- Do you feel burdened, used, resentful, or burned out?
- Are you doing without material goods or free time to meet your child's demands?
- Are you afraid to say "No"?
- Does your child now demand things you once enjoyed giving—gifts or paid vacations?

FOSTERING INDEPENDENCE

Once children graduate from or quit school, it is time for them to become self-sufficient. This does not mean they have to immediately move out, but they need to be working toward this goal. Sometimes, crises occur that send children back home. This is acceptable as long as steps are taken to restore past autonomy. When grown children are not contributing their fair share to finances and household responsibilities, certain steps will motivate them toward healthy independence:[1]

1. Impose household rules for curfew, telephone and TV use, and chores. Give the choice of following the rules or leaving.
2. Require working children to contribute part of their salary for room and board. If parents do not need the money, save it for the child to use for living expenses later.
3. Providing spending money should be contingent on children's efforts toward independence.
4. Set a time limit on how long children can remain at home before you pack their bags and change the locks. Stick to it!
5. If you can afford it, offer to pay the first month's rent and security deposit on an apartment.
6. Set a schedule in writing for decreasing contributions to rent until the child is fully responsible.
7. If you give financial help, pay off past debts rather than assume the never-ending task of providing living expenses.
8. You have the right to say, "I changed my mind" about a previous promise.
9. Make sure both parents are in full agreement on any financial support. Work out disagreements (with a therapist, if necessary) before presenting the child with a plan.
10. Set limits on how much time you spend helping your child resolve crises. Play dumb when your child asks for advice—"Gee I don't know. What are your ideas?"
11. Be prepared for your child to reject you. He or she will most likely come around later.
12. Attend support groups if your child has a substance abuse or emotional problem. Only give spending money to a child involved in needed treatment.

---

[1] Elaboration of ideas can be found in *For Mothers of Difficult Daughters* by Charney Herst (Random House, 1988).

DISAGREEABLE DISTANT ADULT CHILDREN

It is not uncommon for tension that occurred between parents and children in the formative years to continue or to surface when young people leave home. It may take the form of daily battles or total estrangement. Twelve sources of these difficulties are listed in order from the least to the most solvable:[1]

1. The child has difficulty watching parents grow older and withdraws.
2. The child is involved in substance abuse or other illicit activity.
3. The parent's and child's lifestyles, values, or beliefs clash.
4. The child is resentful of or intimidated by the parent's success or embarrassed by the parent's "lack" of accomplishment.
5. Spouses are controlling and hinder contact.
6. The parent and child disapprove of each other's spouses.
7. The child is in an alliance with other family members against the parent or competing with one parent for the other parent's love.
8. The child has difficulty interacting with many people due to feelings of entitlement, sensitivity, blame, and unrealistic expectations.
9. The parent tolerates or overlooks rude, unacceptable behavior.
10. The child is suffering from depression and chronic feelings of unhappiness.
11. The child has unresolved issues from the past.
12. The parent has annoying habits of criticizing, interrogating, offering unsolicited advice, or having unrealistic expectations.

BRIDGING THE GAP

Often, the gulf these problems create can be bridged when parents make a concerted effort. The focus needs to be away from blame, resentment, or approval and on what the parent can do to take charge and make a difference. Develop acceptance and compassion for your child's "flaws." Examine the following strategies and note the sources of the problems that they address (given in parentheses):

Making Initial Changes

- Sympathize with your child. Problem solving and advice can prolong diatribes. (8)
- Set limits on how long you listen to problems. After 20 minutes, say "I really have to go." It's okay to make up excuses. Limit the number and length of phone calls. (8, 9)
- When behavior is disruptive, state the immediate change you would like either directly or indirectly—"I'd like you to say something nice, even if you have to fake it." "Although you're very good at pointing out my flaws, you might surprise yourself and say something kind." (8, 9)
- Arrange some superficial or less intense contact. Discuss the news, movies, and books. Go on outings or complete projects together. (12)
- Revise your expectations. If your children have jobs, a place to live, significant others, interests, and no addictions, they are probably reasonably healthy adults. Expectations for more than weekly phone contact, monthly visits (if they live in town), participation in holiday events, or birthday cards may be unrealistic. (12)

---

[1] Elaboration of ideas can be found in *For Mothers of Difficult Daughters* by Charney Herst (Random House, 1988).

Preparing for Meetings to Mend Tension

- Make a list of questions to get to the root of the problem—"What did I do in the past that still bothers you? Do I advise, pry, or criticize too much? Are you angry with me because . . . ? What would you like me to do differently? What are you willing to do? What do you appreciate about me?" (1, 3, 4, 8, 11, 12)
- Make a list of difficulties you have interacting with your child. Focus on what happens between you, not on his or her lifestyle. Be sure to start each statement with the word "I"—"I feel . . . when you. . . ." (7, 8, 9)
- Make a wish list of what you would like to be different—"Would you stop making fun of me, include me in conversations, not disagree with me so much . . . ?" (7, 8, 9)
- Make a list of what you appreciate or admire in your child. Reframe some dislikes as positives. An arguer can be thought of as a wonderful debater. (12)

Meetings and Encounters

- Give your child your list of questions (see above) at the end of a visit or mail them.
- Plan a meeting no later than two weeks after the child has had time to think over the list. Meet in a public place if neutral ground is needed. Plan for about two hours in person or an hour on the phone if the child lives out of town.
- Show you understand your child's responses to your question list and validate factors that contribute to his or her feelings—"It makes sense that you feel . . . when I (used to). . . . because . . ." (1, 3, 4, 6, 7, 8, 10, 11, 12)
- Express remorse for any of your past actions that caused problems. If the child is willing, help him or her understand the good intentions you had. (11, 12)
- Show your appreciation list to create an atmosphere of safety. Then show your lists of issues that trouble you and requests for change. Ask the child to tell you what makes sense about your concerns or desires. (12)
- Do not push for agreement or solutions. Focus on understanding each other and leave it up to each person to consider the other's requests. (12)

Cases of Estrangement

- Stay away long enough for your child to miss you. Allow time for the child to mature and for life to teach its lessons. (12)
- Write a reconciliation letter. Admit any of your past mistakes, express remorse for ways you might have unknowingly hurt your child, and emphasize your desire to renew your relationship. (11, 12)
- Send cards on holidays and birthdays. Send your child a card on Mother's Day recounting fond memories. (1, 2, 3, 4, 5, 6, 7, 8, 10, 11, 12)
- Plan a meeting with a counselor or mediator when damage to the relationship has been extensive. If you live out of town, state that you are coming to visit and arrange your own accommodations and transportation. (3, 4, 6, 7, 8, 11)
- Get a life! Make sure you don't depend on your child for all your emotional needs. "Adopt" others as adult children when there is no hope of renewing your relationship.

BELIEFS THAT EMPOWER PARENTS

More important than the beliefs you have about child rearing are the thoughts you have about yourself. If you have difficulty using child-rearing skills or if they don't seem to be working, your beliefs about yourself may be getting in the way. To discover thoughts that can cause glitches in taking action ask yourself:[1]

- When my children misbehave, what do I think about myself?
- When did I first have this disturbing thought about myself?
- How do my children "make me" feel when they act up?

Directions: Mark any of the following thoughts that come to you when your children misbehave. Then, mark any of the beliefs you would like to have when your children upset you.

Change Thoughts That Hurt into . . .	Beliefs That Help Parenting Skills
___ I am bad, inadequate, or not good enough.	___ I am still a good parent when my child misbehaves.
___ I am weak, unimportant, or not in control.	___ I can take action to respond to my child's misbehavior.
___ I may be abandoned if I upset my child.	___ I can take care of myself while my child is upset.
___ I have to keep others happy or I'm a failure.	___ I am still a good parent when my child is upset with me.

Negative beliefs that interfere with parenting skills are not actually caused by your child but were instilled from early life experiences that cause two opposite reactions:

- Yelling, blaming, or losing control often come from trying to avoid the awful, helpless, inadequate feelings that occur when your children do not do as you've asked.
- Sinking, unlovable feelings that happen when children are angry suggest that you may have little ability to avoid thoughts that hurt and find that they overwhelm you.

CHANGING NEGATIVE BELIEFS

The first step to changing negative beliefs is to identify positive thoughts you want to have about yourself when your children misbehave. When your children are not causing difficulty, positive beliefs may seem completely true. It will be harder to have this belief when children disobey. To begin to change thinking patterns that rob you of your confidence, start keeping a journal of upsetting incidents.

Journal of Changing Beliefs

Directions: Use the questions and table above to identify the negative belief that each situation triggers. Write a positive belief that you would like to have in its place and affirm this regularly.

Upsetting Incident	Negative Belief	Positive Belief
• Child refused to answer question about homework.	• I'm powerless.	• I can take action that will help my child respond.

[1] See *EMDR: The Breakthrough Therapy* by Francine Shapiro (Basic Books, 1997) for further ideas on how thoughts affect emotions.

EMPOWERMENT

You don't have to wait to acquire positive beliefs about yourself to act powerfully, but you may have to act powerfully to begin to realize that these beliefs are valid. The latter "wakes up" an inner confidence that makes discipline effective and reserves time for enjoying children. The power that is discovered is "power from within" or empowerment of personal abilities, flexibility, and self-control. It is not "power over," which elicits hidden resentments and domination. Truly powerful parents can:

- Listen to their children's complaints and dissatisfactions because they judge themselves by their own standards, not by their children's or others' opinions.
- Consider their children's ideas before making rules and decisions because they extract useful ideas from opposing views without being unduly swayed.
- Stand by their convictions and also admit when they are wrong.
- Control their own lives and, therefore, do not have to control their children's lives.
- Permit their children to have different interests and beliefs from their own because they do not need a clone to confirm their own identity.
- Allow their children to make mistakes because they know they have gained wisdom from their own.

POWER WITH

"Power with" is the power of strong equals to suggest and to listen. A powerful spouse takes time to work through any disagreements over child rearing without giving in or insisting on her way, knowing that a higher truth can be reached by thoroughly understanding the other person's position. She encourages her partners to listen by listening first! When she sees her spouse's taking unconstructive action, she insists on taking time to discuss their differences, focusing first on understanding his efforts before questioning them. A powerful spouse can handle two particularly difficult challenges:

Stepparents:

- Do not take over for spouses who allow themselves to be bullied or manipulated. Instead, they act as a sounding board to help partners clarify their rules and limits and help them think of actions that they are willing to take to enforce decisions.
- Do not step in as an authority until their partner's leadership is firmly established and the stepchildren have bonded to them. They are comfortable allowing the birth parent to do the majority of the discipline and mainly assume this role when he or she is physically absent.
- Offer a special relationship to their stepchildren as a guide, mentor, or wise friend because they are not encumbered by an authority role.

Divorced spouses:

- Make a special attempt to maintain a relationship as parents. This may mean redoubling all of the above efforts in order to act in best interests of the children.
- Put aside past resentments and desires to change the ex-spouses. Understanding is the priority and is used to reach satisfying solutions.

Armed with the above beliefs that you are a good, powerful, loveable person and information about all the ways you can require cooperation, encourage obedience, and reduce anger, you will succeed in being the parent you have always wanted to be.

CHILD-REARING BELIEFS

Child-Rearing Beliefs Checklist

Directions: Mark statements with which you agree. Compare your answers with anyone who is helping you raise your child. Discuss answers that differ to reach an understanding.

Using Power Wisely

___ 1. When parents lecture, nag, plead, or yell, they upset themselves and delay taking action that corrects misbehavior.

___ 2. Parents need to make the final decision in areas of children's lives that affect others or threaten safety. But, they need to allow children "free will" in areas of interests, beliefs, and style.

___ 3. Children do not have to be punished for behavior that affects only themselves and can be given a natural consequence such as doing their own laundry when clothes are not put away.

Incentives That Require Cooperation

___ 4. Withholding all privileges until children do as they are asked is a better motivator than taking away privileges to punish a child for not cooperating.

___ 5. It is more effective to set a deadline for starting a chore or task than to ask a child to do something immediately.

Actions That Encourage Obedience

___ 6. Punishments should be designed to teach good conduct rather than to cause distress or prevent mistakes from ever happening.

___ 7. Punishments need to be intense enough to upset children but brief enough to provide opportunities to show changes in past behavior.

___ 8. Consistently repeating the same punishment is better than one long punishment.

___ 9. One minute per year of age is a useful guideline for the length of time-out.

___ 10. Children should be told how long a restriction will last and can be given a task that shows they have learned from past actions to shorten the length of the restriction.

___ 11. Spankings require parents to be active while the child is passive. Withholding privileges until a task is performed, time-out, essays, or restrictions require children to comply.

Daily Routines, School Problems, and Moral Matters

___ 12. After demonstrating that they know how to keep their rooms neat, teenagers can be allowed some leeway on bedroom cleanliness.

___ 13. When children lie, punishments should be limited to wrongdoing and to help them identify the causes of dishonesty (avoiding punishments, disapproval, rules, or looking bad).

___ 14. Children who are making poor grades do not have to be restricted for a whole grading period if they bring home school reports showing satisfactory progress.

Responses That Reduce Anger, Bad Attitudes, and Back Talk

___ 15. It is acceptable for children to express frustration with rules and consequences by making faces, pouting, crying, or complaining. (Cross out any that you won't tolerate.)

___ 16. Suppressing a child's frustrations makes them build up. Sympathizing with a child's frustrations reduces them and will not undermine punishments as long as parents remain firm.

___ 17. Parents should give children a reason for their decisions but do not need to make them understand the reason.

___ 18. Children do not need to understand their parents' point of view and may not be able to do so until they have followed a rule consistently.

___ 19. Parents can best fulfill their need for understanding by talking to other adults, not by trying to convince their children.

___ 20. Parents need to understand their children's point of view to make good decisions.

CHILD-REARING SKILLS

Child-Rearing Skills Inventory

Directions: Rate how often you use the following skills: rarely (0 points), sometimes (1 point), consistently (2 points). Check any skills that you would like to improve. Focus on one area at a time until you make progress.

		Points
Cooperation and Rules		
___	1. I use deadlines for starting tasks before valued activities that serve as incentives requiring cooperation.	1. ___
___	2. I reinforce deadlines I set by withholding all privileges until the task is started and returning them as soon as the task is completed.	2. ___
___	3. Once I decide on a consequence, I give only one warning before I act.	3. ___
___	4. I think of a variety of actions to take when rules are broken, rather than always using the same consequence.	4. ___
___	5. I use allowance, purchase points,[1] praise, snacks, and verbal recognition to reinforce desirable behavior and reduce the need for corrective action.	5. ___
___	6. I take action to correct my child rather than lecture, nag, plead, or yell.	6. ___
Anger and Attitudes		
___	7. When I correct my children, I remember to express confidence that they will eventually succeed and point out their past and current progress.	7. ___
___	8. When my children are upset, I persistently feedback and reflect their feelings.	8. ___
___	9. When feeding back my children's feelings does not calm them, I repeat my decision and table discussions until later.	9. ___
___	10. When my children are upset with me, I make sure that they eventually express their feelings to me.	10. ___
___	11. I avoid arguments by feeding back my children's viewpoint, rather than try to get mine across.	11. ___
___	12. When I am too upset to understand my child, I suspend all discussion until I can listen.	12. ___
___	13. Sometimes, after feeding back my children's feelings and understanding their point of view, I do not find it necessary to take corrective action.	13. ___
Using Power Wisely		
___	14. I stop myself from interfering or taking any action when my children's behavior is not dangerous and affects only themselves.	14. ___
___	15. When I am uncomfortable with my partner's child-rearing approach, I listen to his or her reasoning and express my own until we reach an understanding.	15. ___
	TOTAL:	___

[1] Points that can be used to purchase a desired object.

BEHAVIOR CONTRACT

For: ______________________________ **Date:** ____________

Chores and Responsibilities—The privileges marked below are withheld until required tasks are completed:

__ Television	__ Electricity[1]	__ Bedroom privileges[2]
__ Computer	__ Visiting with friends	__ Living room privileges[3]
__ Video games	__ Leaving the house	__ Snacks
__ Telephone	__ Stereo, CD, or cassettes	__ Other:

Back Talk or Disrespectful Language—If a parent's efforts to rephrase, label, play with, or exaggerate disrespectful language do not improve the manner of speech, the privileges marked above are withheld until the young person can:

- Restate previous comments with more desirable words and voice tone.
- Demonstrate that he or she understands the parent's point of view.
- Talk about what is really bothering him or her.

Violent or Destructive Behavior

- If necessary, the parents may use a recommended restraining method until the child is calm enough not to engage in violent or destructive behavior.
- If the parent is unable to restrain the child, the authorities will be called (911).

Both Parents and Children Understand: **Initials:**

- Whenever possible, a deadline will be set for starting a task and parents won't take action or make comments until the deadline. _____
- As soon as the task is completed, the above privileges will be restored. _____
- Privileges are not being taken away, they are only being withheld until the task is performed. _____
- The child is in complete control of how rapidly privileges will be returned because he or she chooses when to perform the desired behavior. _____

I have read the above contract and understand it.

____________________ ____________________ ____________________

Parent's Signature Parent's Signature Child's Signature

This Behavior Contract has been recommended by: ____________________

Credentials: ____________________

[1] Circuit breakers can be used to shut off electricity to child's room to allow him or her to remain in the room without use of TV, computers, etc.

[2] Having time alone in one's bedroom, away from the family, other than to sleep.

[3] Spending time in living quarters with the rest of the family.

THE BE-KIND-TO-OTHERS WORKSHEET

Directions: Answer the following and discuss before watching TV, using the telephone, or other activity.

1. When I said: ____ I was (mark all that apply):
   [inappropriate comment child made]

__ Blaming	__ Giving an order or command
__ Criticizing	__ Showing little concern of other's needs
__ Threatening	__ Showing unwillingness to compromise or find solutions
__ Accusing	__ Insulting, name calling, mocking, being sarcastic
__ Generalizing	__ Other:

2. When I said the above comment, I was probably feeling:

__ Tired	__ Annoyed
__ Rushed	__ Other
__ Impatient	

3. When I said the above comment, others probably felt:

__ Angry	__ Scared
__ Hurt	__ Frustrated
__ Sad	__ Shocked
__ Rejected	__ Other:

   . . . and they are not likely to want to (check all that apply):

   ___ Do the following for me: ________________________________

   ___ Help me: ____

   ___ Other:

4. Instead of making the above comment, I could have said:

5. I would have been less likely to make the above comment if others had approached me by saying:

6. If others say I made the above comment and I deny it, the following are possible:

   ___ Being corrected makes me feel bad.
   ___ I have an evil twin.
   ___ I am not aware of my words and behavior.
   ___ Others are hallucinating.
   ___ I am trying to avoid dealing with it.

7. When I don't admit mistakes I make, others feel:

   ___ Frustrated
   ___ Angry
   ___ Confused
   ___ Distrustful
   ___ Other:

8. When I admit mistakes, others feel:

   ___ Relieved
   ___ Trustful
   ___ Proud of me
   ___ Other:

- Assessment tools to identify where to begin focusing treatment: *Exposure Chart, Erasing Embarrassment, Desired Beliefs Chart.*
- Summary of all handouts: *Breaking the Vicious Cycle of Panic, Desired Beliefs Chart, Anatomy of a Panic Attack.*
- Workshops and presentations: Participants can use *Anatomy of a Panic Attack* to identify any symptoms of anxiety or panic that they have experienced and to discuss physiology behind symptoms. *Retraining Reactions* can be used for demonstration, practice, and review of relaxation techniques.

RECOMMENDATIONS

- Do further reading or obtain training to ensure accurate location of acupressure points (see resources below) described in *Retraining Reactions,* although this approach is generally harmless even when it does not benefit clients.

SOURCES AND ACKNOWLEDGMENTS

- Jeffrey M. Schwartz's "4-R's of recovery" to change brain chemistry, explained in *Brain Lock* (HarperCollins, 1996), formed the organizational framework of handouts on relabeling, reattributing, refocusing, and revaluing.
- Claire Weekes's work, summarized in *Simple Effective Treatment of Agoraphobia* (Bantam, 1979), was used as the basis of face, flood, and float techniques.
- Information on physiology of panic come from Reid Wilson's book, *Don't Panic* (HarperCollins, 1986).
- Information on temperament and neurotransmitters that contribute to panic comes from Melvyn Kinder's book, *Mastering Your Moods* (Simon & Schuster, 1995).
- Techniques that utilize acupressure points come from algorithms for treating panic developed by Roger Callahan as presented in *Energy Psychology* by Fred P. Gallo (CRC Press, 1998).
- Information on social phobia comes from *Social Phobia* by David Katzelnick and James Jefferson (Dean Foundation, 1997) and *The Hidden Face of Shyness* by Franklin Schneier and Lawrence Welkowitz (Avon Books, 1996).
- EMDR formulations for negative and positive cognitions as explained in *Eye Movement Desensitization and Reprocessing* by Francine Shapiro (Guilford Press, 1995) were used to develop the *Desired Beliefs Chart.*

RELABELING SYMPTOMS OF PANIC

The worst has not befallen me—It's really just anxiety.

Anyone who has experienced panic or anxiety knows that while an attack is happening, it seems to last forever. Although most episodes endure for less than three minutes, an attack can be prolonged for hours or days by imagining that you are dying, going crazy, or making a fool of yourself. However, the body's natural calming mechanism will always cause the most intense symptoms of panic to pass.

Anxiety attacks are nothing more than the body's natural reaction to a surge of adrenaline. This is the hormone that responds to danger, low blood sugar, and stimulants. It prepares the body for action by increasing blood flow and tensing muscles. When adrenaline effects are experienced without the presence of clear danger, they can be frightening and less easily dissipated. To be convinced of how normally your body is reacting, you need to fully understand the "adrenaline connection" between sensations and panic.

The Adrenaline Connection

Directions: Check any symptoms you experience and study related coping strategies.

Symptoms	To Cope
Increased blood flow:	
__ A pounding, racing heart results from a surge of adrenaline that causes stronger, more rapid contractions to increase blood flow. The heart compensates for quick, forceful beats by taking a pause, creating the sensation of thumping, or "missing beats." Palpitations are a natural reaction to aerobic exercise, infection, exhaustion, caffeine, cigarettes, and troubling thoughts.	Think: The heart muscle is very strong and cannot burst. A "nervous heart" is still in control and will always return to its normal rhythm. Act: Consult a physician to rule out any physical problems: high blood pressure, mitral valve prolapse, menopause, hyperthyroidism, low blood sugar, anemia, or a heart condition. Relabel palpitations as anxiety if physical problems have been ruled out.
__ Hot flashes and sensations of "heating up" result from blood rushing to the center of the body due to increased heart action. To compensate, perspiration helps cool off the body. Coldness in hands and feet may result from blood rushing toward the center of the body.	Think: "Overheating" is a good aerobic exercise. It is identical to what occurs during heavy exercise. Relabel changes in body temperature accompanying palpitations as a side effect of an adrenaline rush and increased heart activity.
Chest muscles contract:	
__ Chest pain that feels like a pinprick or stitch is caused when chest wall muscles become tense. Sharp pain is felt when the lungs expand during inhalation. Deep breaths can be difficult until discomfort passes. A narrowing of arteries causes heart disease.	Act: Have your doctor rule out heart problems, particularly if you have dull pain or pressure in the center of the chest that radiates to the neck, jaw, or left arm. Relabel pain as "chest wall pain" due to stress once heart disease is ruled out.
__ Trouble breathing can happen when tense chest muscles do not allow enough room for lungs to expand. To compensate, some people take large gulps of air or start breathing fast. Trouble breathing can also result from obesity, pregnancy, colds, asthma, and emphysema.	Think: Breathing problems due to anxiety are no different from having trouble catching your breath after heavy exercise. It is impossible to stop breathing—just try holding your breath. Relabel symptoms as the result of tense chest muscles if physical problems aren't present.

__ Hyperventilation happens when too much oxygen collects in the lungs due to rapid breathing and washes out carbon dioxide.	Act: Breath into a paper bag to inhale carbon dioxide if too much oxygen is causing hyperventilation.
__ Giddiness, Tingling, or Numbness can be caused by oxygen collecting in the lungs due to rapid breathing. Physical conditions of anemia and carpal tunnel syndrome can also cause light-headedness or tingling.	Act: See your doctor if symptoms occur at times other than during rapid breathing. Relabel giddiness and numbness that accompanies troubled breathing as the result of too much oxygen from rapid breathing.
Limb muscles tense:	
__ Shakiness is the body's way of releasing muscle tension. It often happens after lifting heavy objects. Trembling can also be caused by hyperthyroidism and low blood sugar.	Think: Shaking can be a way to express joy, as the Shakers and other religious groups did. Act: Unlock knees and let arms hang loosely so they can tremble freely. This allows shaking to pass more quickly.
__ Feeling faint happens when blood flows away from the brain to "feed" tired tense muscles.	Act: Slow down to let any faintness pass. Put your head between your knees to return blood to your brain if necessary.
Throat muscles tense:	
__ Difficulty swallowing can also feel like a "lump in the throat" or choking.	Think: Swallowing is automatic. Act: Try chewing a cracker without swallowing.
Jaw clenches:	
__ Dizziness, disorientation, and floating feelings happen when jaw tension puts pressure on the inner ear. The same symptoms occur when the inner ear is stressed on amusement park rides. Fluid retention from colds, allergies, and thyroid problems can also strain the inner ear.	Act: Notice how far your jaw can drop with your mouth closed when you're not upset. Clenching and letting go of your jaw can help during panic. Give symptoms time to pass. See your doctor for possible inner ear problems. Relabel symptoms as inner ear pressure.
__ Nausea, diarrhea, and blurred vision happen when pressure on the inner ear irritates nerves to the stomach and eyes. Discomfort from fluorescent lighting, cloudy days, loud noises, and freeway driving can stress nerve endings and also aggravate inner ear problems.	Act: Relaxing your jaw may help blurred vision or nausea pass more quickly. Without rushing, you can find a restroom. If you tell yourself it is okay to vomit, nausea often passes. Relabel symptoms that happen during anxiety as irritation of stomach and eye muscles.

THE SECOND FEAR OF PANIC

Panic happens when concern over the above symptoms triggers further adrenaline release that causes a desire to flee. It is experienced in the mind rather than in the body. There is a sense of urgency, with thoughts such as, "I have to get to a place of safety" or, "I have to get outside and get some air." Panic comes in a wave and must pass as adrenaline dissipates throughout the body. What you are feeling is annoying, unsettling, and possibly painful, but it is not harmful! People do not die or "go crazy" from panic. Relabel panic as the fear of fear that inevitably happens before you learn to manage your symptoms.

- Panic is the fear of not being in complete control of physical and mental faculties.
- Generalized anxiety is the fear of not meeting others' expectations or handling responsibilities, such as paying bills or keeping a job.

REATTRIBUTING[1] CAUSES OF PANIC

Adrenaline has many triggers—Studying them helps stop my jitters.

A surge of adrenaline produces all symptoms of panic and anxiety. But, you may wonder, what causes the surge of adrenaline? Whether your symptoms started all at once or developed gradually, you can reattribute their source to one or more of the following factors:

__ **Your physical predisposition:** Each person has his or her own unique chemical balance. Research shows that people who suffer from panic have other family members with the same problem. This suggests that they may inherit a body chemistry that makes them prone to anxiety. People with a sensitive temperament have low levels of the neurotransmitter GABA that inhibits reactions of the nervous system. When people have too little GABA, they are on alert, overreact, and have difficulty calming down. Sensitive people can be nervous, cautious, and shy and may abuse substances (such as alcohol) that increase levels of GABA. By contrast, people who "go crazy" or have psychotic breaks have a completely different chemical balance. They may have high levels of the neurotransmitter dopamine and low levels of MAO.[2] Worry and panic will make you feel miserable but cannot drive you crazy.

__ **Stress:** Pronounced anxiety often occurs first during a period of high physical or emotional stress. Physical conditions such as broken bones, long illness, operations, and strenuous dieting can "shock" the nervous system. Constant conflict, doing things you dread, or trying to accomplish too much in too little time places demands on the body. Under such conditions, the nervous system is persistently alerted and nerves "fire" all the time. During this state of sensitization, usual emotional responses are intensified. Ordinary fears feel like panic. Old conflicts rise to the surface. Typical ways of coping may no longer work. Once you become sensitized, the condition often perpetuates itself unless you understand what is happening. Thus, people who are not sensitive by temperament can become sensitized during stressful times.

__ **Past experience:** Your upbringing and early experiences can give you personality characteristics that make you more vulnerable to the demands of life:

- Overprotected children can develop vivid and fearful fantasies. Imagination is usually worse than the truth. A habit is developed of anticipating, dwelling on, and reacting to imaginary dangers. These thought habits might not be obvious until the first panic attack.
- Overcontrolled children may be raised with constant criticism, standards for perfection, and expectations to conform. As adults, they strive to appear "normal," calm, unperturbed, and perfect. Any situation that triggers "deviant" reactions is particularly upsetting.

Both types of people approach life with a controlling attitude. They need to manage their surroundings and their own internal reactions in a way that reduces "danger," "differentness", or "failure." Often, people who develop panic attacks have been very competent or outgoing, but can no longer live up to their own standards in the face of overwhelming stress.

__ **Emotional difficulties:** When emotional disorders go untreated for long periods of time, they can lead to panic disorder. Often, people are not even aware that they have a problem until they start having anxiety attacks. They may think it is normal to be fearful of giving speeches, (obsessively) tidy, or moody.

---

1 This term is one of Jeffrey M. Schwartz's "4-R's of recovery" for OCD found in *Brain Lock* (HarperCollins, 1996).
2 See *Mastering Your Mood* by Melvyn Kinder (Simon & Schuster, 1995).

- Social phobias make people have excessive, unreasonable fear that others will notice some particular action of theirs. They may imagine that everyone is scrutinizing them and that people will notice all their flaws. When socially phobic people cannot avoid situations that cause them difficulty (talking in public or being in large gatherings), they may have panic attacks.
- Obsessive-compulsive disorder (OCD) causes people to have repetitious, uncomfortable thoughts that are hard to turn off. Common fears are of harming others, threats to self or loved ones, being immoral, not having enough, disorder, germs, and making mistakes. Panic can occur when anxiety-reducing rituals cannot be used or fear triggers avoided.
- Depression is often linked with panic. The major symptoms of (biochemical) depression include loss of energy and interest, withdrawal, poor concentration, and indecisiveness. The simplest tasks can seem overwhelming. During times when life becomes so difficult, a person can be prone to having an anxiety attack.

__ **A physical problem:** Because panic feels so awful, sufferers imagine they have serious illnesses. Doctors can easily conduct tests to find out if dull, radiating chest pains are caused by heart disease. Other very rare conditions are also readily diagnosed: (1) epileptic seizures proceeded by an "aura" or strange aroma can cause attacks of immense fear; (2) strokes may be the cause anxiety if it is accompanied by confusion, difficulty speaking, or loss of movement; and (3) growths on the adrenal glands can cause anxiety during mild exercise, cold weather, or minor upsets. If any physical problem is present, it much more likely to be one of the following nonthreatening conditions. Seek diagnosis, get treatment, and reattribute anxiety to:

- Inner ear problems when loud noises, fluorescent lights, freeway driving, steep hills, or cloudy days seem to cause tension, dizziness, nausea, diarrhea, blurred vision, or headaches.
- Hypothyroidism when tension is due to fluid retention from reduced thyroid activity.
- Hyperthyroidism when shakiness, palpitations, breathlessness, chronic tension, perspiration, and restlessness are accompanied by increased appetite with weight loss.
- Allergies when panic attacks seem more likely to occur during certain seasons or after eating particular foods. Allergens both stress the inner ear and cause a surge of adrenaline, which leads to tension, shakiness, and palpitations.
- PMS when symptoms occur before menstruation. The female hormone progesterone rises to its greatest levels a week before menstruation and can increase the sensitivity of certain chemical receptors, causing tension, restlessness, jitters, and irritability.
- Low blood sugar when fatigue, palpitations, trembling, dizziness, blurred vision, or sweating happens before breakfast or a few hours after meals and eating something with sugar relieves symptoms.
- Anemia when increased respiration and heart rate are due to the body's effort to produce more (iron-carrying) red blood cells.
- High blood pressure when occasional palpitations, tension, dizziness, and fatigue are caused by clogged arteries that require the heart to use more pressure to pump blood.
- Mitral valve prolapse (which may not even need treatment) when dizziness, chest pain, faintness, and palpitations are caused by a ballooning of a valve during heartbeats.

RETRAINING[1] REACTIONS

Practice letting fears go past changes the way my mind reacts.

Over time, panic becomes an automatic conditioned reaction to certain situations or to symptoms of anxiety. Retraining involves desensitizing your reactions to anxiety that seems to come from nowhere. A toddler was conditioned to be afraid of a stuffed rabbit by hearing a loud bang every time he touched it. He was then desensitized to this fear by being given food on which to refocus when the rabbit was present, or he simply faced his anxiety without hearing a bang. These two methods can be used to make the worst panic as harmless as a stuffed rabbit. Practice refocusing during panic and check which strategies are most helpful to you.

WHEN FEARS ARE BOGUS, JUST REFOCUS

__ Refocus on something pleasant—take a walk, knit, shoot baskets, work a crossword puzzle, count backwards from 100 by 3, hum, or recite poems. At first, you may still notice some anxiety. You will need to remind yourself that the effects of adrenaline always pass and that the less concern you give symptoms, the more quickly they fade away. Refocusing is no different from reading an exciting novel even though you hear a siren in the background. Refocus not to avoid anxiety, but to allow sensations to continue as "background music."

__ Refocus on breathing. Taking breaths with awareness is one of the best things you can do for yourself. The following "calming breaths" should be practiced frequently so you can easily execute them when you are feeling anxious:

1. Take a deep, slow breath through your nose to the count of three, completely filling your lungs.
2. Hold for three counts.
3. Exhale through your mouth while counting to six.
4. Pause for three counts.
5. Repeat steps 1–4 two more times.

__ Refocus on a positive image during calming breaths. You can imagine a safe place where you would feel peaceful by yourself. This might be the beach, the woods, a mountain, or a church. You can also imagine yourself doing something you enjoy, such as swimming, playing bingo, or bowling. It's important that you make the details of where you are or what you're doing as vivid as possible: What time of day is it? What is the temperature like? What colors and shapes do you see? What sounds do you hear? What textures do you feel? Make sure your image is the right size and intensity. When people experience panic, they often want to run to a place of safety. You can do this instantaneously by imagining such a place in your mind.

__ Refocus on a spot. Concentrating on a focal point will spontaneously cause a relaxation response. You may notice becoming still, your jaw and shoulders dropping, your eyes blinking, your eyelids getting heavy, and your eyes wanting to close. Like focusing on breathing or imagery, staring switches you from being a thinker to being an observer. The only thing that produces tension is thoughts. Repeating a comforting word when thoughts dare to enter your mind helps maintains a state of observance that makes panic impossible.[2]

__ Tapping acupressure points may go further than refocusing by removing an imbalance in the body's electrical flow that "holds negative emotions in place." The most important treatment points to tap (about seven times each) during a panic attack are:

---

[1] This term is one of Jeffrey M. Schwartz's "4-R's of recovery" for OCD found in *Brain Lock* (HarperCollins, 1996).
[2] *Trans-Formation in Everyday Life* by Kate Cohen-Posey (Golden Nuggets Press, 800-440-1773), www.psych-assist.net.

1. The bony ridge directly under the eye pupil (ue)
2. Four inches under the armpit (ua)
3. Where the nose meets the ridge of the eyebrow (eb)
4. An inch under the collarbone (cb) and an inch to the side of the sternum
5. Inside the little fingernail (lf).

After noticing some calming effect, further reduce anxiety by moving your eyes in a horizontal figure 8 while tapping the outside points of your eyebrows, humming a few notes, counting to three, and humming again. This is supposed to balance the emotional and logical brain hemispheres.[3] Then repeat steps 1–5.[4]

__ The floor-to-ceiling eyeroll combines the use of acupressure points with automatic eye closure that is a sure sign of relaxation. While tapping the back of your hand between the little and ring finger knuckles, hold your head still and look down until your lids are almost shut. Slowly roll your eyes up as if you were trying to see your own eyebrows. When it is too tiring to look up anymore, allow your lids to flutter closed. Take a deep breath, stop tapping, and exhale while your eyes rest.

WHEN YOU FACE A FLOOD OF TENSIONS IT LOSES ITS DIMENSION

__ Flooding is the opposite of trying to control symptoms. If you face your sensations, encourage them (flood), and float past them, panic will last less than 60 seconds and go through you like a wave. When you try to control your symptoms, you are actually trapping anxiety inside yourself. Attempting to hide what is happening or holding still are ways of trying to control. Even worse, some people run from panic to a "place of safety." This pumps adrenaline into their systems and is like pouring gasoline on a fire. Shaking, allowing a racing heart to run its course, and doing the following allows anxiety to pass through:[5]

- Challenge your symptoms by encouraging them—"Come on, Panic—do your worst. Let's see how bad you can get." Try making yourself shakier. Inviting anxiety makes it back off. Remember that peace is always on the other side of panic. The faster you get into the worst part of panic, the more quickly you will reach peace of mind!
- Change your tone of voice to say your worst fears in pig Latin, sing them, pinch your nose, or use a Donald Duck accent.
- Use a support person to help you discover the power of reverse psychology to flood away tension. Outrageous comments can be made in a soothing tone of voice to outwit fear—"Oh good, you're panicking. Let's see what happens. If you don't come out of it, I'll let all the people who have recovered know that their worst fears can come true."

---

[3] The brain balancing approach has numerous relaxation exercises used here was developed by Fred Gallo to modify Callahan's original "Algorithm." Contact fgallo@energypsych.com or see *Energy Psychology* by Fred P. Gallo (CRC Press, 1998).

[4] Algorithm for treating panic disorder was developed by Roger Callahan. Contact Callahan Techniques at 760-345-4737 or www.tftrx.com.

[5] Flooding is further described in *Simple, Effective Treatment of Agoraphobia* by Claire Weekes (Bantam, 1979)

EXPOSURE TO DIFFICULT SITUATIONS

The more fears I look at in the face, the more they leave without a trace.

Over time, people with anxiety can develop agoraphobia and begin limiting daily activities to avoid experiencing panic when they are not in a "safe" place. People who appear to have mastered anxiety attacks, only to have them return later, never fully recovered in the first place. When panic decreases, do not become complacent! Use the following Exposure Chart to see if you are avoiding difficult situations. Then, choose a circumstance that causes you minimal distress. Practice exposing yourself to it with one of the methods below until you are comfortable. Let your symptoms know you intend to wait for them to pass.

- Refocus on a spot, safe-place image, details around you, your breathing, or a pleasant activity, or tap acupressure points if symptoms of panic start during a practice period.
- Flood by focusing on sensations of anxiety and talking yourself through them—"Oh good, this is just what I wanted to happen. The more times I float through symptoms of panic (without adding a second fear), the more quickly I will become desensitized to them."
- Retreat/repeat by walking or driving away from a place of safety. At the first sign of tension, retreat. Calmly turn around and go toward safety. When you start to feel comfortable, repeat. Walk or drive away again. Continue this procedure throughout the practice session. Do not walk or drive in a random fashion. Plan your route in advance and work on it regularly until you are comfortable.[1]

POINTERS FOR EXPOSURE

- Intentionally expose yourself for a practice period of 10–45 minutes without other obligations or distractions. Do not wait until you have to deal with a difficult situation.
- Practice for the designated time period even if panic passes quickly. Often, people have one or two waves of panic and then feel surprisingly comfortable.
- Practice even when you are stressed. Set your goals lower but practice regularly. The sense of accomplishment from practicing for 10 minutes may help you feel better.
- Take a moment to relax before starting. Doing this even when you are not tense will review calming techniques that you can use with any anxiety that does come.
- In public places, be sure to look at your surroundings and other people. When you avoid looking at people, you may imagine that they are staring at you.
- You may become bored and "get in your head" as situations become more comfortable. If you notice you are thinking too much, switch back to noticing your surroundings.
- Do not rush if symptoms of anxiety start! This only pumps adrenaline into your system.
- Progress will not always be even. Do not get discouraged if you have plateaus. Practicing the same activity over and over will build a platform for later growth.
- You may regress after making steady progress. This is to be expected. Success can be frightening. Review a previous accomplishment until it becomes comfortable again to gain confidence that setbacks can be overcome with practice.
- Identify new challenges that involve greater levels of distress after mastering one situation. This gives you opportunities to continue practicing until you are confident in your ability to "float through" symptoms of panic in any situation.

---

[1] The retreat/repeat method of exposure is further described in *Simple, Effective Treatment of Agoraphobia* by Claire Weekes (Bantam, 1979).

EXPOSURE CHART

Directions: Begin to eradicate panic attacks from your life by identifying situations that you avoid. Rate the degree to which you avoid each item (0 = not at all, 10 = completely). Add any other situations not listed. Systematically expose yourself to situations with a rating of 5 points or less until they are no longer a problem. Then continue to decrease anxiety in other difficult situations through exposure. Columns are provided so you can rerate yourself over time.[2]

Situations I Avoid	Degree Avoided: 0–10 Points		
Home — Date:			
• Taking showers or baths without anyone nearby			
• Remaining at home alone			
• Being in my yard by myself			
• Walking away from my home ___ blocks			
• Other:			
Travel			
• Driving in and out of my driveway			
• Driving in my neighborhood			
• Driving where there are traffic lights			
• Driving in traffic			
• Driving on interstate highways			
• Traveling over bridges or through tunnels			
• Traveling on buses			
• Traveling on trains, subways, or trams			
• Traveling on planes			
• Other:			
Public places			
• Supermarkets			
• Restaurants			
• Parties, social gatherings			
• Theaters			
• Churches			
• Malls			
• Amusement parks			
• Football games/stadiums			
• Other:			
Confinement			
• Lines in stores			
• Elevators			
• Prolonged conversations			
• Barber's/hairdresser's chair			
• Dentist's chair			
• Other:			

[2] Some of the items for this exposure chart were taken from *Don't Panic* by R. Reid Wilson (Harper & Row, 1986) p.30.

REVALUING[1] PROBLEMS

With a little change in attitude, fears loose all their magnitude.

Symptoms of panic can be subdued and eliminated with knowledge about how your body responds to an adrenaline surge and with practice refocusing on something pleasant or floating past anxiety during episodes. However, recovery will not be complete until you have changed your attitude toward panic by revaluing it. In the following example, insecurity became an intoxicating experience:

> One young man began imagining a beautiful peaceful place when he first started to feel his heart pound. He was surprised that this actually made him feel euphoric. Of course, as soon as he began looking forward to symptoms of anxiety so he could get "high," he no longer had panic attacks. His recovery continued as long as he remembered that he could turn a frightening adrenaline rush into a pleasant experience.

With practice, anyone can minimize panic reactions and adopt a whole new viewpoint about them. The first step to changing your attitude is to identify the self-defeating thoughts you currently have about panic. Then, you can compute opposite, positive beliefs that will help you recover by revaluing your symptoms. Notice that the difference between destructive and helpful beliefs can be very subtle:

Change Thoughts That Hurt into ...	**Beliefs That Reduce Panic**
• I put up with symptoms of panic and hope they pass as soon as possible.	I welcome symptoms of panic as opportunities to retrain reactions by floating or refocusing.
• My goal is to stop having panic attacks.	My goal is to become an expert at minimizing panic reactions.
• Getting through one panic attack without difficulty will make the next one easier.	Getting through one panic attack prepares me for any future, more severe, episodes.
• Once I've faced a situation without panic, I no longer need to practice it.	I give panic opportunities to surface by facing situations that used to be or still are hard.
• Recovery means that I have to face every situation that is hard for me.	I find new situations to practice without having to master everything that is hard for me.

The first statement in each pair stresses "success" and suggests that you have to try to prevent or avoid panic. The second statement shows that you have revalued anxious symptoms as opportunities to practice making peace with panic. When you have truly changed your outlook, you will not have a problem if panic returns after a period of being symptom-free. Therefore, it is very important to practice affirming *Beliefs That Reduce Panic* (above) until they are true for you.

[1] This term is one for Jeffrey M. Schwartz's "4-R's of recovery" for OCD found in *Brain Lock* (HarperCollins, 1996).

SETBACKS

Although many people stop adding the second fear of panic after understanding what is happening to them, others have more difficulty retraining their reactions or find their symptoms return after a period of doing well. This can happen for several reasons:

- Success can be frightening. After a good period, people often think: "I hope I never have to go through that again!" "I wonder if this will last." "Am I cured?" "What if I start having problems again?" Any of these thoughts can invite panic!
- Success allows fewer opportunities to practice dealing with panic. People can fall into old patterns of thinking scary thoughts or trying to control symptoms.
- Coming back from a vacation or being in the hospital can cause people to feel stressed by the demands of their daily routine. Brief retraining may be necessary to again become desensitized to certain situations. Even people without panic disorders often feel anxious on Mondays or when coming home from vacations.
- Underlying emotional problems of depression, social phobia, obsessing, and perfectionism that have not been addressed can cause panic to return.
- Symptoms from undetected minor medical problems such as inner ear dysfunction, allergies, PMS, low blood sugar, thyroid dysfunction, anemia, high blood pressure, or mitral valve prolapse can trigger anxiety after periods of doing well.
- Multiple factors contributing to problems with anxiety (sensitive temperament, chronic illnesses, traumatic experiences, family or work conflicts, perfectionistic or avoidant traits, depression, phobias, or obsessions) will create many challenges to not add the second fear of panic to stress.
- Relying solely on medication for recovery can cause symptoms to return when drugs are discontinued. Although some use of medication may be helpful, it is important to gradually replace medication with behavioral techniques, such as refocusing on pleasant activities and floating past anxiety to desensitize panic reactions.

The return of panic is almost a necessary part of full recovery. You need to show yourself that you can deal with symptoms if they do return to lose the fear of problems recurring. Because you may reexperience panic from time to time, it is essential to adopt a final attitude that revalues any "setbacks" in your life.

Change Thoughts That Hurt into . . .	Beliefs That Reduce Panic
A setback means that everything I've tried in the past does not work.	If I've desensitized myself to triggers of panic in the past, I can easily do it again!

BREAKING THE VICIOUS CYCLE OF PANIC

People may be predisposed to experience panic because of a sensitive temperament, high levels of stress that sensitize nerves, emotional disorders (social phobia, obsessions, and depression), a hyperactive imagination, or a perfectionist personality. The actual first episode or trigger incident will be caused by a surge of adrenaline due to one of three things:

- A tense situation: conflicts with people, giving a speech, dealing with painful memories, being in a place where a person feels trapped, or a recent death—"What if I die like my aunt Mary did three weeks ago?"
- A conditioned reaction to certain triggers that bypasses thinking processes—A young girl had a near-drowning experience. A year later, in a submarine ride, she had her first panic attack.
- A nonthreatening physical condition that causes unexplained symptoms (dizziness, nausea, blurred vision, sweating, shaking, faintness, rapid breathing, palpitations, or hot flashes) that are not fear, but feel like fear.

Once the first panic attack happens, it can quickly develop a life of its own. People begin to think, "What was that? Is it going to happen again? Do I have some terrible illness? Am I having a nervous breakdown? What if people notice me?" Negative thoughts that flash through the mind almost below the level of awareness can trigger subsequent incidents until they start happening with increasing regularity.

> A woman with high standards was physically stressed from a miscarriage. She first became panic-stricken while grocery shopping in the aisle of baby products. Later, she began having anxiety attacks anywhere in the store, and then, even when driving past the store—just because these cues were associated with her first attack.

TWO ADDITIONAL PROBLEMS

When panic is not understood as a part of anxiety, episodes can increase in intensity due to two additional problems. Once these are recognized, they can be eliminated by learning coping strategies.

Coping Stategies

Symptom	To Cope
__ Feeling unreal or depersonalized is due to racing thoughts. Brain waves can cycle very rapidly in situations that require "quick thinking." When thinking is converted into action people have a sense of being in charge. If the source of danger in unclear, thinking has no place to go and people feel "trapped " in their heads.	Think: Racing fearful thoughts will not "drive you crazy." Act: Refocusing on your surroundings or even on troubling sensations will help you feel more real and connected to yourself. Relabel unreal feelings as a natural consequence of brooding.
__ Poor memory, indecision and loss of confidence come from a mind over crowded with brooding. Little energy is available for making decisions or remembering routine details. These symptoms can be worse in the morning when blood sugar is low. You may have gone to bed the night before hoping to wake up a new person and then despair at being your same old self. People begin to wonder, "Will I ever be normal again?"	Think: "I am not losing my mind." As you learn to manage symptoms, thinking will become clearer and confidence will return. Be easy on yourself and appreciate little accomplishments. Act: You may need anti-depressant medication to "jump start" your system if you have become with-drawn and have little motivation to do anything, Relabel symptoms as the natural consequence of brooding and early morning blues.

THE VICIOUS CYCLE OF PANIC

Even when stresses, depression, tense situations, or a temporary physical condition have passed, people can continue to have panic just because they fear it will happen. This is the fear of fear. People become afraid of their own bodily reactions—"I've been doing pretty well lately, I wonder if panic will come back." "What if I really do have a nervous breakdown this time?" "What if people can tell that I am perspiring?" This aggravates predisposing factors of temperament, emotional disorders, and personality traits and creates on-going stress that produces the vicious cycle of panic:

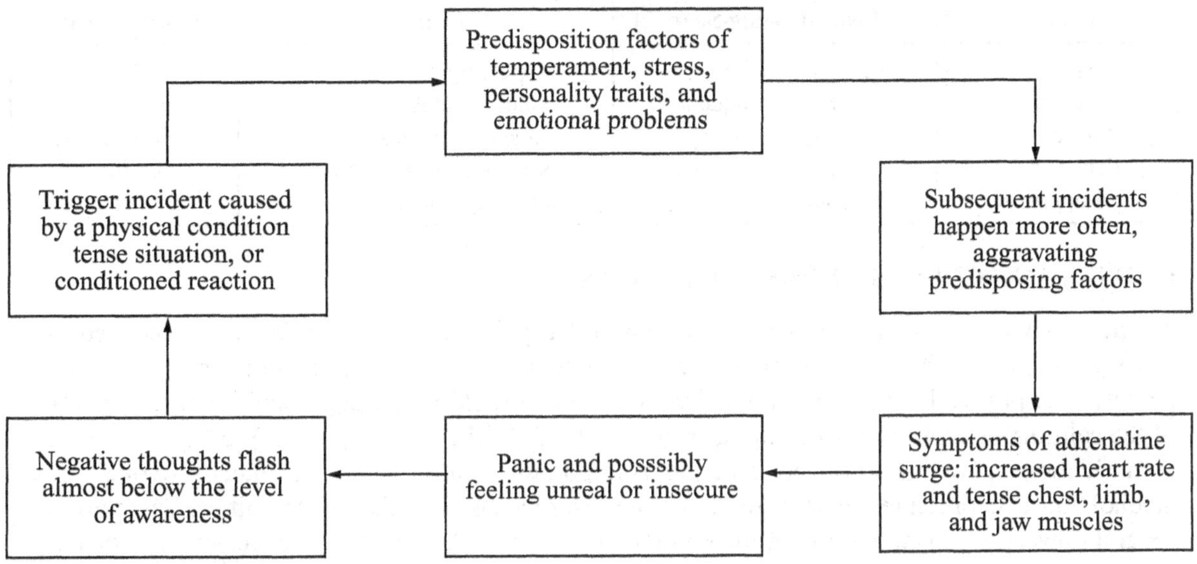

BREAKING THE CYCLE

The steps of recovery from panic can restore peace with calming swiftness and make each link in the "vicious" cycle an opportunity for change:

- Reattribute predisposing factors to minor physical conditions (ear or thyroid problems, PMS, allergies, low blood sugar, anemia, high blood pressure) and unrecognized emotional problems (temperament, stress, overactive imagination, perfectionism, depression, social phobia, obsessions) that are little cause for concern once they have been treated and/or identified.
- Relabel troubling "symptoms" as a surge of adrenaline. This eliminates fears of dying, going insane or making a fool of yourself. People who have anxiety are overly concerned with reality while people who become psychotic are out of touch with reality. They may think they are Jesus, hear voices or speak in a way that makes no sense. Although people with anxiety can have vivid imaginations, they know who, what and where they are.
- Retrain yourself not to react to anxiety triggers and negative thoughts by refocusing on pleasant activities or facing, flooding and floating past the worst sensations of panic.
- Revalue panic episodes as opportunities to practice coping with and minimizing symptoms.
- Expose yourself to difficult situations to increase your comfort zone as panic attacks reduce in frequency. Friends and family can help until you can face triggers alone.
- Get additional help if needed to reduce stress from conflicts or painful memories..
- Reread information on panic disorder at the first sign of reoccurrence of symptoms or after intense episodes of anxiety.

ERASING EMBARRASSMENT

People with social phobia fear embarrassment and negative evaluations by others. Among children, 10% to 15% are shy, and 8% to 11% of adults develop social phobia, which usually begins in mid- to late-adolescence.[1]

Rating Social Phobia

Directions: For a quick check of whether or not you have social phobia, rate how often or intensely you experience any of the following fears on a scale of 0–10, with 10 the most intense fear.

Fear of	Fear of Being Seen	Fear of	Fear of Being
__ Shame	__ Choking on food	__ Appearing foolish	__ Inept
__ Ridicule	__ Using poor etiquette	__ Voice sounding funny	__ Inferior
__ Rejection	__ Spilling something	__ Forgetting an answer	__ Unappealing
__ Criticism	__ Shaking, sweating, or blushing	__ Not knowing an answer or knowing what to say	__ Humiliated
__ Disapproval			__ Embarrassed

CAUSES AND CURES FOR SOCIAL PHOBIA

Shyness may be an inherited trait. Studies suggest that genetics account for 22% to 50% of social anxiety. People may have this problem due to worrisome thoughts about how they are being perceived or physical factors: extra blood vessels under the skin (causing blushing) or low levels of the calming or excitement-seeking neurotransmitters (GABA and dopamine). Early identification and treatment of social anxiety is important because it can eventually provoke alcohol abuse, depression, panic disorder, eating disorders, or avoidant personalities. There are several powerful ways to modify it, including taking medications that help reduce any physical causes:

- Beta-blockers, used in the 1960s to reduce high blood pressure, are effective in reducing heart palpitations and shaky hands that can interfere with performance. They are less effective when taken regularly or in less intense social situations.
- Antidepressants that increase the flow of serotonin improve social phobia in 50% to 75% of cases. It may take 8–12 weeks to achieve the full benefit, and gains may be lost if medication is discontinued. Mild side effects may occur initially.
- Tranquilizers such as Valium and Xanax can reduce social jitters for 78% of people. They work in 15 minutes to reduce anxiety, but they can cause drowsiness, forgetfulness, and dependency, and aggravate depression in some cases.

Choose helpful beliefs and dare to take action that changes false thinking:

- "Physical symptoms will . . . cause panic vs. decrease the longer I stay." Dare to wait 15 minutes before leaving or try making symptoms worse.
- "Everyone is . . . staring at me vs. paying little attention to me." Dare to look around and make a survey of how many people notice you.
- "If I make a mistake, people will think . . . I'm stupid vs. I'm human." Dare to intentionally be foolish—ask where the lettuce is in a hardware store.
- "If I shake, sweat, or blush, people will . . . think I'm pathetic vs. be compassionate." Dare to tell people you shake when you're nervous and watch their reaction.

---

[1] Statistics come from *Social Phobia* by David Katzelnick and James Jefferson (Dean Foundation, 1997) and *The Hidden Face of Shyness* by Franklin Schneier and Lawrence Welkowitz (Avon Books, 1996), www.shyness.com.

- "If I talk to someone . . . I won't know what to say vs. questions and comments will naturally come to me." Dare to ask "nosy" questions to start conversations.

Avoid avoidance to reduce or eliminate social phobia permanently:

- Change body chemistry by exposing yourself to fearful situations. This gives the neurotransmitter that reduces fear reactions (GABA) a chance to build potency.
- Expose yourself to situations you moderately avoid. Pick daily goals and wait for anxiety to lessen. Repeat tasks to neutralize fear and face other tough situations until you can tackle your worst problem. Use positive thoughts (above) during practice.
- Develop hierarchies for difficult tasks. Prepare a speech on shyness. Practice it with a tape recorder, close friends, first-graders, and in your imagination, and then give it.

Rating Avoidance

Directions: Mark situations you avoid and rate the degree to which you dodge them with people you know and don't know on a 0–10 scale: 0 (none) or 10 (complete) avoidance.

	Degree Avoided with People	
Avoidance Situations	**I Know Well**	**I Don't Know**
Occupational or educational activities		
__ Working while being observed	__	__
__ Asking or answering questions at classes or meetings	__	__
__ Attending or speaking up at meetings	__	__
__ Taking a test or giving an oral report or speech	__	__
__ Talking to teacher, boss, or other authority figure	__	__
Interaction		
__ Asking for information or directions	__	__
__ Calling someone on the phone	__	__
__ Leaving messages on answering machines or e-mail	__	__
__ Meeting people and introducing myself	__	__
__ Talking to people of the same sex	__	__
__ Talking to people of the opposite sex	__	__
__ Making eye contact	__	__
__ Expressing disagreement or disapproval	__	__
Social situations		
__ Small or large gatherings	__	__
__ Going out for drinks	__	__
__ Going to or giving a party	__	__
__ Asking someone for a date	__	__
__ Kissing or making sexual contact	__	__
Public scrutiny		
__ People noticing acne, cerebral palsy or other condition	__	__
__ Making telephone calls	__	__
__ Eating or writing with others around	__	__
__ Using a public restroom	__	__
__ Entering a room when others are already seated	__	__
__ Being the center of attention	__	__
__ Giving a performance	__	__

EXTRA HELP FOR PANIC DISORDER

Recovering from panic attacks may include talking with support groups, family, friends, a therapist, or your doctor. In most cases of anxiety, heart palpitations and chest pains have nothing to do with heart disease. However, you may have difficulty completely eliminating this fear until you have had appropriate diagnostic tests. Family and friends who are willing to read information on panic disorder can help in many ways:

- Become thoroughly familiar with information about panic disorder and anxiety.
- Do not tell people their fears are silly, that it's "all in their heads," or that they're "not trying hard enough." Instead, help them understand how an adrenaline rush can make symptoms feel so awful.
- Discuss beliefs that will reduce concerns about symptoms of anxiety. Offer feedback that panic episodes are barely noticeable or information about other family members who have experienced problems with anxiety or depression. This can help people realize that an (inherited) sensitive temperament is a contributing factor.
- Help relabel and reattribute symptoms when a person is not thinking clearly during a panic attack—"You may not have realized how stressful that visit from your mother was."
- Help people refocus on their breathing, something interesting in their surroundings, or silly trivia questions if sensations of panic start.
- Do not constantly try to divert people's attention to prevent panic, but encourage them to find out if panic will come and offer reassurance that you will help them refocus if it does.
- Help people "flood out" anxiety by offering to "worry for them" in your silliest Mickey Mouse voice.
- Encourage people to expose themselves to difficult situations and offer to go with them to help them through any panic that occurs.
- Do not suddenly withdraw support, but find clever ways to gradually help people gain confidence in their independence after helping them refocus, float through, and face panic. Let them know you will be in another room, in the yard, at a neighbor's house or following behind in your car in case you are needed.

FRIENDLY CAUTIONS

- Avoid asking for help from friends and relatives who are pushy, disinterested, inept, or rigid. Attempts to involve them in your recovery or make them change will hinder you.
- Do not argue with people who give you bad advice or try to make them understand. Let them know that you are glad they are concerned and just feedback what they are saying—"So you think it's silly that I keep driving around the block and that by now I should be able manage downtown traffic. It must be frustrating for you to see me struggle and not be able to fix things for me." Even if comments are cutting, respond to them as if they had been kind! Then find someone understanding with whom you can talk or write to yourself in a journal.
- Watch out for friends and family who discourage recovery because they benefit from the limitations that panic places on your life. They may be afraid of losing you or need you to be "weak" so they can be strong. As you start to recover, they may become suspicious, jealous, accusatory, irritable, or even start to develop panic themselves!

NATIONAL NETWORKS AND SUPPORT GROUPS

If you are fortunate, you will be able to find one or two people who will give you assistance. However, this is not necessary. Many people do fine on their own or working with a therapist. You may also be able to find a support group in your community. There are national networks, web sites, and books that can offer additional assistance:

- TERRAP (Territorial Apprehension) INC., 932 Evelyn Street, Menlo Park, CA 94025 (800-2-PHOBIA) offers a nationwide network for panic disorder and agoraphobia.
- Anxiety Disorder Association of America, 6000 Executive Blvd., Suite 513, Rockville, MD 20852, Anxdis@aol.com (301-231-9350) has a newsletter and can provide information about therapists, research, and self-help groups.
- Anxiety-Panic Internet Resource is a self-help network dedicated to overcoming and curing overwhelming anxiety: www.algy.com/anxiety/menu.shtml.
- Treat Your Own Panic Disorder reviews self-treatment for panic disorder: http://e2.empirenet.com/~berta/.
- General Internet sites and links: www.athealth.com/, www.cmhc.com.
- Books: *From Panic to Power* by Lucinda Bassett (HarperCollins, 1997).

MEDICATION

Both antidepressants and anti-anxiety medications are commonly used in the treatment of panic disorder. Antidepressants such as Prozac, Zoloft, and Paxil increase serotonin levels in your brain, which makes problems less likely to happen without preventing them entirely. In mild cases, the herb, Saint-John's-Wort has been shown to relieve both depression and anxiety. Anti-anxiety medication such as Xanax, Valium, and Ativan may prevent panic attacks and keep you from learning how to refocus or float through reactions. Refocusing and floating actually desensitize anxiety triggers. However, medication can be an important part of treatment when:

- Depression is suggested by indecisiveness, withdrawal, and reduced concentration, energy, interest, and pleasure. Often, this is a physiological condition and with current medications, is more treatable than many other illnesses! An antidepressant may be necessary to "jump-start" your body's chemistry so you can return to your usual level of functioning.
- Reassurance is needed that you can take a pill if you are not able to reduce symptoms on your own. Knowing that you can take anti-anxiety medications will ease your mind enough to get through the worst moments of panic. Taking this medication when you are not actually experiencing panic can cause drowsiness. If taken during an episode, anxiety will "absorb" the medication and sleepiness will not occur.

PROFESSIONAL HELP

If thoughts of panic or memories of some of your episodes are overwhelming, a therapist can help you reexperience and "work through" your anxiety in the office setting. This can give you the confidence to know that you can diminish anxiety on your own. By exploring your first, worst, and most recent panic attacks with a therapist, you may discover the origin of your problem and make real strides in changing your reactions. Therapists can also identify and treat any depression, obsession, or social phobia that is contributing to your problems.

DESIRED BELIEFS

Desired Beliefs Chart

Directions: Rate how valid the following beliefs about yourself and your symptoms of anxiety are for you: (1 = completely false, 7 = completely true.) Columns are provided so you can rerate yourself over time.[1]

Desired Beliefs	**Validity: 1:7 points**		
Date:	____	____	____
Relabel—Even if I have a full blown panic attack, I know:			
• I am safe from severe physical consequences.	____	____	____
• I will remain conscious even if it feels as if I might faint.	____	____	____
• I will remain sane and in touch with reality.	____	____	____
• I will appear "normal," rational, and sane to others.	____	____	____
• I can drive safely or take my time to pull off the road.	____	____	____
Reattribute—I know my symptoms can result from:[2]			
• A highly reactive nervous system due to a sensitive temperament, too much stress, an overactive imagination,	____	____	____
perfectionism, social phobia, obsessions, or depression.	____	____	____
• Minor or treatable physical conditions such as inner ear or thyroid problems, allergies, PMS, low blood sugar, anemia, high blood pressure, or mitral valve prolapse.	____	____	____
• Overuse of coffee, colas, chocolate (containing caffeine), nicotine, or other substances.	____	____	____
• Facing a threatening situation, flashing on a negative though, or having a conditioned reaction.	____	____	____
Retrain—I know I can retrain my brain by:			
• Floating through the worst of my symptoms or refocusing on something pleasant.	____	____	____
• Exposing myself to situations that might cause panic and using floating, refocusing or retreating and repeating to become comfortable.	____	____	____
Revalue—I know I can:			
• Welcome symptoms of panic as opportunities to retrain my brain.	____	____	____
• Become an expert at minimizing panic.	____	____	____
• Prepare myself for any future, more severe attacks by minimizing symptoms of panic.	____	____	____
• Give panic plenty of chances to surface by practicing situations that used to be and still are hard.	____	____	____
• Find new situations to practice without having to "conquer" every difficult situation.	____	____	____
• Desensitize myself to any panic that resurfaces if I've done so in the past.	____	____	____

[1] See *EMDR: The Breakthrough Therapy* by Francine Shapiro (Basic Books, 1997) for further ideas on how thoughts affect emotions.

[2] Rate only items that apply in your case.

ANATOMY OF A PANIC ATTACK

First Fear or Conditioned Reaction

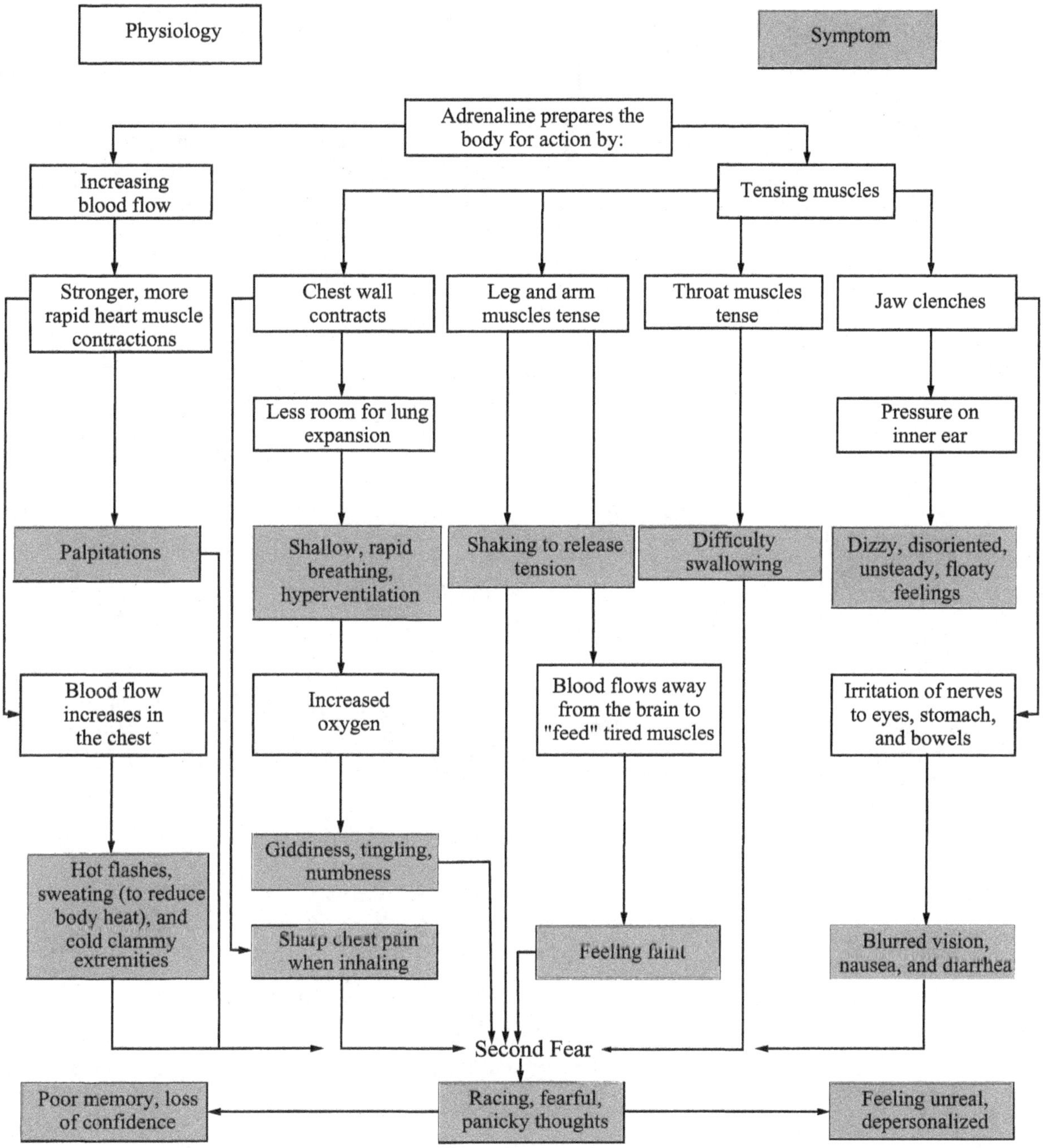

Chapter 6

Not Again

NOT AGAIN

OBJECTIVES FOR TREATMENT PLANNING

1. Identify worries and rituals that are part of obsessive-compulsive disorder (OCD).
2. Understand that impulses, obsessions, and compulsions are neither realistic nor signs of "mental weakness," insanity, or sin.
3. Describe tactics that decrease the intensity of obsessions and compulsions.
4. Describe tactics that decrease or eliminate Trichotillomania (TTM).
5. Report feeling comfortable with situations or objects that previously triggered OCD.
6. Express confidence in ability to manage impulses, obsessions, and compulsions.

MINI INDEX FOR CHAPTER 6

USING THE HANDOUTS

- Assessment tools: *Relabeling Worries and Habits, OCD Checklist, Reattributing the Cause of OCD, Weekly Progress Record for TTM.*
- Literature on treatment methods: *Refocusing and Modifying, Practicing with Imagery, Practicing Exposure, Preventing Rituals.*
- Visual aid that helps clients understand OCD at a glance: *OCD Checklist.*
- Review sheet for behavior strategies: *Planning Recovery, Trichotillomania.*
- Preparation for processing cognitions that interfere with recovery: *Beliefs That Help OCD, Imagery Practice Chart.*
- Handouts for family and friends: *Extra Help for OCD, Trichotillomania.*

- Workshops and presentations: Participants can use *OCD Checklist* to identify any of their own, family members', or friends' obsessions and compulsions. The *Reality Check Chart* can be used to list participants' or family members' obsessive concerns and speculate on the chance of each one happening. Small groups can brainstorm a scenario for the *Imagery Practice Chart* that exaggerates a participant's or family member's obsessive fear.

CAUTIONS AND RECOMMENDATIONS

- Use items marked on the *OCD Checklist* for concerns to rate on the *Reality Check Chart,* to develop scenarios for the *Imagery Practice Chart,* and to identify difficulties to list on the *Avoidance Identification Chart* and *Ritual Identification Chart.*
- Supplement competing responses for TTM (8.25–8.26) with acupressure points described in *Refocusing and Modifying.*
- Do further reading or obtain training to ensure accurate location of acupressure points (see resources below) described in *Refocusing and Modifying,* although this approach is generally harmless even if it does not benefit clients.
- *Practicing with Imagery, Practicing Exposure, Preventing Rituals,* and *Beliefs that Help OCD and TTM* may be best to use with clients actively involved in treatment who are willing to make the time commitment for these intense approaches.

SOURCES AND ACKNOWLEDGMENTS

- Jeffrey M. Schwartz's "4-R's of recovery" to change brain chemistry, explained in *Brain Lock* (HarperCollins, 1996), formed the organizational framework of handouts on relabeling (6.4), reattributing (6.8), and refocusing (6.10) and the preparatory work in plans for recovery (6.18).
- Intense behavior treatments found in the work of Edna Foa and Reid Wilson in *Stop Obsessing!* (Bantam Books, 1991) were used to develop imagery practice, exposure, and ritual prevention described in charts for reality checks (6.9), exposure (6.15), and rituals (6.17).
- Techniques that utilize acupressure points come from algorithms for treating OCD developed by Roger Callahan as presented in *Energy Psychology* by Fred P. Gallo (CRC Press, 1998).
- EMDR formulations for negative and positive cognitions explained in *Eye Movement Desensitization and Reprocessing* by Francine Shapiro (Guilford Press, 1995) were used to develop *Beliefs That Help OCD and TTM.*

RELABELING WORRIES AND HABITS

This isn't me—it's OCD.[1]

Do you have thoughts that repeat themselves over and over? Are you plagued by repetitious habits that are getting out of control? If so, you may have a problem called obsessive-compulsive disorder (OCD). Just by distinguishing constructive worries from unfounded obsessions and healthy habits from unnecessary compulsion, you can start to change! Excessive concern about doing something wrong, being sick, hurting others, looking just right, saving things, being clean, orderly, or germ-free, and preventing misfortune are common sources of obsessions and compulsions. Relabeling concerns and tiresome habits as obsessions and compulsions reduces their power and sets the stage for change:

> I know my fear that dirt will infect me is just an obsession and that my hands aren't actually contaminated, even though I'm compulsively washing them.

DISTINGUISH OCD FROM RELATED DISORDERS

OCD is easy to confuse with related disorders. Misdiagnosis can cause additional worries and delay proper treatment. Knowing what OCD is not will help relabel what actually is troubling you or help you find additional needed treatment:

- Depression can cause people to have repetitive thoughts of being bad, defective, or unworthy. Excessive feelings of guilt, self-hate, and shame are a part of depression. In more severe cases, people may seriously consider suicide. Although, people with OCD fear that they may hurt themselves, they have no desire to do so. The stress of OCD can lead to symptoms of depression: decreased energy, interest, and desire to be with people and even crying spells.
- Panic disorder can cause people to have constant concern about dying, going crazy, or appearing foolish because of unnecessary concern about symptoms that result from a surge of adrenaline. When people with OCD are unable to (perform rituals that) ensure cleanliness, safety, and security, they may feel such intense anxiety that they panic.
- Trichotillomania causes people to repeatedly pull out their hair resulting in noticeable loss. Because low levels of the neurotransmitter serotonin may be a factor in trichotillomania, OCD, panic disorder, and depression, the same medications can reduce symptoms in each of them.
- Problems with impulse control can cause people to give in to urges. Yielding to cravings to overeat, have sex, spend money, or gamble temporarily relieves stress. People with OCD strive for perfection and are constantly battling the possibility of "undesired" impulse. Rather than indulging impulses, they are often overcontrolled.
- Personality disorders can cause people to act compulsively. They may clean, wash, check, or hoard unnecessarily. Instead of feeling exhausted, they feel good about their rituals or they place many demands on others. Their compulsions may help them avoid feeling worthless or having contact with others.
- Neurological tics cause repetitive movements and sounds. These happen automatically and have no thought or intention associated with them. Compulsions are purposeful and attempt to relieve anxiety related to an obsessive thought. Often, people with tics also have obsessions and compulsions. In both conditions, the part of the brain that controls muscle movement and error detection may not be properly regulated. However, obsessions and compulsions can fade when they are postponed, but the "urge" to tic increases when it is delayed. Therefore, each of these problems requires different treatment approaches.

---

[1] Jeffrey M. Schwartz identifies relabeling as one of the "4-R's of recovery" from OCD in his book *Brain Lock* (HarperCollins, 1996). The rhyme "This isn't me, it's my OCD" also comes from *Brain Lock.*

Sometimes, people can be trained to substitute an inconspicuous toe twitch for more obvious tics. "Practicing" a tic at a convenient time may reduce the need to produce it when it would be bothersome. The same medications are not generally used to treat tics and OCD.

Tic Checklist

Directions: Help recognize repetitious behaviors that are tics rather than compulsions. Check any of the following that you do.

Simple motor:			
__ Eye blinks	__ Eye widening	__ Nodding	__ Head turning
__ Jaw jerks	__ Hand jerks	__ Shoulder jerks	__ Stomach jerks
__ Arm movements	__ Finger movement	__ Leg movements	__ Other:
__ Grimacing	__ Tongue thrusting	__ Tensing body parts	
Complex motor:			
__ Tapping	__ Hitting self	__ Funny expressions	__ Obscene gestures
__ Hopping	__ Slamming things	__ Cracking joints	__ Picking at things
__ Stomping	__ Pushing on eyes	__ Touching body parts	__ Other:
__ Squinting	__ Grooming hair	__ Counting	
Simple vocal:			
__ Coughing	__ Snorting	__ Throat clearing	__ "Aaaaaa"
__ Hawking	__ Grunting	__ Gnashing teeth	__ "Ttttuh"
__ Squeaking	__ Squealing	__ Blowing across upper lip	__ "Uh uh uh"
			__ Other:
Complex vocal:			
__ "Uh huh"	__ Swearing	__ Repeating sentences after others	__ Repeating one's own sentences
___"You bet"	__ Racial slurs		
__ "All right"	__ Common insults		__ Other:
__ "Yeah, yeah"	__ Obscene noises		

TOURETTE RESOURCES

Tourette Syndrome (TS) is a neurological disorder characterized by tics—involuntary, rapid, sudden movements, or vocalizations that occur repeatedly in the same way. The cause is genetic and may be related to how the neurotransmitters, dopamine and serotonin are used in the body. For further information see:

Http://members.tripod.com/~tourette13
www.fairlite.com/trich
alt.support.tourette—an online newsgroup dedicated to Tourette Syndrome.
Living with Tourette Syndrome by Elaine Shimberg, (Simon & Schuster, 1995).
Children with Tourette Syndrome, A Parent's Guide by Tracy Haerle and Eisenreich, (Woodbine House, 1992).

OCD CHECKLIST

DIRECTIONS: You may have a problem with obsessive-compulsive disorder (OCD) if you mark several items in the following table. If so, identify your specific worries or rituals in the questionnaire to relabel them as obsessions and compulsions. Underline all concerns that apply in each item.[1]

Obsessions	Compulsions
__ Unpleasant thoughts that come into my mind against my will often upset me.	__ I spend more time than most people cleaning, showering, or checking.
__ I usually have doubts about the simple, everyday things that I do.	__ Other people have difficulty meeting my standards for order, cleanliness, safety, hard work, or decency.
__ I have little control over my thoughts.	__ It's hard for me to be sure I've done something even when I know I've done it.
__ I worry that my bad thoughts will come true.	__ I repeat certain actions over and over.
__ When I start worrying, I can't easily stop.	__ People think I'm a perfectionist, a "neat freak," a hypochondriac, superstitious, rigid, or a "pack rat."
__ Insignificant events worry me too much.	

General Obsessions

__ I worry (with little reason) that my partner is doing something behind my back.
__ I worry too much about hurting others' feelings or making people mad.
__ I worry too much about household noises, how things feel, or other sensations.
__ I worry about losing my wallet or unimportant objects, such as a scrap of notebook paper.
__ I worry that I won't say things just right or use the "perfect" word.
__ I worry about always doing "the right thing" or being honest, fair, or on time.
__ I worry about salvation, having sinful thoughts, blaspheming, or other religious concerns.
__ I am superstitious that saying or doing certain things can cause bad luck.
__ I avoid "unlucky" numbers, places, or animals.
__ I worry that some part of my body is hideously ugly despite reassurance to the contrary.

Aggressive or Sexual Obsessions

__ I fear losing control with sharp objects, while driving, in high places, and in other ways.
__ I fear I will harm others or hurt babies, or I get violent images in my mind.
__ I avoid sharp or breakable objects such as knives, scissors, or glass.
__ I worry that I will blurt out or write obscenities or insults, even though I never have.
__ I worry that I might (accidentally) steal something.
__ I have unwanted sexual thoughts about strangers, family, friends, children, or others.
__ I get violent sexual images that I would never act out.
__ I worry about being a homosexual for no actual reason.

Thinking and Counting Rituals

__ I often have to repeat "good" thoughts or words to "erase" bad ones or to feel safe.
__ I often find myself praying for nonreligious reasons or have to pray "the right way."
__ I feel the need to confess to things I never did.
__ I try to remember events in detail or make mental lists to prevent bad consequences.
__ I count floor tiles, books, nails in walls, my teeth, or other things to relieve tension.

[1] Checklist was adapted from the questionnaire in *Stop Obsessing!* by Edna Foa and Reid Wilson (Bantam, 1991).

OCD Checklist

Checking and Repeating Rituals

___ I worry that lack of due caution will cause some misfortune, such as a fire or burglary.
___ I repeatedly check locks, windows, stoves, or other things to prevent misfortunes.
___ I repeatedly search for news about any accidents caused by others or myself.
___ When driving, I stop to check that I haven't (accidentally) hurt someone.
___ I repeatedly ask or phone others for reassurance that everything is OK, that I haven't made them mad, that I haven't forgotten an appointment, or for other concerns.
___ I repeat activities such as combing my hair or going in and out of doorways.
___ I make sure I've repeated such activities the "right" number of times.
___ I repeatedly check for mistakes while doing bookwork and worry about it later.
___ I repeatedly check my body odor or appearance to make sure I'm acceptable.

Ordering and Cleaning Rituals

___ I must have certain things around me set in a specific order or pattern.
___ I always want my papers, pens, books, collections, or closets arranged just right.
___ I spend much time putting things in the right place, and I reposition rugs, pictures, etc.
___ I notice at once if things are out of place and get upset if others have rearranged them.
___ I vacuum my house, dust, change sheets, or wash floors more than once a week.
___ I spend a lot of time cleaning such things as faucets, counters, utensils, or my collections.
___ I eat foods in a particular order for nonnutritional reasons.
___ I follow a set order during baths or grooming and start over if that order is interrupted.

Germs, Dirt, Danger, or Contamination Rituals

___ I worry about getting diseases from my own saliva, urine, feces, or other things.
___ I worry about getting contaminated or contaminating others by coming in contact with radon, radioactive materials, toxins, dirt, insects, animals, or other substances.
___ I avoid shaking hands, public restrooms, doorknobs, raw meat, cleansers, dirt, sticky substances, emptying the garbage, changing kitty litter, or other problem situations.
___ I wash my hands many times a day or for long periods of time.
___ I often take very long showers or baths and wash to decontaminate rather than to clean.

Hoarding Rituals

___ I save old newspapers, notes, cans, paper towels, napkins, wrappers, or other items.
___ I pick up useless objects from the street, garbage cans, garage sales, or other places.
___ I have difficulty throwing things away for fear I may need them some day.
___ Over the years my home has become cluttered with collections (that bother others).
___ I worry excessively about saving money or food, even when I don't need to.

Health and Illness Rituals

___ I repeatedly take my pulse, blood pressure, or temperature, or check for injuries.
___ I worry that I have (or might get) an illness despite reassurance from doctors that I'm okay.

Rate the Impact of Obsessions and Rituals on Your Life

1. How much distress do your obsessions/rituals usually cause you? (0 = none; 10 = intense): ___
2. How often or how much do your thoughts or rituals interfere with social or work functioning?
   ___ Never   ___ Slightly   ___ Somewhat   ___ Frequently   ___ Severely

REATTRIBUTING THE CAUSE OF OCD

It's just a chemical, so don't get polemical.[1]

As the rhyme suggests, people often get "polemical" and attempt to dispute, defend, analyze, and control their obsessions. Obsessive-compulsive disorder is not caused by a weak mind, insanity, a sinful nature, or actual danger. Nor is it hopeless. Once you can reattribute repetitive thoughts and urges to your brain physiology and chemistry, you will be able to simply observe false thoughts—it is pointless to reason with them.

BRAIN PHYSIOLOGY

Research suggests that there is a physical basis for OCD whether that is abnormalities in neurotransmitters or other causes:

- The part of the brain where error detection happens is shown to "overheat" in PET scans. Many people have had the thought "What if I jump?" when they are someplace high. Then they think "What a silly idea." However, when the brain's "error-detection circuit" is stuck, fear seems to make false thoughts repeat.
- There is a strong tendency for OCD to run in families. Malfunctioning (inherited) brain physiology may cause repetitive thoughts, and traumatic life experiences or stress may contribute to the content of obsessions. Thus, the "germ freak" may have had a near-death experience, and a hoarder may have been chronically deprived.

ANSWERS THAT RELIEVE OCD CONCERNS

Having OCD can be thought of as a faulty set of brakes that makes it hard to stop repeating a thought or action. Just as slamming a set of defective brakes makes them fail, attempts to stop disturbing thoughts seem to make them stronger. People with OCD need to find ways to gently discourage their thoughts and habits. Mark any of the following questions that trouble you and study the answers to prepare yourself to make needed changes.

___ Does OCD mean I have a weak mind? It is a misconception to think that a "strong mind" can control obsessions and compulsions. Due to the brain physiology discussed above, people with OCD don't have an "off button" to stop anxiety-provoking thoughts. Attempts to use "will power" can sometimes make problems worse. However, a set of "brakes" can be built through learning techniques that postpone, modify, or focus away from disturbing thoughts and urges. Reattribute causes of OCD to physical factors rather than a lack of effort.

___ Does OCD mean I am crazy? OCD is entirely different from a thought disorder or psychosis. People with the latter speak in a way that makes no sense, think they are Napoleon, or hear voices. Although people with OCD may have the faulty belief that they can get sick from a speck of dirt, they are in touch with reality and know who, what, and where they are. OCD is considered an anxiety disorder because repetitive thoughts or habits attempt to relieve or cause anxiety. Reattribute OCD to overconcern, rather than a lack of concern with reality.

---

[1] Reattributing is one of the "4-R's of recovery" found in *Brain Lock* by Jeffrey Schwartz (HarperCollins, 1996). The mnemonic rhyme is from the same book.

__ Do "awful" urges or thoughts mean I'm sinful? The greatest concern of some people with OCD is that they are committing a sin or jeopardizing their salvation. It is their very desire to be a good person that makes them worry about offending God. If this is your fear, remember that God is the master psychologist who knows the difference between obsessions that cause people to dwell on the very thoughts they dread and a lack of conscience. Reattribute OCD to being overconscientious rather than an absence of conviction and morals.

__ Does the return of obsessions and compulsions mean I won't recover? After a few days of peace, people with OCD often start to worry, "What if those thoughts comes back?" It is the fear of obsessions that strengthens them. When a troubling thought or urge returns, it just means it is time for a "tune-up." You can learn to use techniques that desensitize, postpone, modify, or focus away from disturbing thoughts and gradually change brain chemistry. Reattribute reoccurrence of obsessions or compulsions to the need to practice strategies that regulate unwanted thoughts.

__ How can I tell when my concerns are legitimate? Some people with OCD are slow to realize that they have a problem because they are convinced that their concerns are realistic. It is only when thoughts or rituals begin to interfere with their lives that they realize they have a problem. The facts about OCD concerns may surprise you:

- Many people use public restrooms without worrying about disease and don't get ill.
- It is a medical fact that "fresh" urine is germ-free. In some cultures, people never wash their hands after going to the bathroom and do not get sick.
- A curling iron can be left on all day without causing a fire.
- Often, people are more at ease visiting someone whose house isn't perfectly neat.

You can distinguish exaggerated fears from realistic problems by using the Reality Check Chart below to compare your forecasts of "disaster" with those of friends or professionals.

Reality Check Chart

Directions: List all the consequences you fear and rate how much distress each concern causes you (0–10 units). Then, rate the chance of its happening (0–100%).

Concerns	Level of Distress 0–10 units	Chance of Happening 0–100%
Examples:		
If I touch a doorknob without washing my hands, I'll get a disease.	8	1%
I might lose control and stab my child.	10	0%
People will think I'm a slob if my house isn't in perfect order.	7	3%

Adapted from chart in *Stop Obsessing!* by Edna Foa and Reid Wilson (Bantam Books, 1991), p. 59.

REFOCUSING AND MODIFYING TECHNIQUES

After many repetitions, concerns about leaving the house, touching a speck of dirt, or disorder can cause the minds of people with OCD to obsess. When checking locks, washing hands, or straightening stops these obsessions, people are also trained to engage in rituals. As soon as another trigger event is anticipated or experienced, the whole cycle starts again. Vague feelings of anger or tension can also trigger obsessions. Any attempts to resist and fight troubling thoughts just create more anxiety and perpetuate the cycle:[1]

Compulsive Cycle

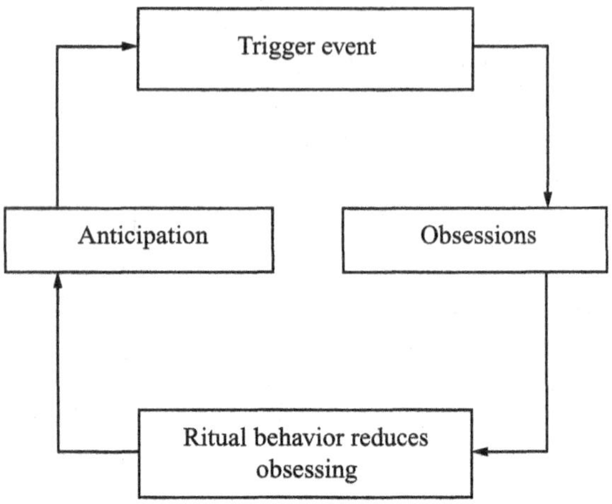

Obsessive Cycle

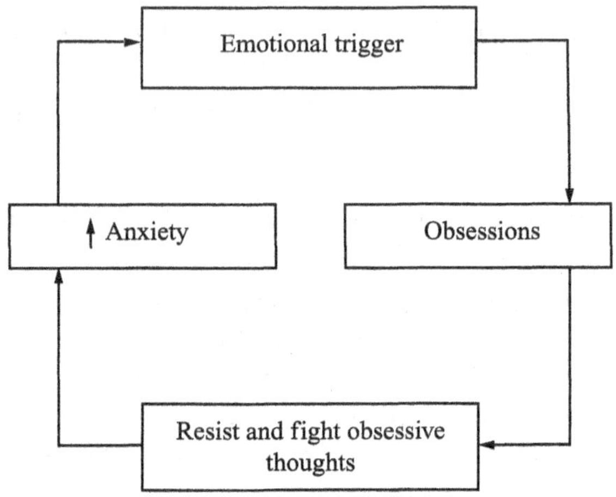

Since the 1980s, this problem has become treatable, both through medication and behavior therapy. After learning to recognize obsessions and compulsions and realizing that OCD is harmless, you can start to interrupt the above cycles by postponing or modifying techniques.

POSTPONE AND REFOCUS

When thoughts are bogus, I change my focus.

Repetitious thought/urges —> Postpone & refocus —> ↓ Obsessing/ritualizing

When you notice obsessions or urges, tell them that they will have to wait a couple of minutes. Then, actively refocus your attention. This is the same as continuing to read even though you hear a siren in the background. Do not keep busy to prevent obsessions or compulsions. Take time to relax and then refocus if unwanted thoughts or urges come. There are numerous creative and powerful ways to refocus:

- Refocus on something pleasant: take a walk, knit, tap complex rhythms, count backwards from one 100 by 3, recite a poem, shoot baskets, or work a puzzle.
- Refocus on calming breaths: (1) slowly breathe in through your nose; (2) hold for three counts; and (3) exhale through your mouth while counting to six. Repeat steps 1–3 two more times. Practice when you are not obsessing. Then, when you notice tension building, breathe!

[1] Flow charts were adapted from *Stop Obsessing!* By Edna Foa and Reid Wilson (Bantam, 1991).

- Repeat a positive thought during your calming breaths to plant it deeply in your mind. Thoughts such as "This isn't me, it's OCD," "It's just a chemical, so don't get polemical," and "When thoughts are bogus, I just refocus" are good for starters.
- Focus on a positive image during calming breaths. Imagine antibodies protecting you from germs; your house guarded from intruders by a shield; a loving person accepting you with all your flaws; or your obsessions floating away like helium balloons.
- Tap acupressure points when obsessions or urges start. This may go further than refocusing by removing an imbalance in the body's electrical flow. Tapping the following points (about seven times each) can reduce or eliminate obsessions and urges to ritualize:

1. Tap an inch to the side of the sternum and an inch under the collarbone (cb) and the bony ridge directly under the eye pupil (ue).
2. Use the sequence cb, ue, cb.
3. After noticing some calming, further reduce anxiety by moving your eyes in a horizontal figure 8 while tapping the outside points of your eyebrows, humming a few notes, counting to three, and humming again.
4. Then, repeat the sequence.[2]

Set a goal to postpone rituals or thoughts with one of the above methods for one to five minutes and gradually increase your time. Keep a chart of how long you postpone and the refocusing activity used. If you succeed at postponing for your goal time, give yourself a treat. If you are not able to postpone for the planned length of time, set your goal lower.

MODIFY RITUALS AND OBSESSIONS

Obsessive thought or ritual	—>	Modification	—> ↓	Obsessions and compulsions

Any time you change something about a habit, you weaken it. The following offer easy ways to reduce obsessions and rituals:

- Modify obsessions by saying your worries out loud, writing them, speaking them in pig Latin, pinching your nose, or singing them to the tune of your favorite song.
- Modify images that accompany obsessions by picturing yourself dancing on the side of the road instead of jumping out of the car, or "stabbing" your husband with a rose.
- Modify compulsions by changing when, what, how, or where you do your rituals. You can change the order of the steps in your rituals, the objects you use, or the number of times you repeat them. Perform your rituals in slow motion, with your eyes closed, standing on one foot, or with your non-dominant hand, or add a consequence. Every time you indulge your thoughts, make yourself do sit-ups or copy sentences from this handout.

[2] Using acupressure points to treat OCD was developed by Roger Callahan. Contact Callahan Techniques at 760-345-4737 or www.tftrx.com. It has been further modified by Fred P. Gallo, fredgallo@aol.com.

PRACTICING WITH IMAGERY

I repeat my fears until I'm bored to tears.

Even when you learn that your repetitive worries and habits are illogical, you may continue to obsess because your mind has been trained to react to certain trigger events. The way to "untrain" your mind is to intentionally expose yourself to the trigger event without trying to resist anxiety with rituals. Tension eventually lessens and the association of the trigger with obsessing is broken. Often, it is best to start exposure through imagery.[1]

Obsessive thought	—>	Imagery practice	—>	↓	Obsessing

Instead of waiting for distressing thoughts to pop into your mind, intentionally think them. This works for two reasons: (1) obsessions are reactions to a trigger; when you choose to have them, you increase your control over them; (2) avoiding things that distress you increases anxiety; if you feared the color purple and imagined sitting in a purple room, you would feel tremendous tension initially, but eventually it would pass. There are two ways to practice obsessing:

1. Pick a specific time each day to spend obsessing. Give yourself a full 10 minutes to think of or write down all your worries. When unwanted obsessions come at other times, tell them they will have your full attention during your practice period. If you tend to obsess while trying to fall asleep, you are using bedtime for practice. This is poor timing. Worry earlier in the evening. Just as you become less aware of a bad odor the longer you are exposed to it, by bedtime, "interest" in your worry will diminish. Fighting obsessions intensifies them. Allowing time to obsess, de-energizes them.
2. Create scenarios that exaggerate your obsessions. Write a story and/or record one. Listen to or read your story over and over for an entire practice period of 45–90 minutes. Focus your attention on physical sensations of anxiety to release tension. Continue imagining the scenario until your fear reduces. Rate your distress on a 0–10 scale (0 = no distress, 10 = intense distress) each time you say, write, or listen to your story. Daily practice sessions for three weeks can dramatically alter brain chemistry. When spontaneous obsessions and rituals decline or stop, you can have practice periods as needed. Instead of being upset if a worry comes back, you can simply tell yourself, "My brain must be 'heating up' because I'm under stress. It looks like I need a practice session." The following are examples of possible imagery scenarios:
   - Doorknob germs crawling all over your body and causing a gruesome disease.
   - People coming into your house when it is not perfectly clean and scolding you.
   - A crowd of people making fun of you because a few hairs are out of place.
   - Your friends talking about you because you made a mistake on your checkbook.
   - Having an empty closet 10 years from now because you threw out an outfit.

If the thought of imagining your scenario terrifies you, work with a partner. Hearing your worries from someone else's mouth or developing them to their "illogical" extension makes them seem absurd and can give immediate relief.

---

[1] Method for imagery practice is adapted from *Stop Obsessing!* By Edna Foa and Reid Wilson (Bantam Books, 1991).

IMAGERY PRACTICE CHART

Directions: Write a story that exaggerates one of your obsessions or fears. Make the story as detailed as possible. Do not hesitate to use humor as you follow these steps:

- Spend 45–90 minutes reading, singing, listening to, writing, or imagining your story.
- Rate the degree of anxiety you feel after each time your read or imagine your story on a subjective unit of distress (SUD) scale (0 = no distress, 10 = intense distress).
- Continue to practice for 21 days or until you feel no distress imagining your scenario. Then write a scenario for another obsession and work on it.

WEEKLY PRACTICE SHEET

Sample Scenario:

Instead of avoiding my favorite restaurant out of fear that I might hurt someone, I decide to go in. I order a delicious steak. Just as I start to cut into it, the waiter sets bread on the table and I stab his hand instead. When I see blood starting to come out of his hand, a strange compulsion comes over me and I stab him again and again. Then I turn around looking for other hands to stab. People are moving their hands wildly to avoid my attempts to lurch at them. By now, the authorities have been called. They know just how to deal with me. They pretend to put out their hand for me to stab and quickly pull it back as I start to lunge. I am caught off balance and the knife is wrestled from me. As I am being taken away to jail, the arresting officer says, "Oh she must have caught that hand-stabbing virus that the astronauts brought back from outer space."

My Scenario:

1st Practice	2nd Practice	3rd Practice	4th Practice	5th Practice	6th Practice	7th Practice
1. ___ SUD	1. ___ SUD	1. ___ SUD	1. ___ SUD	1. ___ SUD	1. ___ SUD	1. ___ SUD
2. ___ SUD	2. ___ SUD	2. ___ SUD	2. ___ SUD	2. ___ SUD	2. ___ SUD	2. ___ SUD
3. ___ SUD	3. ___ SUD	3. ___ SUD	3. ___ SUD	3. ___ SUD	3. ___ SUD	3. ___ SUD
4. ___ SUD	4. ___ SUD	4. ___ SUD	4. ___ SUD	4. ___ SUD	4. ___ SUD	4. ___ SUD
5. ___ SUD	5. ___ SUD	5. ___ SUD	5. ___ SUD	5. ___ SUD	5. ___ SUD	5. ___ SUD
6. ___ SUD	6. ___ SUD	6. ___ SUD	6. ___ SUD	6. ___ SUD	6. ___ SUD	6. ___ SUD

PRACTICING EXPOSURE

When fears are faced, they get erased.

Intentionally facing irrational fears ultimately reduces them. Rational fears usually are associated with specific dangers. Irrational fears mushroom in size and generalize to the most harmless acts or objects. Most people proofread a letter once before mailing it. When you fear making mistakes (and being "incompetent"), you might find yourself proofreading 5, 10, or even 20 times. Then your checking ritual could generalize to reading your shopping lists over and over for mistakes.

Exposure —>	↑ Anxiety —>	↓ Anxiety —>	↓ Rituals/obsessions

To "decondition" anxiety reactions, you need to face the things you fear. When you intentionally provoke anxiety but imagined consequences do not happen, the association between your fear and the trigger event is broken. You can learn that no harm will come by deliberately:

- Making mistakes
- Holding sharp objects
- Touching "germs"
- Petting a black cat
- Putting something out of place
- Leaving an iron plugged in for 15 minutes
- Throwing out a useless item
- Going out without all your makeup on

PRACTICING EXPOSURE

Taking the following steps will help you learn that putting yourself "in harm's way" can be healing:

1. Make a list of all the things you avoid. Generally, people with OCD fear being harmed, harming others, or being negligent/unacceptable. Examine your rituals to find out which of these you are trying to prevent or undo and list the specifics.
2. Rate how completely you avoid each item on your list (0 = never, 10 = always).
3. Arrange your list in order of the degree to which you avoid—Leaving the front door unlocked without checking for a 15-minute walk vs. leaving it unlocked all day.
4. Choose a situation that you avoid somewhat (level 5)—Leaving a dining room chair out of place or throwing out your collection of tin cans. Expose yourself to it.
5. Focus on the physical sensations of fear rather than your thoughts during exposure.
6. Confront the situation until you notice a marked decrease in distress. Continue to practice facing a situation until you experience minimal or no distress.
7. Practice 45–90 minutes daily for one to three weeks to achieve the best results.
8. Pick a situation that causes more distress from your list. Repeat steps (5) and (7) until you have eliminated distress in a level 10 situation. Use a partner or therapist to help you if your discomfort does not decrease during a practice session, or work on the same situation the next day for a longer period of time.
9. Practice highly distressing situations with imagery before actual exposure.
10. Be sure to identify all the ways you avoid so that you can expose yourself to and eliminate obsessions and compulsions. If you do not ultimately face all situations that cause you distress, you can lose gains you've made on easier items!

AVOIDANCE IDENTIFICATION CHART

Directions: Make a list of all the things you avoid. Rate the degree to which you avoid each item (0 = not at all, 10 = completely). Include items that are somewhat uncomfortable (4–7) along with ones you must completely avoid (9–10).	
Situations or Objects Avoided	**Degree Avoided (0–10)**
Examples:	
• Using a public laundry	10
• Using the laundry in my apartment complex	6
• Touching a doorknob in a high-class restaurant	7
• Touching a doorknob in a fast-food restaurant	8
• Buying items that I saw someone else touch	8
• Checking out a book from the public library	4
• Picking up litter	10
What I avoid:	

Chart adapted from information in *Stop Obsessing!* by Edna Foa and Reid Wilson (Bantam Books, 1991), p. 61.

PREVENTING RITUALS

I must refrain to untrain my brain.

Exposure +	Ritual prevention	—>	↑ Anxiety	—>	↓ Anxiety	—>	↓ Compulsions

Ritual prevention is an integral part of exposing yourself to situations that provoke obsessions or compulsions. Concerns about external danger, negligence, incompetence, imperfection, bad luck, and scarcity usually have elaborate rituals associated with them. Identify your rituals and the amount of time you spend performing them to alleviate concerns. Examine the following for ideas:

Negligence—>Checking:

- Stove—30 times/day
- Trash can—3 times/ day
- Faucets—5 times/day
- Shower curtain closed—5 times/day

Disorder—>Straightening:

- Desk—10 min./day
- Drawers—30 min./day
- Books—30 min./week
- Collections—30 min./day
- Pictures—30 min./day

Germs

- Wash hands—20 times/ day
- Shower—90 min./day
- Scrub counters—30 min./day

Scarcity

- Clipping/filing newspaper Articles—30 min./day
- Collecting discarded items—2 Hrs./day
- Shopping—8 hrs./week

Bad luck

- Praying—50 times/day
- Repeating the "right" thought—30 times/day
- Patting my heart—100 times/day

Appearance

- Showering—5 times/day
- Putting on makeup—2 hrs./day
- Ironing underwear—10 min./day

PRACTICE PREVENTION

Tendencies to ritualize can be turned into opportunities to practice prevention by practicing the following steps:

- Plan in advance how you will prevent rituals when you expose yourself to triggers. This gives you time to prepare yourself to change patterns. Sufficient time spent practicing exposure will take the edge off anxiety and make it easier not to ritualize. Your past attempts to stop rituals have probably been made on the spur of the moment.
- Use techniques for postponing rituals and refocusing on a pleasant activity to assist in ritual prevention.
- Do not engage in rituals to reduce anxiety when you begin exposure practice. Initially, this may involve "overkill"; for example, do not wash your hands all day; take one 10-minute shower a day; or do not save anything for a week.
- Clarify realistic standards by consulting with friends or professionals. Hands need to be washed only after using the toilet, before handling food, or when they're visibly dirty. Stoves and front doors need to be checked only once before bed or leaving the house. Vacuuming, changing sheets, and dusting can be done weekly.
- Practice "symbolic" ritual prevention on a regular basis. Make it a point to carry a pocketknife. Leave one corner of a room disorganized. Rearrange decorative items regularly. Intentionally think "dangerous words." Throw out unnecessary items frequently. Occasionally go to the store without brushing your hair or wearing lipstick.
- Be sure to identify all your rituals. You can use the above steps to eliminate them.

RITUAL IDENTIFICATION CHART

Directions: Identify the rituals you perform to undo or prevent harm, mistakes, deprivation, or other problems. Calculate the amount of time you spend performing these rituals. Make sure you have examined all of your repetitious habits to determine if they are compulsions.

Repeated Habits and Actions	Performance/Time
Examples:	
• Repeating what I am doing to "undo" a bad thought	30 minutes/day
• Counting the number of times I am repeating to make sure is not three times or a multiple of three	60 minutes/day
• Washing my hands	40 times/day
• Calling my husband to make sure he hasn't been hurt	50 minutes/day
• Counting rolls of toilet paper, canned goods, etc.	20 minutes/day
• Buying things from garage sales	10 hours/week
• Putting two periods after every sentence I write	10 minutes/day
My Rituals:	

Chart adapted from information in *Stop Obsessing!* by Edna Foa and Reid Wilson (Bantam Books, 1991), p.62.

PLANNING FOR RECOVERY

The plans below can be used to help you think about how to take action to transform your obsessions and compulsions. If possible, choose a family member or friend to work with you. They can help you stay in contact with feared objects or situations, refocus on body sensations of anxiety, playfully exaggerate your imagery stories, and postpone or prevent urges to ritualize. Before getting started it is necessary to prepare by:

- Identifying repetitious thoughts or habits and making lists of them.
- Examining how realistic your fears are by rating the distress each concern causes (0–10 units) and the chance of it happening (0%–100%).
- Relabeling these thoughts and habits as a part of obsessive-compulsive disorder (OCD).
- Reattributing the causes of OCD thoughts and habits to your unique physiology.
- Revaluing the occurrence of OCD thoughts and habits as opportunities to practice strategies that can change brain chemistry.

GENERIC PLAN 1

This plan relies on postponing and refocusing and generates gradual but steady reduction in OCD thoughts and habits without requiring large time commitments.[1]

1. Practicing observing your obsessions and compulsions. Tell yourself, 'I'm repeating this 'What if worry' or silly ritual because my brain cannot detect that it is irrational (even though my mind knows better).'
2. Use rhymes and positive thoughts to replace repetitious thoughts and habits—This isn't me, it's OCD, I'm still complete when I need to repeat, It's just stress that makes my mind regress, When thoughts are bogus, I change my focus, I repeat my fears till I'm bored to tears, When fears are faced, they get erased.
3. Begin refocusing whenever you catch yourself obsessing or acting out rituals. Put your attention on something enjoyable that takes concentration: play with a yo-yo, work a crossword puzzle, recite a poem or Bible verse, breathe with awareness, go for a walk, or tap acupressure points.
4. Do not be concerned if your mind is only half on your chosen activity. At first, OCD thoughts and urges will seem to 'fight' to get your attention. You have still begun the process of refocusing. You will gradually get better at it.
5. Do not stay busy to keep OCD thought and urges away! This will deprive you of opportunities to practice refocusing. Instead, tell yourself, 'I can relax and only get busy if any thoughts come.'

GENERIC PLAN 2

This plan makes use of special behavioral techniques that can produce rapid change. It involves a three-week recovery program in which you intensely practice up to two hours a day. This may mean rearranging daily commitments, obtaining child-care, or even taking time off from work.[2]

1. Write or make tape recordings of stories exaggerating the details of one thing you fear (rejection, humiliation, defectiveness, disorder, being harmed, harming people, or other concerns). Identify any catastrophic fear behind your obsession or compulsion and incorporate it into your story. Start with concerns that cause moderate distress.

---

[1] This plan is based on ideas in the book, *Brain Lock* by Jeffrey M. Schwartz (HarperCollins, 1996).
[2] This plan is based on the book, *Stop Obsessing!* by Edna Foa and Reid Wilson (Bantam Books, 1991).

2. Use imagery practice to repeatedly read, listen to, or imagine the story you created until it no longer causes you distress. Do your best to practice 45 minutes daily for three weeks. Start with moderately upsetting situations and proceed to the most distressing. Do not use imagery practice to avoid exposure (number 3).
3. Systematically, expose yourself to upsetting concerns by acting out or coming in contact with the things you have already practiced through imagery:
   - Send a letter to your support person with several missing periods.
   - Watch violent movies, hold knives, and go to restaurants.
   - Go to the grocery store without taking a shower and examine people's faces to see if they notice.
   - Throw out hoarded items, little by little.
   - Touch 'unclean' objects and focus on anxiety until sensations decrease.
   - Have a friend create a disorder and look at it for ten minutes, 4–5 times a day.
   - Stop yourself from checking to see if the stove is off or the door locked.
   - Stand on a sidewalk crack without crossing your fingers to prevent bad luck.
   - Intentionally think 'dangerous' thoughts or imagine a misfortune.
4. Immediately focus on your catastrophic fantasy until anxiety lessons or you stop obsessing.
5. Do not engage in rituals that accompany your concerns during and after practice.
   - Make it impossible to avoid 'contamination' by touching a tissue with an 'unclean' object and rubbing it over your clothes, counters, or sheets and use imagery practice until distress lessens.
   - Symbolically reinfect your hands with your 'contamination' tissue after washing them.
   - Keep your house disorganized or go through the kitchen often without checking the stove when you first start your recovery program.
   - Make sure all of your routines for cleanliness, caution, and order are within normal limits.
   - Do not let yourself cross your fingers or repeat 'good' words to 'undo' misfortunes you are imagining.
6. Be alert to situations or objects that you avoid and face them with imagery and exposure until you have markedly reduced anxiety and frequency of obsessions.
7. Regularly do 'risky' things (disorganize a corner of a room, use 'dangerous' objects, throw something out, leave a faucet dripping, imagine something awful, or 'infect' yourself with your 'contamination tissue' to symbolically show your obsessions that they can no longer worry you.
8. Repeat this plan with all of your obsessive concerns or compulsive habits until they are no longer distressing. Gradually focus on more upsetting concerns.
9. If obsessive thoughts return, postpone them, refocus on enjoyable activities, or modify something about them and schedule an imagery practice session as soon as possible.

EXTRA HELP FOR OCD

Recovering from obsessive compulsive-disorder (OCD) may include talking with a support group, family, friends, and a therapist and taking medication. Family members and friends who are willing to read information on OCD can be of great assistance by acting as 'support persons.' At every stage of recovery, they can offer important input or action:

- Help relabel repetitious thoughts and rituals as obsessions and compulsions. The best approach is to ask 'Do you think that's a ritual or realistic?' It is more important to help people observe and 'play with' their obsessions than to tell them to stop—Sing their obsessive thoughts or perform their rituals for them as a ballet.
- Do not try to accommodate to OCD standards. Do what you think is reasonable in the way of cleanliness, orderliness, or safety and allow loved ones to do whatever else they need to do to satisfy themselves.
- If you are continually asked for reassurance, refuse to answer unless the person will write down what you are saying word-for-word —'My husband states he is not mad at me.' This applies to telephone calls for reassurance as well.
- Help explain brain chemistry that makes it hard for an 'off button' to block false thoughts from repeating. Reassure people that no matter how bizarre their thoughts and rituals seem, they are not crazy, immoral, weak, or hopeless.
- Offer information about family members who have experienced problems with OCD or related disorders to place the 'blame' on genetics.
- Help people rate the possibility of fears and concerns actually happening—Point out that a stray cat on the side of the road has about a 1% chance of becoming road kill.
- Help people refocus when they report they are obsessing or when they want to postpone rituals—Have them recite poems to you, ask silly trivia questions, play hand clapping games with children, or take calming breaths.
- Help create scenarios that exaggerate obsessions in vivid detail with humor. Read, sing, or dramatize scenarios with loved ones and help them rate the distress they feel after each performance.
- Offer to accompany people while they expose themselves to difficult situations. Help them tune in to sensations of anxiety and notice signs of calming—Touch the washing machines in a public laundry and remain there for 45–90 minutes until tension lessens.
- Help loved ones prevent rituals after they have exposed themselves to an OCD trigger—Threaten to join them in the shower if they bathe over 10 minutes.

FRIENDLY CAUTIONS

Avoid asking for help from friends and relatives who are pushy, controlling, inept, disinterested, or rigid. Attempts to involve them in your recovery or make them change will only slow you down. Be cautious of bad advice. Input that makes you obsess even more is probably incorrect. Watch out for people who discourage recovery. They may be too helpful and offer to do things for or with you so you won't have to 'get upset.' As you start to recover, they may become suspicious, jealous, accusatory, irritable, or even start to obsess themselves!

NATIONAL NETWORKS AND SUPPORT GROUPS

If you are fortunate, you will be able to find one or two people who will give you appropriate assistance. However, this is not necessary. Many people do just fine on their own or working with a therapist. You may also be able to find a support group in your community. There are national networks, web sites, and books that offer additional assistance:

- Obsessive-compulsive information: Dean Foundation, www.deancare.com, 8000 Excelsior Drive, Suite 302, Madison, WI 53717-1914.
- Our Courage Defines Us, International Newsletter for OCD: PO Box 9123, Niskayuna, NY 12309-0123.
- Anxiety Disorder Association of America, 6000 Executive Blvd., Suite 513, Rockville, MD 20852 (301-231-9350) has a newsletter and can provide information about therapists, research, and self-help groups.
- OC Foundation, Inc., www.ocfoundation.org, PO Box 70, Milford, CT 06460-0070, 203-878-5669.
- General Internet sites and links: www.athealth.com/, www.cmhc.com.
- *Brain Lock* by Jeffrey Schwartz (HarperCollins, 1996).
- *Stop Obsessing* by Edna Foa and Reid Wilson (Bantam Books, 1991).
- *Tormenting Thoughts, Secret Rituals* by Ian Osborn (Pantheon, 1998).

MEDICATION

Antidepressants such as Prozac, Zoloft, and Paxil increase serotonin levels in the brain and have been very effective in treating OCD. Luvox is similar to these medications and is more helpful in treating OCD than depression. The herb Saint-John's-wort helps in some cases. At times, medication completely relieves symptoms of OCD or makes them 'livable.' Often, behavior treatment is needed in addition to medication. It is especially important that women who plan to become pregnant at some time in their lives learn how to reduce or eliminate symptoms without medication. In mild to moderate cases of OCD when depression is not present, behavior strategies may be the treatment of choice. Behavior treatment can change brain chemistry but initially requires discipline and effort.

PROFESSIONAL HELP

Therapists are especially helpful when using aggressive behavior therapy techniques of exposure and ritual prevention. First exposing yourself to OCD triggers through imagery can make actual contact with difficult objects and situations much easier. There are several treatment approaches that can make imagery practice less painful when first starting your recovery program. Therapists can also identify and treat any depression, panic disorder, or impulse control disorder that is contributing to your problems.

TRICHOTILLOMANIA

The Greek words *thrix* (hair) and *tillein* (to pull) name an impulse disorder in which people feel mounting tension that can be relieved only by pulling out their hair. Many people with trichotillomania (TTM) also bite nails, suck their thumb, chew their tongue, pick scabs, cut themselves, or bang their head. People with TTM can have obsessive-compulsive disorder or have relatives with OCD. Both conditions may be related to problems with the neurotransmitter serotonin. Although stress can aggravate or cause the first onset of hair pulling, TTM is most likely a biochemical, inherited disorder. The following questionnaire supplies information needed prior to starting treatment for this problem.[1]

HAIR PULLING QUESTIONNAIRE

1. Why is hair pulling a problem for you:
   - How much time do you spend pulling hair per day?
   - What changes have you had to make in your hairstyles because of hair pulling?
   - What do you avoid because of hair pulling? Does it cause you to be dishonest?
   - How does it affect your relationships with family, friends, and coworkers? How do others react to your hair pulling?
2. What "risky" activities are likely to lead to hair pulling:

___ Watching TV	___ Reading	___ Studying	___ Talking on the phone
___ Class Work	___ Falling asleep	___ Driving	___ Other:

3. What behaviors or feelings come just before you start to pull your hair:

___ Touching your face	___ Looking in the mirror
___ Propping your head on your hand	___ Touching/stroking hair
___ Other behavior or feelings:	

4. What behaviors would make hair pulling more difficult or impossible:

   ___ Doing a craft or playing with clay, Koosh balls, Velcro, or velvet, etc. during risky times.
   ___ During class, holding a pen in one hand and a notebook in the other.
   ___ Reading a book until falling asleep.
   ___ Wearing gauze gloves, acrylic nails, or putting gel on affected areas.
   ___ Making tight fists or snapping a rubber band on your wrist until the urge to pull has passed.
   ___ Brushing hair when scalp tingles.
   ___ Other:

5. What rewards can you give yourself for days or hours when you resist urges to pull?

___ Going out to dinner or the movies	___ Taking a bubble bath
___ Buying myself a gift	___ Eating a mint
___ Adding to my collection of stones, CDs	___ Other:

TREATMENT PROGRAM

Behavior therapy can be very effective in eliminating hair pulling. Antidepressant medications that increase serotonin levels may first be needed if depression, panic disorder, or OCD accompanies TTM. This helps people gain the motivation and focus needed for behavior treatment. Beware of tranquilizers and sedatives that can prevent practicing or learning the following urge-reducing strategies:

---

[1] Ideas for the questionnaire and the treatment program are adapted from *Trichotillomania: A Behavioral Approach Video and Manual* by Carol Novak (Pioneer Clinic, 1995) and *Trichotillomania: A Guide* by Anders and Jefferson (Dean Foundation, 1994).

1. Awareness training:
   - Record incidents of hair pulling on a chart prior to starting and throughout treatment to increase awareness of behavior and progress being made.
   - Observe hair plucking in a mirror or on videotape to monitor movements involved. Describe out loud exactly what you are doing.
   - Practice positive grooming after any incidents of pulling: brushing hair, repairing eye makeup, or scalp massage.
2. Relaxation training. Practice each of the following and decide which is most useful:
   - Take three calming breaths by breathing in through your nose to the count of three and exhaling through your mouth to the count of six.
   - Imagine a safe place (the beach, woods) or enjoyable activity (swimming, dancing) during your calming breaths. Notice what you would see, hear, smell, and feel in each situation to switch from thinking to observing.
   - Focus on a spot and observe signs of relaxation: becoming still, jaw and shoulders dropping, eyes blinking, muscles relaxing, and heavy eyelids.
   - Repeat a comforting word or phrase during calming breaths, imagery, or staring to block thinking that interferes with the (peaceful) state of observation.
   - Roll your eyes from the floor to the ceiling by holding your head still and looking down until your lids are almost shut. Slowly roll your eyes up toward your eyebrows. When it is too tiring to look up anymore, allow your lids to flutter closed. Take calming breaths, imagine a safe place, or repeat a comforting word.
3. Competing response (imagery) training: Choose a behavior from #4 on the Hair Pulling Questionnaire to substitute for hair pulling. Imagine being in a situation in which hair pulling occurs and see yourself practicing a competing behavior.
4. Exposure training to high-risk situations: Practice substituting a competing response (#4 on questionnaire) through imagery and then expose yourself to the actual situation. Give yourself a reward if you are able to resist any urges to pull. Continue to practice deliberate exposure in various situations until urges to pull are absent or reduced. Use relapses to clarify high-risk situations and practice exposure.

HELPING CHILDREN

When hair pulling starts before the age of 4, it is often outgrown. Parents need only use simple interventions such as rewards for not pulling and distractions (competing responses) described above and on the questionnaire. TTM that starts at 13 or older may need intense intervention as described above. When young children are still pulling hair by age 6, they may have the later-onset type of TTM that requires behavior treatment.

RESOURCES

- TTM Learning Center, 1215 Mission St., Suite 2, Santa Cruz, CA 95060, trichster@aol.com.
- Pioneer Clinic, 2550 University Ave., St. Paul, MN 55114.

WEEKLY PROGRESS RECORD FOR TTM

Week of: ___________________

Behavior therapy can be even more effective than medication in reducing or eliminating hair pulling. However, it requires time, discipline, and dedication. Make a commitment to practice your program consistently for three weeks. The following chart will help you stay motivated and on track as you turn urges to pull into opportunities to heal.

Hair Pulling Record

Directions: This chart should be filled out daily for one week prior to officially starting your treatment program. Continue to fill it out once you start using relaxation, imagery, competing responses, delaying urges, and rewards. For each incident, record:

- The date and time or situation when hair pulling did (or did not) occur.
- Emotions you were feeling: restless, anxious, bored, depressed, or angry.
- Intensity of your urge to pull (0 = none; 10 = extreme).
- The time spent and number of hairs pulled (these may be taped to the chart).

Date	Time or Situation	Emotions	Urge to Pull (0–10 units)	Time Spent Pulling Hair	Number of Hairs Pulled

Chart adapted from *Trichotillomania: A Behavioral Approach Video and Manual* by Carol Novak (Pioneer Clinic, 1995.)

BELIEFS THAT HELP OCD AND TTM

The more you understand that your obsessions, compulsions (OCD), or repetitive impulses (TTM) are not weaknesses, crazy, sinful, realistic, or signs of failure, the easier it is to change the beliefs you have that perpetuate your problem.[1]

Directions: Mark any of the negative faulty beliefs you have had about yourself or your problem. Then, identify the positive beliefs you would like to have about yourself, in spite of your current repetitive thoughts and habits.

Change Thoughts That Hurt into . . .	**Beliefs That Help OCD**
__ My obsessions, rituals, or impulses mean I am weak, crazy, bad, sinful, dangerous, or not trustworthy.	__ I have obsessions, rituals, or impulses because part of my brain gets blocked from stopping false thoughts from repeating.
__ The standards I set for myself are necessary to be a good, decent, safe, clean, healthy, or an attractive person.	__ I am good, sane, moral, attractive, or safe even when I don't meet my (unrealistic) standards.
__ I would be overwhelmed with anxiety if I attempted to stop my rituals or impulses.	__ I will survive any anxiety I feel from stopping my rituals and it will eventually subside.
__ Thought, rituals, and impulses are signs that I am not getting better.	__ Obsessions, rituals, and impulses are opportunities to practice recovery techniques.

You may notice that when you are calm or not faced with a particular challenge, your positive beliefs seem valid. It will be harder to maintain them when obsessive thoughts or urges come. Therefore, it is important to practice your new set of beliefs every day to help them become part of a mind-set that promotes making actual changes.

Desired Beliefs

Directions: Rewrite each of the positive beliefs you want to have in a way that addresses your particular problems. Then rate how valid the belief now seems to you (1 = totally false; 7 = completely true). Columns are provided so you can rerate yourself over time.

	Validity: 1–7 Points		
Examples: **Date:**	3/4	4/4	5/4
• I am competent even if I leave the period off the end of a sentence.	3	5	7
• I will survive the anxiety I feel when I don't act on an impulse to pull hair.	1	3	5
• When I use my fear of germs to pick up something "dirty," I heal myself.	3	5	6
• I can feel secure even if I throw away my collection of strings.	4	6	7
Beliefs I would like to have: **Date:**			

[1] See *EMDR: The Breakthrough Therapy* by Francine Shapiro (Basic Books, 1997) for further ideas on how thoughts affect emotions.

SECTION II DISORDERS

Chapter 7

Balancing Your Moods

BALANCING YOUR MOODS

OBJECTIVES FOR TREATMENT PLANNING

1. Identify and recognize symptoms of depression or mania.
2. Describe temperament and genetic factors that lead to mood disorders.
3. Make a decision to take medication if it is indicated.
4. Take medication responsibly as prescribed by physician.
5. Describe using tactics that decrease intensity of depression or mania.
6. Report that beliefs that relieve grief or guilt are valid.
7. Describe three ways symptoms of mania or depression have cleared.

MINI INDEX TO CHAPTER 7

USING THE HANDOUTS

- Assessment tools: *Types of Temperament, Sadness and Depression.*
- Literature for unipolar disorders: *Sadness and Depression, Banishing the Darkness of Depression, Women and Depression.*
- Literature for mood cycling: *Mood Roller Coasters, Getting Down When You're Too High, Women and Depression (PMS).*
- Visual aid that explains mood disorders at a glance: Chart in *Mood Roller Coasters.*
- Preparation for processing cognitions that interfere with recovery: *Good Grief, Getting a Grip on Guilt.*
- Review sheets for behavior strategies: *Banishing the Darkness of Depression, Getting Down When You're Too High.*

- Handouts for family and friends: *Extra Help for Mood Disorders;* literature for unipolar disorders, mood cycling, and review sheets.
- Workshops and presentations: *Types of Temperament* and chart can lead into a discussion on chemistry, moods, and predisposition for various disorders. *Sadness and Depression* can help people differentiate healthy reactions from disorders in themselves, family, and friends.

CAUTIONS AND RECOMMENDATIONS

- The chart *Identifying Your Temperament* is not standardized. It offers a general idea of how people function. Clinicians may need to help clients with suggested scoring. Introversion/extroversion and overreactivity/underreactivity can be used as *x* and *y* axes to plot where a client would fall on a chart of types of temperament.
- General unhappiness and frustration with life are *not* addressed in this section. Handouts from *Relationship Skills* (Chapter 1) and *In Search of Self* (Chapter 10) can be used with troublesome thinking and behavior that can contribute to depression.

SOURCES AND ACKNOWLEDGMENTS

- A biochemical, behavioral, and solution-focused approach explained in Melvyn Kinder's book *Mastering Your Moods* (Simon & Schuster, 1995) contributed to *Types of Temperament, Banishing the Darkness of Depression,* and *Getting Down When You're Too High.*
- The biochemistry of depression and the importance of assessing medication needs before using other treatment approaches are stressed in *Sadness and Depression, Mood Roller Coasters,* and *Women and Depression.* Information and statistics were drawn from *A Mood Apart* by Peter Whybrow (HarperPerennial, 1997) and *You Mean I Don't Have to Feel This Way* by Colette Dowling (Bantam Books, 1993).
- Criteria for mood disorders and proposed criteria for PMS from the *Diagnostic and Statistical Manual,* 4th edition (American Psychiatric Association, 1994) were used to develop *Sadness and Depression, Mood Roller Coasters,* and the *PMS Symptom Chart.* Aaron Beck's five manifestations of depression found in *Depression: Causes and Treatment* (University of PA Press, 1967) helped organize the chart, *Depression vs. Sadness Checklist.*
- Cognitively oriented approaches described in *The Grief Recovery Handbook* by John James and Russell Friedman (HarperPerennial, 1998), *Breaking the Patterns of Depression* by Michael Yapko (Doubleday, 1997), and *Feeling Good* by David Burns (Avon Books, 1980) contributed to *Good Grief* and *Getting a Grip on Guilt.*
- EMDR formulations for negative and positive cognitions as explained in *Eye Movement Desensitization and Reprocessing* by Francine Shapiro (Guilford Press, 1995) were also used in *Good Grief* and *Getting a Grip on Guilt.*

TYPES OF TEMPERAMENT

Everyone has his or her own unique chemical balance, rather than imbalance. At one time, it was thought that all behavior was learned. Since the 1980s, much has been discovered about how chemicals released by glands (hormones) and nerves (neurotransmitters) influence feelings and behavior. Other substances (enzymes) regulate chemical reactions. The major players that mold your temperament are:

- GABA (gamma-aminobutyric acid) inhibits neural activity. Alcohol and tranquilizers increase levels of GABA in the brain.
- Testosterone is the male hormone that is also found in women to lesser degrees. High levels of testosterone may be associated with increased aggression.
- Norepinephrine enables the nervous system to respond to incoming stimuli.
- MAO (monoamine oxidase) is an enzyme that regulates norepinephrine. Too little may result in a barrage of incoming stimuli, causing agitation and inattention. High levels reduce responsiveness to incoming stimuli, leading to depression.
- Dopamine is a neurotransmitter linked to pleasure and self-stimulation. Dopamine, serotonin, and norepinephrine have chemical structures similar to such drugs as LSD.
- Serotonin balances the action of dopamine and norepinephrine.

FOUR BASIC TEMPERAMENTS[1]

1. Sensors or on-edge people may have low levels of nature's tranquilizer, GABA, causing them to be very reactive to their surroundings but to back away from triggers due to a limited comfort zone. They can be sensitive and perceptive or anxious and fearful. Panic attacks, social phobias, and avoidant disorders can become problems.
2. Focusers or low-keyed people may have high levels of MAO and low levels of serotonin and norepinephrine. This causes them to underreact to external stimuli and turn inward to find interest through fantasy, pondering, reading or ruminating. They can have great powers of concentration and task orientation or brood and feel empty. Obsessions, compulsions, dependency, and depression can become problems.
3. Seekers or go-getters may have an abundance of nature's pleasure pill, dopamine, and low MAO. This leads to underreactivity to threat and may cause them to seek excitement and even danger to feel alive. They can be friendly, high achievers, and courageous or restless and dissatisfied. Attention deficits, addictions, and cycles of elation and despair can be problems.
4. Dischargers or quick-triggered people may have low levels of serotonin and MAO and high levels of nature's antagonist, testosterone, causing them to overreact to external stimuli. Because they are outgoing, they lash out at what bothers them. They can be passionate, sensuous, energetic, and lively or explosive and unpredictable. Personality disorders with poor insight and blaming others can be problems.

The chart on the following page can help you identify your temperament. The temperament with the most points may be your type. If the sum of your sensor plus focuser points in the left column is high, you may be introverted. If the sum of your discharger plus seeker points in the right column is high, you may be extroverted. If the sum of sensor plus discharger points is high, you may be over-reactive. If the sum of focuser plus seeker points is high, you may be under-reactive. If your point total for all types is similar, you may be evenly balanced or cycle in moods. It can help to have others rate you.

[1] See *Mastering Your Moods* by Melvyn Kinder (Simon & Schuster, 1995) for more on biochemistry and description of temperaments.

Identifying Your Temperament

Directions: Give yourself 1–4 points for each item that describes you. Score items that list more than one quality according to how many traits characterize you. For instance, if you both worry and expect the worst, score that item 2 points. If you are a pessimist but don't worry, give yourself 1 point.

Introverted **LIMITED** **<— COMFORT ZONE —>** **EXTENSIVE** **Extroverted**

OVER R-REACTIVE

Sensors (SN)—Low GABA

__ I *worry* or *expect* the worst. (2)
__ My worries exhaust me.
__ I can be anxious and not know why.
__ It's hard to calm down when I'm anxious.
__ I notice details others would find trivial.
__ I don't like to be the center of attention.
__ I push myself and then get overwhelmed.
__ When uncomfortable, I get sweaty/shaky.
__ I find it difficult to relax.
__ I try to avoid confrontation.
__ I seek reassurance.
__ I often feel like an outsider.
__ *Security* or *safety* is important to me. (2)
__ I use *alcohol* or *drugs* to calm down. (2)

I am:

__ *Sensitive*, *perceptive*, or *empathetic*. (3)
__ Tense in new situations or easily startle. (2)
__ Very aware of bodily sensations.
__ *Shy*, *quiet*, or a "*peoplepleaser*." (3)
__ Most at ease with family or close friends.
__ Drawn to exciting but comforting people.

Total Points: __ (28)

Dischargers (D)—High testosterone, low MAO

__ I react quickly when others upset me.
__ I don't hold back angry feelings.
__ Sometimes I don't know why I'm angry.
__ I get angry about things others find trivial.
__ It's hard to calm down when I'm mad.
__ I use alcohol or drugs to help my anger.

I am:

__ Easily *irritated*, *frustrated*, or *impatient*. (3)
__ *Critical*, *complaining*, or *rigid*. (3)
__ *Intense*, *sensuous*, *lively*, or *passionate*. (4)
__ Drawn to tolerant or calming people.

I can:

__ *Confront* others or *intimidate* people. (2)
__ Take out my anger on anyone.
__ Be *aggressive*, *forceful*, or *explosive*. (3)

Holding back anger:

__ Makes me feel tired or depressed. (2)
__ Can lead to an explosion.

After an outburst:

__ I feel regretful.
__ I don't feel sorry or I make up excuses.

Total Points: __ (28)

UNDER-REACTIVE

Focusers (F)—Low serotonin, high MAO

__ I often *ponder*, *imagine*, or *dream*. (3)
__ I can focus and ignore my surroundings.
__ I attend to details in my work.
__ I focus on problems to try to feel better.
__ Often, my brooding does not help me.
__ I *dwell* on criticisms or cry easily. (2)
__ I pursue exciting or unavailable partners.
__ I get *angry* or *bored* when my partner doesn't "make me" happy. (2)
__ I eat to relieve *boredom* or *sadness*. (2)
__ I use caffeine or drugs for energy.

I easily feel:

__ *Sad*, *exhausted*, *lonely*, or *unimportant*. (4)
__ *Dissatisfied* with myself, *guilty*, *hopeless*. (3)
__ *Tense*, *bored*, or *indecisive*. (3)

My concerns can:

__ Make it hard to enjoy life.
__ Keep me from sleeping.

Total Points: __ (28)

Seekers (SK)—High dopamine, low MAO

__ I seek *achievement* or *pleasure*. (2)
__ I rarely get bored but tire of repetition.
__ Once I've finished a project, I move on.
__ It's hard for me to relax and slow down.
__ I've had many *jobs* or *partners*. (2)
__ I idealize people and can be let down.
__ I prefer caffeine or stimulants to downers.

I enjoy:

__ Attracting *attention* or *shocking* others. (2)
__ *Excitement*, *parties*, or *travel*. (2)
__ *New* experiences, people, or *variety*. (3)
__ Intense romance and later get bored.
__ *Debates* or *competition*. (2)
__ *Scary rides* or *fast driving*. (2)

I can be:

__ *Unconventional*, *spontaneous*, or *rash*. (3)
__ *Energetic* or a *leader*. (2)
__ *Bold* and brave or *restless* and dissatisfied. (2)

Total Points: __ (28)

SADNESS AND DEPRESSION

AS DIFFERENT AS NIGHT AND DARK

Everyone has experienced sadness and unhappiness. These may result from (1) the loss or absence of a valued person, object, or situation, or (2) troublesome thinking, behavior, and interaction patterns. Depression is a disturbance in the flow of neural information due to changes in brain chemistry. The body's ability to feel, think, move and even digest is literally depressed! An estimated 15% to 25% of the population will experience depression at some time in their lives. Thoughts of defeat, deprivation, and self-devaluation that accompany depression suggest it is a "mental problem." Even these may result from brain chemistry rather than life experiences.

GLOOMY CHEMICAL GREMLINS[1]

Depressed people have low levels of norepinephrine and serotonin. These chemical messengers enable us to respond to and transmit incoming neural information. When serotonin is lacking, everything in the body slows down. Studies have shown that the brains of people who commit suicide have fewer "binding sites" that permit proper distribution of serotonin. There are several ways to disturb the delicate chemical balance needed for mood stability:

- Heredity can affect the body's ability to produce and use serotonin. Genes are particularly suspect when depressed people have a close relative with a mood disorder.
- Illnesses such as anemia, cancer, chronic pain, and immune deficiencies can physically influence mood. Thyroid problems are present in 10% to 15% of depressed people.
- Some medications for high blood pressure, heart problems, Parkinson's disease, hormone replacement, and birth control can trigger depression.
- Hormone levels of estrogen, progesterone, and melatonin change dramatically monthly or seasonally and may be major players in the chemistry of depression. Both serotonin and melatonin are found to be lower in some women suffering from PMS.
- Abuse of alcohol and drugs may ultimately lead to depression even though they are initially mood enhancing. Studies show that women and children are often depressed before they begin abusing alcohol or drugs.
- Traumatic experiences early in life may actually alter body chemistry. People who have lost a parent in childhood are twice as likely to have major depression as adults.
- Prolonged stress can wear down the body's reserves and lead to depression. People also acquire beliefs during trauma and high stress that influence moods. About 25% of depressed compared to 5% of nondepressed people are experiencing serious stress.

Experiments with mice show that a combination of factors is the most likely cause of depression. Some strains of mice exposed to inescapable electric shocks develop "depressed" eating, sleeping, mating, and learning habits. They continue to deteriorate even after shocks are stopped. Other strains of mice bounce back to normal when they are no longer subject to shocks. This may suggest that even prolonged stress will not result in depression unless people are genetically predisposed.

THE DIFFERENCE BETWEEN BLUE AND BLAH

Sadness can be caused by any change in familiar patterns of behavior that is experienced as loss: death, divorce, moving, retirement, graduation, and illness. Grief is far different from the

---

[1] See *You Mean I Don't Have to Feel This Way* by Colette Dowling (Bantam Books, 1993), p. 37, 41, 92.

inability to experience pleasure that accompanies depression. It may be barely noticeable with minor disappointments or an outpouring of feelings during major loss. When sadness is mistaken for depression, feelings can be compounded and frightening. When depression is mistaken for sadness, people may not receive proper medical attention. Therefore, it is important to make the distinction:

- Sadness is an e-motion, or energy-in-motion. Focusing on sad feelings, allowing them to build, and releasing them through crying and/or talking leads to a healing outlook. Avoiding painful feelings suppresses them and can eventually lead to depression. When properly weathered, daylight follows these "dark nights of the soul."
- Depression is a motionless, vacant state. Struggling to release feelings that aren't there can be exhausting and add to the problem. An energizing distraction or medication may be needed to banish the darkness.

Depression versus Sadness Checklist

DIRECTIONS: Mark items that best describe your experience. Although sadness and depression can be mixed, the more pronounced condition needs to be addressed first.

Depression Indicators	Grief Reactions
Inability to feel:	**Feelings of:**
___ Pleasure, hope, love, or attachment	___ Sadness, missing, disappointment, or love
___ Emotionally "flat"	___ Numbness in the first few hours
Thinking:	**Thinking:**
___ Poor concentration due to difficulty pulling thoughts together, slow thinking	___ Poor concentration due to preoccupation
	___ Increased thinking (about loss)
Thoughts:	**Thoughts:**
___ "I'm disgusting, worthless, inadequate."	___ "I'm alone, incomplete, empty, abandoned."
___ "I've done something wrong; I'm at fault."	___ "I didn't do enough. I should have. . . ."
___ "Nothing will work out."	___ "I cannot trust anyone."
___ "I cannot do anything. Nothing helps."	___ "I have no purpose. I cannot go on."
___ "Death would be a relief."	___ "Death would be an escape."
Motivation:	**Motivation:**
___ Loss of will, desire, interest	___ Avoidance of or desire to talk about loss
___ Avoidance of people, work, and activity	___ Focus on loss interferes with other pursuits
Physical:	**Physical:**
___ Disrupted sleep: too much or too little	___ Disrupted sleep: too much or too little
___ Poor appetite or overeating	___ Poor appetite or over eating
___ Weight loss or gain	___ Weight loss or gain
___ Reduced or no ability to respond sexually	___ Sexual responsiveness varies
___ Possible crying spells without knowing why	___ Likely bouts of sobbing over loss
Activity:	**Activity:**
___ Restless or slowed activity/speech	___ Emotional roller coaster: up and down
___ Reduced talking, smiling, motion, energy	___ Drained or exhausted

Information in the chart is organized around Aaron Beck's five indicators of depression found in *Depression Causes and Treatment* (University of Pennsylvania Press, 1967).

MOOD ROLLER COASTERS

People who experience polar opposites from elation or agitation to despair are said to have bipolar mood disorders. This term includes any significant up-and-down cycles in moods and makes it easier to recognize the problem before it reaches the incapacitating stages that warranted a (now out-of-date) diagnosis of manic-depressive illness. Low periods are often confused with "unipolar" disorders of major depression, recurrent depression, and dysthymia (low energy, pessimism, and withdrawal). Medication that treats one disorder may not be effective for the other. The table below can help distinguish these two branches of the same biochemical tree.

Unipolar Mood Disorders	Bipolar Mood Disorders
Course of illness • Likely to begin in late 20s or early 30s • Two-thirds of all cases will have recurring depression. • Can be triggered by illnesses, stress, grief, hormonal changes (in women), or nothing. • Frequency and intensity of depression can increase over the years.	**Course of illness** • Likely to begin in late teens or early 20s. • Almost all cases have recurring highs and lows. • Can be triggered by changes in seasons, jet lag, sleep loss, grief, stress, or nothing. • Frequency and intensity of highs and lows can increase over the years.
During depressed periods • Shallow sleep and early waking more likely. • Interest in food is reduced.	**During depressed periods** • Lengthened sleep (12+ hours) more likely. • Increased desire to eat.
Genetics and biochemistry • There is a 43% chance of identical twins having episodes of depression.[1] • Depression may be due to overregulation or depletion of chemical messengers that enhance mood. • Lithium alone will not relieve depression but may boost the effect of other antidepressants.	**Genetics and biochemistry** • There is greater than 70% chance of identical twins having bipolar disorder.[2] • Possibly due to poor regulation of neurotransmitters that excite the brain, causing "high" periods followed by depletion. • Lithium alone can sometimes stabilize mood by reducing brain excitability and strengthening serotonin.

[1] See *A Mood Apart* by Peter Whybrow (Harper Perennial, 1997, p. 113). Other research shows a 0–13% chance of both fraternal twins having depression, suggesting a strong genetic link in unipolar depression.
[2] Ibid.

DETECTING BIPOLAR DISORDER AND ITS COUSINS

The best way of identifying a bipolar disorder is by careful observation of mood over time. The 0–100 scale on the *Mood Chart* is offered for that purpose. It can also be used to classify several varieties of mood disorders:

- Normal mood: Moods vary from 40 to 60 except for periods of grieving a loss.
- Cyclothymia: Mood cycles from 30 to 70 over a period of hours or days.
- Dysthymia: Mood has been in the range of 30 to 45 for over a two-year period.
- Hypomania: Mood stays in the 55 to 70 range most of the time but can have manic episodes.
- Bipolar II disorder: Mood is most often in the 30s or 40s, with periods of relief in the 60s.
- Bipolar disorder: Mood can swing from the 30s or below to the 70s or above.
- Major and reoccurring depression: Mood is below 40 for two or more weeks.

Mood Chart

Directions: Use the 0–100 scale below to rate your mood on a daily or weekly basis. Note the date when you start your ratings. Put a dot in the box that describes your mood for that day. Eventually connect the dots to make a graph.

	Date: ______							Date: ______							Date: ______							Date: ______							Date: ______						
	S	M	T	W	T	F	S	S	M	T	W	T	F	S	S	M	T	W	T	F	S	S	M	T	W	T	F	S	S	M	T	W	T	F	S
90																																			
80																																			
70																																			
60																																			
50																																			
40																																			
30																																			
20																																			
10																																			

Depression > > > > > > > > > > > > > > > **"Normal"** < < < < < < < < < < < < < < < < **Elation**

0–15 Extreme	15–25 Severe	25–35 Moderate	35–45 Mild	45–55	55–65 Mild	65–75 Moderate	75–85 Severe	85–100 Extreme
Totally withdrawn, doesn't talk; unable to eat, respond; suicidal or too depressed to harm self; hears voices of guilt, doom; hospitalizaation needed	Needs prodding to function; serious sleep disorder; weight loss or gain; suicidal ideas; very withdrawn; feels guilt, self-hate, paranoia; may need hospitalization	Loss of energy, interest, movement, desire to work; disturbed sleep, appetite, ability to function; withdrawn; desire to stay in bed; life not worthwhile	Feels unsure, unfocused, slowed down; lack of energy, optimism, pleasure, desire, sexual interest; crying spells	Normal	Feels wonderful, confident, perceptive, creative; Increased interest in travel, business, projects, sex, religion, spending money	Excessive confidence, activity, talking, thinking, travel, sex, irritability, controlling, spending money; decreased eating, caution, sleep (4–6 hours/ night)	Very rapid talking, thinking; Very little eating, sleeping, control; Unusual ideas, behavior; Religious fervor; Hostile; May need to be hospitalized	Restless/hyper; Hostile/violent; Nonstop talking; Paranoid Hears voices Incoherent Can't function Elated or wild Little or no: eating, sleeping, control, organization; Hospitalize

WOMEN AND DEPRESSION

Depression is the disorder that discriminates: 10% of all men and 25% of all women will experience it at some time in their lives. This unhappy statistic is true for all women regardless of race, income, education, or occupation. Although women are more likely to be undervalued, victims of sexual abuse, or live below the poverty level (all of which could contribute to depression), there may be other factors. Puberty, after childbirth, and prior to menses (PMS) are particularly vulnerable times for women:

- Girls 13–14 years old are most likely to experience depression. Prior to puberty, slightly more boys than girls become depressed.
- After a child is born, 10% of all mothers become seriously depressed. Five days after giving birth, there is a dramatic drop in estrogen and progesterone. The lower progesterone drops, the more likely a new mother will become depressed.
- Women ages 45–64 have a lower incidence of depression than at other ages. Any moodiness, poor concentration, and insomnia occur a couple of years after periods become irregular, not after the final menses. However, women are at greater risk for low thyroid prior to menopause. Hypothyroidism is the great imitator of depression. Weight gain, tiredness, dry/coarse hair, and intolerance to cold are indicators of problems. Even when thyroid counts are low normal, women may experience symptoms of depression related to thyroid function. A complete thyroid battery is essential for detection.

PREMENSTRUAL SYNDROME (PMS)

Of all the times when women are most vulnerable to depression, PMS deserves honorable mention. It is estimated that 40–60% of women are affected in some way. Symptoms begin 2–10 days before the onset of menses and stop shortly afterward. They can vary in intensity from month to month. Noting when symptoms occur for 3–4 months is the only way to diagnose PMS. In addition to problems noted on the *PMS Symptom Chart,* a woman may experience acne, clumsiness, feelings that are out of control, violence, panic, and even epilepsy. Spasmodic cramps are not a symptom of PMS. There are several theories about possible causes and cures for periodic blues:

- Too little progesterone or too much estrogen in relation to progesterone: Estrogen builds the uterine lining by retaining body fluids and progesterone clears them out. Brain tissue swollen with water could explain migraines and depression. Progesterone suppositories taken 10 days before menses are controversial but can be enormously helpful in extreme cases.[1]
- Low potassium and blood sugar levels: This may be a result of hormonal imbalances rather than a cause of PMS. Avoiding salt, caffeine, and alcohol while increasing complex carbohydrates, potassium, magnesium, and calcium can help.
- Lower levels of serotonin premenstrually but not postmenstrually (and lower general levels): Estrogen may influence serotonin production and the ability to regulate serotonin. Treatments for depression such as lithium, antidepressants, and Saint-John's-Wort can help PMS.

---

[1] Contact Bair PMS Center, 1125 Gage Blvd., Suite C, Topeka, KS 66604, www.bairpms.com.

PMS SYMPTOM CHART

Month:

Mark days of menstruation (Mns) with a red X. Note symptoms with suggested lower-case letters.

Day	1	2	3	4	5	6	7	8	9	10	11	12	13	14	15	16	17	18	19	20	21	22	23	24	25	26	27	28	29	30	31
Mns																															
SYMPTOMS																															

Month:

Day	1	2	3	4	5	6	7	8	9	10	11	12	13	14	15	16	17	18	19	20	21	22	23	24	25	26	27	28	29	30	31
Mns																															
SYMPTOMS																															

SYMPTOMS[1]

Psychological
- a. Depression, hopelessness
- b. Crying spells, moodiness
- c. Irritability, anger, rage
- d. Tense, anxious, keyed up
- e. Exhausted, tired, withdrawn

Physical
- f. Head, joint, or muscle aches
- g. Over- or undersleeping
- h. Breast tenderness, swelling
- i. Bloating, binging, hunger
- j. Other:

Reproductive Cycle[2]

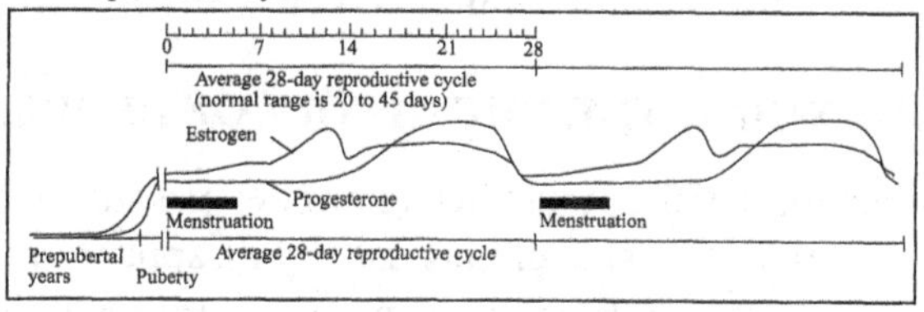

---

[1] Symptoms are adapted from "Research criteria for Premenstrual Dysphoric Disorder" with permission from the *Diagnostic and Statistical Manual of Mental Disorders,* Fourth Edition. Copyright 1994, American Psychiatric Association.

[2] Reproductive Cycle Chart adapted with permission from *Body and Self* by George J. Bloch, William Kaufmann, Inc. 1985.

BANISHING THE DARKNESS OF DEPRESSION

Due to advances in medication, depression is now more treatable than many physical illnesses. However, only one out of three seriously depressed people ever seeks help! Although counseling can teach thinking and people skills that improve mood, the need for medication should be addressed first. The more of the following conditions that are present, the greater the need for antidepressants:

- Other physical problems or medication reactions have been ruled out. A complete thyroid battery should be done if a person has gained weight, feels exhausted or is sensitive to cold.
- Routine activities are becoming increasingly difficult: problems concentrating, making decisions, working, sleeping, or carrying out daily tasks.
- Suicidal thoughts are causing problems.
- Concentration and energy are not sufficient to counsel on past trauma or recent loss.
- A family history of depression is present.
- More than one previous episode of significant depression has occurred.
- Medication has been helpful in the past and has not caused prolonged side effects.
- Interest in or ability for self-examination is lacking.
- Therapy to change thinking, behavior, or interaction patterns has not helped.

CHANGING THE CHEMISTRY OF DEPRESSION

Since the 1950s, nonaddictive antidepressants have helped 60–75% of people with depression find relief. Any side effects usually disappear or become tolerable after a couple of weeks. These medications act directly on various neurotransmitters:

- Dopamine—linked to pleasure and self-stimulation.
- Norepinephrine—enables the nervous system to respond to incoming stimuli.
- Serotonin—balances the action of dopamine and norepinephrine.
- MAO (monoamine oxidase)—an enzyme that breaks down adrenaline and serotonin.

The variety of options is steadily growing: tricyclics (TCAs), MAO inhibitors (MAOIs), selective serotonin reuptake inhibitors (SSRIs), and other "designer" antidepressants that target very specific neurotransmitters with fewer and fewer side effects:

Antidepressants	Used for	Side Effects
TCAs—Elavil, Sinequan, Tofranil: Increase flow of norepinephrine and serotonin	Depression and to safely treat insomnia, but may have unwanted side effects.	Dry mouth, rapid pulse, constipation, weight gain, grogginess, or mania.
MAOIs—Nardil, Parnate: Increases level of adrenaline and serotonin by stopping their breakdown by MAO.	Atypical depression with low energy, anxiety, overeating, and poor sleep without low mood. First used for TB.	Nausea, high blood pressure, and headaches when taken with incompatible medication or food.
SSRIs—Prozac, Paxil, Zoloft, Celexia, Luvox: Act directly on serotonin flow.	Mild–severe depression. Also used for OCD, panic disorder, PMS, bingeing.	Difficulty with orgasm or arousal, nausea, agitation, or confusion.
Designer meds—Desyrel, Asendin, Serzone, Effexor, Wellbutrin, Remeron.	Best for mild–severe depression. Wellbutrin is also used to help stop smoking.	Penile erection, headaches, high blood pressure, restlessness, or insomnia.

Other options besides medication may be needed or preferred:

- Electroconvulsive therapy (ECT) can stabilize the "beat" of the brain when people are immobilized by depression. This is similar to a pulse of electricity resetting the rhythm of a heart that has stopped beating. Ninety percent of people who don't respond to medication improve with ECT.
- Saint John's wort is an herb with as many as 50 active chemicals. It may slightly increase the flow of serotonin and dopamine and suppress MAO and interlukin-6 (an immune cell found in excess in some depressed people). The proper amount (300–600 mg. 3 times/day) may relieve depression with fewer side effects than medication. This may not be the best option if a person is sun-sensitive, at risk for cataracts, or needs rapid results.

TAME YOUR TEMPERAMENT[1]

People who are introspective and underreactive can be prone to brooding and feeling empty. If stagnation is allowed to continue, it can lead to serious problems. Understanding your temperament and modifying your habits can help manage low periods without antidepressants or boost the power of any medication you are taking:

1. Recognize and reframe your mood: When you are brooding or feeling empty, tell yourself that your body is signaling the need for outside stimulation. Reattribute any thoughts of hopelessness, helplessness, and regret to sluggish body chemistry.
2. Postpone worry and apathy: Set limits on how long and when you allow yourself to ruminate or vegetate. Do not permit more than two separate hours a day. If you feel a mood coming on, tell yourself it will have to wait till your "down time."
3. Modify ruminations: Say worries out loud, pinch your nose, write, sing, or speak them in pig Latin. Avoid thought-stopping methods that hinder needed stimulation.
4. Get a light: Spend time outdoors, especially in the early morning. Replace fluorescent fixtures with full-spectrum bulbs that have the same rays as the sun.[2] This resets production of melatonin, which causes hibernationlike states that mimic depression.
5. Sleep deprivation can be the fastest way to alter mood if you are oversleeping.
6. Gain a sense of your state of underarousal: Shift from brooding and apathy to noticing physical sensations: aches, heaviness, emptiness, or trouble smiling.
7. Refocus to break the vicious cycle of gloom: Do not withdraw from people or activities that provide needed stimulation. Without expecting too much of yourself, do something! Break tasks down into small parts. Be proud of anything you accomplish.
   - Get your attention outside yourself: Smell perfume, examine a leaf, listen to music, feel textures, or take a bath. Engage senses that help you turn outward.
   - Exercise your body: Pick activities that will get your metabolism in gear without being exhausting: leisurely walks, slow dancing, window-shopping, or bike riding.
   - Exercise your mind: Read engaging books, do crossword puzzles, or play cards.
   - Reach out to others: If you don't want people to know you are depressed, make excuses for your lack of energy and even tearfulness by saying you're not feeling well. That is the truth! Find at least one or two people with whom you can be open. Get a telephone or e-mail buddy or find (online) support groups.

---

[1] See "Focusers" in *Mastering Your Moods* by Melvyn Kinder (Simon & Schuster, 1995).

[2] www.appollolight.com, 800-545-9667 or www.lighttherapyproducts. com, 800-486-6723—product information. Full-spectrum bulbs are also available at some hardware stores, nurseries, and health food stores.

GETTING DOWN WHEN YOU'RE TOO HIGH

There was a time when people died from feeling too good. The brain burns 25% of a person's calories. The racing thoughts and lack of desire for food that occurs during manic episodes made it impossible to provide enough nutrients to keep the body alive. Two chemical messengers are responsible for this condition:

- Norepinephrine (which promotes responsiveness to incoming stimuli) is overactive, causing intrusive curiosity and an excess of ideas in the early stages of mania.
- Dopamine (which produces heightened pleasure and self-stimulation) later becomes dominant. This further increases energy, unusual strength, and euphoria.

CHANGING THE CHEMISTRY OF MANIA

In 1949, an amazing discovery was made that lithium salts could calm a wildly racing mind. Due to safety concerns, its usage was not allowed in the United States until the 1970s. Currently, lithium prevents reoccurrence of mania in 70% of all cases. It may reduce brain excitability by slowing down transmission of impulses along and between nerves and by boosting serotonin. Lithium can take two weeks to have an impact and may not be effective with rapid cycling moods. Therefore, other options are sometimes used:

- Electroconvulsive therapy (ECT) can stabilize the "beat" of the brain just as a pulse of electricity through the heart resets its rhythm when it is fibrillating (shivering).
- Antipsychotic medications used to treat thought disorders quickly block dopamine, slowing flights of ideas and stiffening movement. Due to long-term side effects, they are not usually used once lithium or anticonvulsants start working.
- Hormone replacement therapy used for thyroid problems can stabilize mood or augment antidepressants, particularly if the thyroid is not functioning properly.
- Anticonvulsants such as Depakote, Tegretol, Lamictal, and Neurotin started being used for bipolar disorders in the 1980s and 1990s. They reduce brain excitability by slowing the speed at which nerves recover after transmitting electrical impulses. These medications are best with rapid cycling and mixed symptoms of mania and depression. They can be combined with lithium to manage the most difficult mood disorders.

Anticonvulsants and lithium require careful monitoring. Blood levels need to be high enough to be therapeutic without producing toxic reactions. Although some people will initially experience side effects, these usually disappear within a month. Any inconvenience from taking these medications is far less disruptive to careers, finances, relationships, and safety than symptoms of mania!

THE BLESSING OF HYPOMANIA

People who are blessed with mild elevations in mood, or hypomania, have an inexhaustible supply of energy, enabling them to live adventurous, successful lives. However, they may be underreactive to internal stimuli and need excitement and even danger to feel alive. Periods of calm or low anxiety can feel intolerable. Serious problems happen when they engage in high-risk behavior or "overcharge" their minds with constant activity. The following ways of modifying habits can sometimes help manage high periods without medication:[1]

---

[1] For further information, see *The Depression Workbook* by Mary Ellen Copeland (New Harbinger Publications, 1992) and *Mastering Your Moods* by Kinder (Simon & Schuster, 1995).

Getting Down When You're Too High

1. Balance sources of excitement: Recognize your need for activity but have diverse focuses (work, love, sports, or community) rather than becoming overcharged by or addicted to one source of stimulation.
2. Recognize the early warning signs of "overenergy": sleeping or eating less; getting too busy; increased conflict or irritability; urgent needs to spend money, travel, or have sex; obsessing on religion; talking or thinking too much.
3. Set firm limits for yourself during high periods: Don't commit yourself to extra activities outside your usual routine. Turn spare cash and credit cards over to a trusted person. Put off decisions until you have slowed down. Force yourself to have down time (see #6) before you do something exciting or try to resolve a conflict.
4. Avoid foods or drugs that make you hyper: sugar, caffeine and alcohol. Eat regular meals. Do not eat too much of any one thing. Herbs such as grape seeds that may help control dopamine and norepinephrine can provide added focus.
5. Have a bedtime routine: Do not engage in stimulating activity after 7 P.M. Avoid staying out late or up all night. Take sleeping aids if necessary.
6. Postpone some activities: Arrange "down time" in low-stimulation, nonstressful environments. Gradually increase the amount of time you can spend alone or relaxing. Balance moderately exciting activities with down time.
7. Focus on your sense of underarousal during down time: Describe your experience of boredom or aloneness to a tape recorder or in writing to increase your tolerance of low stimulation.
8. Get out of your head and come to your senses: Smell perfume, examine a leaf, listen to calming music, feel textures, or take a bath. Engage senses that help you slow down constant mental chatter.
9. Focus on others' thoughts rather than your own: Do not do all the talking. Ask people questions and repeat or rephrase what they say. Memorize and recite poems. Play a musical instrument. Boring books and slow movies are better than exciting fiction, romance, or religious material.
10. Slow down your mind: Meditation is a must. A few brief periods throughout the day of observing your breathing, a relaxing image, your thoughts, or the way you drum your fingers may be better than one long period of quieting your mind.[2]
11. Slow down your body: Pick activities that require concentration or release energy without overcharging you. Relaxing swims or weight lifting are better than exercise that makes you hyper. Do tedious, repetitious chores such as scrubbing the floor, knitting, weeding, painting, and cleaning out closets.

If you are not able to slow down with these strategies, do not blame yourself! Medication can be essential to stop the runaway locomotive of your mind. Get help from your doctor immediately!

[2] See *Trance-Formation in Everyday Life* by Kate Cohen-Posey (Leighton's Sales Co) to teach yourself to meditate. 877.956.2998 or www.psych-assist.net.

GOOD GRIEF

Sadness and grief are natural reactions to changes in familiar habits due to death, divorce, moving, graduation, retirement, illness, and even vacations. All of these involve loss that can be painful for two reasons:

- They bring up core beliefs about the nature of existence—"I'm alone." "I'm responsible." "I'm lost." "I have no purpose." "I'm incomplete." "I'm vulnerable."
- They make us face "unfinished business" from a situation or relationship: resentments, regrets, unspoken appreciation, and unmet expectations.

It is not time or keeping busy that heals the painful wounds of loss, but creating a new definition of yourself and completing what was not finished in the relationship.

COMPLETE UNFINISHED BUSINESS[1]

No matter how good a relationship or a situation is, it is a work in progress and therefore incomplete. As soon as you experience a loss, your mind reviews and searches for what was never communicated. This review continues intermittently until it is completed. The following show how you can help the process by communicating your regrets, resentments, unspoken appreciation, and unmet dreams to a mental image of the person who is gone, in a letter that you may never send, or to the eyes of a friend in role play.

Make Amends

- Pinpoint your mistakes: Take responsibility for your contribution to any problems in the relationship, but only for your part! There are usually some positive consequences from even the worst blunders.
- Express your regret: "I am sorry for . . ."
- Express the (unrealistic) wish behind regrets: "I wish I had (could have) . . ." Identify a specific action that could have made the situation different.
- Change your pattern: In future situations, act out any realistic wishes you identified. Even if you are unable to do this with the person who is gone, you still make amends by being different with others.
- Do not ask for forgiveness: Forgiveness is entirely the choice of the "injured" party. If the other person is deceased, you can imagine how they would respond to you.

Let Go of Resentments

- Identify any power you gave up or lost: Resentment comes from a loss of power.
- Identify the power or choices you now have: As you grow, you gain options. It may be difficult to let go of resentment until you know you can fulfill past unmet needs.
- Express your past resentment and newfound power as a statement: "I resented you for . . . but now I can (plan to) . . ."
- Do not tell people you forgive them. Often, this is perceived as an attack. Instead, let them know when you are doing OK. This releases both you and them. It is your responsibility to recover from any of your past hurts.

Express Unspoken Gratitude, Dreams, and Future Plans

- "I want you to know. . . ."

---

[1] From *The Grief Recovery Handbook* by Joan James and Russell Friedman (Harper Perennial, 1998).

AFFIRM BELIEFS THAT REDEFINE YOURSELF

All relationships and situations develop their own set patterns and routines. When you become disconnected from these, it is natural to feel as though you are in free fall. Unless you are an expert "sky diver," such experiences will trigger your most painful beliefs. To discover them, take a mental snapshot of the worst part of the ending of the relationship. As you look at that memory or mental image of the person who is gone, ask yourself:

- "What does this mean about me?"
- "How does this make me feel about myself?"
- "When did I first have this disturbing thought about myself?"

Directions: Mark any hurtful thoughts that are linked to your current or past losses. Then mark any healing beliefs that you would like to have to help you negotiate this difficult time in your life.

Change Hurtful Thoughts into ...	**Healing Beliefs**
__ I'm alone or abandoned. I don't belong.	__ I can find others to love and care for (me).
__ I'll never love (be loved) again.	__ If I've loved (been loved) once, I will be again.
__ There is only one right person for me.	__ I can love more than one person in a lifetime.
__ I cannot trust again.	__ As I grow, I can become more discerning.
__ I should have been there when he died.	__ The sun rises and people die without my help.
__ I'm responsible. I didn't do enough.	__ I did my best or enough.
__ I'm unlovable or defective.	__ I'm lovable or good enough.
__ I'm lost. I have no purpose.	__ I can find new joy and meaning in life.
__ I'm empty or incomplete.	__ I am complete and can go on.
__ I'm vulnerable. I can't handle this	__ I can learn or find strength from this.
__ I can't take care of myself or go on.	__ I can (learn to) take care of myself and go on.

POINTERS FOR TURNING LOSSES INTO GAINS

Identifying new ideas, affirming them regularly, and using some of the following pointers will give you the compass you need to land on your feet on solid ground:

- Do not bury your feelings in food, alcohol, anger, TV, or work.
- Do not be strong for others. It may help them to see your pain.
- Be with your sadness when it comes. Accept it, but don't invite it.
- Use emotional moments to mentally communicate unspoken words to your loved one or affirm beliefs that heal. This may intensify feelings and help release them.
- Stay with the pain of a negative memory but purposely follow it with a good one.
- Find a support group or person with whom you can share feelings.[2]
- Dispose of belongings gradually. Periodically review items you can release.
- Plan activities for anniversaries that are enjoyable and comforting or use "special days" to mentally communicate how your "heart" plans to go on.
- Do not force yourself to feel pain that's not there. It is okay to enjoy life after loss.

[2] Contact your local hospice or GriefNet at http://rivendell.org or http://divorce.internetworld.net.

GETTING A GRIP ON GUILT

Guilt, self-depreciation, and shame are an integral part of depression. Whether they are the cause or a by-product is not known. A combination of both life experience and biochemistry help explain why some people constantly put themselves on trial.

Guilt and Shame	
Early experience of:	**Creates a mindset of:**
Abandonment or massive rejection	"I'm defective, bad, or unlovable."
Being given too much responsibility	"I'm responsible (for things I can't control)."
Constant criticism	"I don't do enough." "I have to be perfect."
Being told not to feel a certain way	"My feelings are wrong."
Being blamed for others' problems/feelings	"I have to keep people happy."
Repeatedly having your needs put aside	"Others' feelings come before my own."
A family trauma: divorce, illness, abuse	"I'm responsible (for things I don't cause)."
Having a family where little goes wrong	"I can prevent bad things from happening."
Biochemistry:	**Leads to:**
An underreactive temperament	Introspection and excessive self-analysis
The sluggish biochemistry of depression	Difficulty responding to new information

FALSE GUILT

If you are predisposed by life experience or biochemistry to self-condemnation, it is easy to have a false or disproportionate sense of responsibility for anything that goes wrong. You may magnify what you've done, take personal responsibility for everything that goes wrong, "should yourself" instead of understand yourself, and unrealistically expect yourself to only have positive feelings. Rarely is an undesirable state of affairs all one person's fault or as bad as it seems at the moment. Make your introspection work for you by reexamining your "wrongdoings" and putting them in perspective.

GUILT TEST

Directions: Identify something you feel bad about. Determine a percentage for your intention of causing the event, your contribution to it, the amount of control you had over it and the degree to which it was bad. Get a second opinion on all your ratings in case you have not yet learned that guilt comes in shades of gray.

I feel bad about:

1. I had ___% intention of making this turn out the way it did.
2. I am ___% responsible for the other person's distress or negative outcome.
3. The other person is ___% responsible for his or her distress or negative outcome.
4. I had ___% control over achieving the outcome I wanted.
5. I was ___% capable of preventing what happened when it happened.
6. Other factors (lack of experience information) contributed to ___% of the outcome.
7. I was ___% successful in achieving the outcome I wanted.
8. The world or other person was ___% damaged by what I did.
9. The ultimate outcome of what happened was ___% negative and ___% positive.

Some people seem to prefer to condemn themselves rather than place responsibility where it is due. Just recognizing what you are doing is the first step of change. Decide if you are guilty of the following false guilt payoffs:

- If I cannot do anything right, than I do not need to try to improve or act differently. Change means I would have to make an effort and possibly fail.
- If I am responsible for the bad things that have happened to me, then I can control future misfortunes. Change means I would have to give up my "illusion of control."
- I am not sure what it will mean to change negative views. Therefore, I look at life events in a way that reinforces my current perceptions.[1]

PROPER GUILT

Most people don't learn to skate without falling, and it is impossible to go through life without making blunders. It is proper to feel remorse when you have unnecessarily or willfully acted in a hurtful manner toward yourself or another person in a way that violates your standards.[2] However, no matter how bad your transgression, you are not innately bad or evil. Good people do wrong things! The very fact that you feel regret means you have a conscience. It is better to take one or more of the following actions to relieve your distress than to wallow in "poor-awful-me-ism":

- Pinpoint your mistakes: Take responsibility for your contribution to a problem, but only for your part!
- Express your regret: "I am sorry for. . . ." Do not make excuses by saying "I'm sorry I . . . , but . . ." This is a sneaky attempt to gain absolution. You can explain why you did something only if you are asked!
- Express the wish behind the regret: "I wish I had. . . ." Identify a specific action that could have made the situation different. This will help you learn from your mistakes.
- Change your pattern: In future situations, change your actions. Even if you are unable to do this with the person you hurt, you still make amends by being different with others.
- Do not ask for forgiveness: forgiveness is entirely the choice of the "injured" party.

Most people feel either too much or too little guilt. The chronically guilty take responsible for everything bad that has ever happened to them or their loved ones. The forever innocent do not hold themselves accountable for the bad consequences of their actions or how they respond to others' blunders. It is easier to tone down a sense of overresponsibility than to build one in people who have little. However, by owning your part of a problem and only your part, you model how to make amends and make it more difficult for others to shift blame.

[1] See "Cognitive Dissonance" in *Breaking the Patterns of Depression* by Michael Yapko (Doubleday, 1997), p. 224.
[2] See "Guilt" in *Feeling Good: The New Mood Therapy* by David Burns (Avon Books, 1980), p. 199.

EXTRA HELP FOR MOOD DISORDERS

The more serious the mood disorder, the more essential family members and friends are to recovery. Depressed people may be too indecisive or hopeless to seek treatment. When people are elated, they may fear that medication will take away their creativity and energy. Becoming thoroughly informed and using the following steps can help people with mood disorders understand what is happening to them and how treatment can help:

- Recognize what is happening: The easiest way to spot a mood disorder is by noticing your own reaction. If you feel pushed away, criticized, or as though you're the only one making an effort, the other person may be depressed. If you feel annoyed by constant chatter, late hours, or recklessness, the person may be manic.
- Offer feedback: Assure people that their disinterest, indecisiveness, pessimism, poor hygiene, tiredness, and even difficulty feeling love are symptoms of depression and not just because they aren't trying hard enough. Elated people may not be receptive to feedback. During less euphoric intervals, they may be able to understand how they are putting themselves or others in jeopardy.
- Communicate your conviction that help is available and that the person will feel better. Get a pep talk from a professional if you have your own doubts.
- Arrange and accompany people to initial therapy appointments: Before treatment takes effect, depressed people may have trouble articulating their difficulties and absorbing what has been discussed. Take notes and ask questions that loved ones might overlook.
- Give professionals feedback on early signs that medication is helping: Often, the family notices changes before depressed or manic people do.
- Maintain as normal a relationship as possible: Don't give in to wishes to withdraw. Engage loved ones in leisurely walks, massages, card games, and small talk or read to them. Remind them that enjoyment and interest will come in time.
- Assure people that they are still valued: Express affection. Remind them that their mood is separate from who they are, that their "old self" will return and that they will be able to overlook their manic mistakes or temporary lack of accomplishment.
- Avoid criticisms and anything that will aggravate self-condemnation. Break tasks into small, achievable steps. Offer to clean with them to keep them focused or shampoo their hair. Let hygiene go to minimum standards until treatment takes effect.
- Interrupt excessive sleep when people are depressed: Sleeping more than nine hours a day can aggravate the problem.
- Avoid cliché questions and advice: "What's wrong?" "You're not trying hard enough." "Think positively." "Try to relax." "Slow down." Depressed people may be incapable of positive thoughts or of verbalizing what is wrong. Such advice makes them feel worse. Seriously manic people cannot slow down without medication.

FRIENDLY CAUTIONS

Avoid asking friends and relatives for help who are pushy, disinterested, inept, or rigid. Attempts to involve them in your recovery can delay progress. Be cautious of bad advice. Input that makes you feel worse about yourself is probably not correct. Be especially careful of people, self-help groups, and even professionals who tell you that medication is a crutch. Do not argue with bad advice or try to make others understand. Thank people for their concern and tell them you'll consider what they are saying.

MEDICATION

Antidepressants and mood stabilizers are safe and nonaddictive. Side effects will go away with time and "experimenting" to find the most effective medication. Sedating antidepressants are important when insomnia accompanies depression. Tranquilizers such as Valium, Xanax, and Ativan can aggravate depression, but when prescribed with an antidepressant can be helpful. Stimulants such Ritalin and Dexedrine are energizing but should be prescribed only under special circumstances in conjunction with antidepressants. The herb Saint-John's-wort can be taken when people are reluctant to use medication if they are not sun-sensitive, at risk for cataracts, or need rapid results. However, prescription medication is necessary for many depressed people and most people who have had a manic episode.

PROFESSIONAL HELP

Counseling is very important when depression is related to a past trauma, a recent loss, or troublesome thinking, behavior, and interaction patterns. Even when medication alone eliminates all symptoms of depression or mania, some counseling is important to help people understand the nature of their disorder, future need for medication, and ways to reduce stress.

NATIONAL NETWORKS AND SUPPORT GROUPS

Because mood disorders often cycle or reoccur, it can be enormously helpful to share experience and wisdom with others who have traveled the same path. Many communities have a local chapter of Depression and Manic-Depressive Association listed in the newspaper or phone book. Resources can be found by calling local mental health centers. There are national networks, newsletters, Websites, and books that offer additional assistance:

- National Depressive and Manic-Depressive Association and newsletter: 730 North Franklin St., Suite 501, Chicago, IL 60610-3526, 800-826-3632, www.ndmda.org.
- American Association of Suicidology: 4201 Connecticut Ave. NW, Washington, DC 20008, 202-237-2280.
- SPAN (Suicide Prevention Advocacy Network): 5034 Odin's Way, Marietta, GA 30068, 888-649-1366, www.spanusa.org.
- National Depression Screening Project: 800-573-4433.
- Bipolar Network News: 5430 Grosvenor Lane, Suite 200, Bethesda, MD 20814.
- National Foundation for Depressive Illness: PO Box 2257, New York, NY 10116, www.depression.org.
- Polars' Express (a newsletter): MDDA-Boston, 115 Mill St., PO Box 102, Belmont, MA 02178, 617-855-2795, mmddabps@sprintmail.com.
- General Internet sites and links: www.athealth.com/, www.cmhc.com.
- Books: *The Depression Workbook* by Mary Ellen Copeland (New Harbinger Publications, 1992); *His Bright Light* by Danielle Steel, her son's story; (Delaarte, 1998); *Darkness Visible* by William Styron (Vintage Books, 1992).

SECTION II DISORDERS

Chapter 8

Taming Your Temper

TAMING YOUR TEMPER

OBJECTIVES FOR TREATMENT PLANNING

1. Identify temperament or disorders that contribute to destructive anger.
2. Identify risk factors for potential violence.
3. Identify patterns of anger avoidance and take steps to change them.
4. Identify people and situations that trigger temper and signs of losing control.
5. Report using tactics that decrease intensity and frequency of anger.
6. Report that beliefs that ease rage or allow (appropriate) anger are valid.
7. Describe tactics that reduce explosiveness in significant others.

MINI INDEX FOR CHAPTER 8

USING THE HANDOUTS

- Assessment: *Profiles of Anger, Anger and Violence, Types of Temperament* (7.4).
- Reducing avoidance or intensity of anger: *Claim It and Aim It, Taking Danger out of Anger.*
- Reducing frequency of anger: *Practice Makes Peace, Beliefs That Ease Anger.*
- Preparation for processing cognitions (following EMDR protocols) for clients who are actively involved in treatment: *Beliefs That Ease Anger, Claim It and Aim It.*
- Review sheets for behavior strategies: *Taking Danger out of Anger, Practice Makes Peace, Inflexible-Explosive Children.*
- Handouts for family and friends: *Profiles of Anger, Inflexible-Explosive Children, Anger and Violence, Practice Makes Peace, Extra Help for Anger.*
- Workshops and presentations: Assertive language circles (1.2) are an ideal way to start workshops on anger. Participants can use *Taking Danger out of Anger* and *Practice Makes Peace* to identify temper triggers and write brief scenarios of upsetting incidents. These can be role-played in pairs or in front of the group using guides from *Practice Makes Peace.* The use of

acupressure points or guided imagery to reduce anger can be demonstrated with participants who are able to access anger by thinking of a mad moment.

CAUTIONS AND RECOMMENDATIONS

- Its is a priority to assess risk factors of physical abuse when anger is the presenting problem. The handout *Anger and Violence* can help such evaluations; however, it may not be wise for possible offenders to see the second page, which discusses safety plans. When violence has occurred, handouts on anger can be used in conjunction with group therapy but should not replace domestic violence programs.
- Do further reading or obtain training to ensure accurate location of acupressure points (see resources below) described in *Taking Danger out of Anger,* although this approach is generally harmless even if it does not benefit clients.
- Supplement *Profiles of Anger* with *Types of Temperament* (7.4), handouts from *In Search of Self* (Chapter 10), and *Women and Depression* (7.10) when PMS is a suspected cause of anger.
- Supplement *Taking Danger out of Anger, Practice Makes Peace, Claim It and Aim It,* and *Extra Help for Anger* with handouts from *Waltzing through Emotional Landmines* (Chapter 1).
- Supplement *Inflexible-Explosive Children* with handouts from *Powerful Parenting* (4.8).

SOURCES AND ACKNOWLEDGMENTS

- Criteria from the *Diagnostic and Statistical Manual,* 4th edition (American Psychiatric Association, 1994) were used to describe attention deficit, mood, and personality disorders that can contribute to problems identified in *Profiles of Anger.*
- Literature on domestic violence taken mainly from *Spouse Abuse* by Michele Harway and Marsali Hansen (Professional Resource Exchange, 1994) contributed to *Anger and Violence.*
- Guided imagery and behaviorally oriented strategies from *Letting Go of Anger* by Ron and Pat Potter-Efron (New Harbinger, 1995) and *Mastering Your Moods* by Melvyn Kinder (Simon & Schuster, 1994) were used in *Taking Danger out of Anger.*
- Techniques that utilize acupressure points described in *Taking Danger out of Anger* were developed by Roger Callahan (Callahan Techniques, 760-345-4737, www.tftrx.com) and are also explained in *Energy Psychology* by Fred P. Gallo (CRC Press, 1998), fgallo@energypsych.com.
- Strategies for cognitive rehearsal in *Practice Makes Peace* draw heavily on *Tongue Fu* by Sam Horn (St. Martin's Griffin, 1996), www.samhorn.com.
- EMDR formulations for negative and positive cognitions explained in *Eye Movement Desensitization and Reprocessing* by Francine Shapiro (Guilford Press, 1995) were used to develop *Beliefs That Ease Anger* and *Claim It and Aim It.*
- The *Physiology of Anger and Related Treatment Strategies* come from the work of Ross Green, Ph.D. explained in *The Explosive Child* (HarperCollins, 1998).

PROFILES OF ANGER

Anger is a protective mechanism against a real or perceived loss of power. It energizes people to take needed action. However, many people have anger that works against them. Although these people are often said to have "bad tempers," this term is far too general and does little to further the understanding of destructive anger. The following profiles of people who have difficulty with anger suggest different treatment approaches. Although types overlap, pick the one that best describes you or your loved ones. Finally, examine the explosive temperament that may underlie all the others.

DEFIANCE

Defiant people are irresponsible, impulsive, reckless, dishonest, unfaithful, unlawful, self-centered, or violent. They may see themselves in others and be jealous and on guard.

- Cause: Their basic needs may not have been met in the first two years of life, or caregivers may have anticipated needs before any frustration was experienced.
- Effects: They never bonded with nor developed trust in caretakers, causing rejection of authority and lack of internalized controls. Other people are considered possessions, and relationships serve to achieve some end (sex, money, or power).
- Anger: Accumulated rage from early unmet needs can be triggered any time or on anyone due to frustration or not getting their way.
- Treatment: Because they don't care about others' feelings or rules, they will have little desire to change unless there is legal intervention.

HYPERACTIVITY

Hyperactive people can be restless, distractible, moody, underachieving, and disorganized and have difficulty completing tasks. Poor impulse control can lead to legal problems.

- Cause: The frontal (thinking) cortex does not receive enough stimulation from the lower area of the brain, possibly causing self-stimulation through constant activity. "Sluggish" frontal lobes may also have difficulty inhibiting incoming stimuli, creating the effect of attending to everything.
- Effects: Continual activity and problems focusing creates an abundance of disturbing triggers and difficulty moderating reactions to them.
- Anger: Outbursts may be frightening but are usually short-lived.
- Treatment: Stimulants and some antidepressants can be very helpful, along with learning anger management techniques.

HYPOMANIA AND PMS

Hypo(mild)mania and Premenstrual Syndrome (PMS) can cause people to have episodic anger. The "highs" of hypomania are more intense and inconsistent than overenergy of hyperactivity and can be followed by "lows" in which energy vanishes.

- Cause: Hypomania may be due to poor regulation of neurotransmitters that excite the brain. During PMS, fluid retention may put pressure on the brain.
- Effects: Increased excitability (and anger) of hypomania can last days or weeks. PMS anger begins 2–10 days before menses and stops shortly afterwards.
- Anger: In extreme cases, violence can occur. As people become more manic, hostility and paranoia increase. During PMS, women can be keyed up and explosive.
- Treatment: Mania is highly responsive to mood-stabilizing medication that can eliminate anger problems. Antidepressants and hormone treatment can help PMS.

ERRATIC PERSONALITIES

Erratic people have intense or stormy relationships with many people; often feel empty and bored; are uncertain about abilities, worthiness, or desires; have rapid and radical shifts in moods; and are impulsive in ways that can be self-damaging.

- Cause: Parents may have failed to meet needs for support or autonomy.
- Effects: They alternate between fears of suffocation and abandonment, cannot deal with mixed emotions, and see people as all good or all bad.
- Anger: Outbursts can be unpredictable and out of proportion to trigger events. They may be fueled by fears of abandonment or control, disappointment in others' inability to live up to idealizations, and feelings of victimization.
- Treatment: Mood stabilizers and antidepressants may help. Anger management techniques can be learned through considerable repetition over time.

HYPERSENSITIVE PERSONALITIES

Inflated, hypersensitive people feel self-important and entitled to special treatment; exaggerate their achievements; seek constant attention or admiration; and have difficulty understanding others' feelings.

- Cause: They may have had parents who were overindulgent, failed to set limits, or saw children as an extension of themselves and only valued them for their abilities.
- Effects: They must be all good to keep from feeling all bad. They can swing from feeling superior, powerful, and smug to feeling worthless, incompetent, and empty.
- Anger: Rage is a means to avoid feeling shame and humiliation from criticism and absence of complete approval from others. They may hold long grudges.
- Treatment: They may be motivated to learn anger control techniques during crises when they are in jeopardy of losing significant others or jobs that supply self-esteem.

PERFECTIONISTIC PERSONALITIES

Perfectionists can be preoccupied with details, rules, and order; inflexible about matters of morality and cleanliness; and insist that others submit to their way of doing things.

- Cause: They may be biochemically predisposed to feeling displeasure, or could have had critical parents with similar unrealistic standards.
- Effects: They can swing from feeling competent and in control to feeling vulnerable and unsettled when things aren't "right."
- Anger: Frequent outbursts can happen when others do not comply with their efforts to control. They may be easier on people who aren't "extensions" of themselves.
- Treatment: Antidepressants and mood stabilizers can sometimes help. Their high standards justify their anger and they may seek help only in a crisis.

EXPLOSIVE TEMPERAMENT

Explosive people have temperaments that can be extroverted, bold, passionate, intense, sensuous, energetic, lively, critical, complaining, and outspoken.

- Cause: A lack of the enzyme MAO may cause underregulation of neurotransmitters that respond to incoming stimuli. Too much testosterone may cause aggression.
- Effects: They can be very reactive to environmental stimuli, whether with positive feelings of passion or negative feelings of annoyance.
- Anger: They are excitable about things others find trivial and may have trouble calming down or recognizing the source of their anger.
- Treatment: Antidepressants that balance the function of different neurotransmitters and mood stabilizers that reduce brain excitability can be enormously helpful. However, medication is not always needed to master anger management techniques.

INFLEXIBLE-EXPLOSIVE CHILDREN

Some children never seem to outgrow the terrible twos. Although they only appear happy and cooperative when they are getting their own way, they may actually have trouble thinking through problems and shifting gears from what they are doing to what others want them to do. This happens for a variety of physical reasons, including:

Phsysiology	Behavior
• The frontal (thinking) cortex does not receive enough stimulation from lower areas of the brain.	**Hyperactivity** Self-stimulation through constant activity, thinking and talking, causing frequent reprimands. Difficulty tempering reactions to upsetting events.
• Underactive frontal cortex cannot regulate incoming stimuli. • Stimulation overload. • Poor blood flow to the right brain, which manages cause-and-effect relationships, spatial perception, and decision making.	**Attention deficits** "Ability" to attend to everything at once. Poor short-term memory, planning, anticipating, and difficulty separating thoughts from feelings. Trouble learning from mistakes. Trouble seeing the whole picture: poor spelling, thinking in black and white (You always, never . . .), difficulty understanding others, getting lost or losing things and adapting to unexpected situations.
• Low levels of serotonin are unable to counterbalance neurotransmitters that respond to incoming stimuli and produce self-stimulation.	**Depression, Aggression and OCD** Explosiveness or inflexibility about the way things look, feel, taste or smell, and about the order in which things are done.
• Dysfunction in the left brain.	**Learning disabilities** Trouble expressing thoughts and problem solving.

HELPING INFLEXIBLE-EXPLOSIVE CHILDREN

Discipline that stresses consistency, consequences and complimenting good behavior works well with children whose ability to focus, plan, anticipate, remember, and verbalize is maturing appropriately. Inflexible children with little frustration tolerance need a low-stress approach that teaches skills, prioritizes demands, and pre-empts explosions. This begins when caretakers examine their own behavior. Mark items that you need to concentrate on changing:

Self-examination.

__ Are you taking misbehavior personally? Saying children are willful implies that they are intentionally being uncooperative. It is more likely that their low frustration tolerance and difficulty shifting gears cause problems with anger than "willfulness."

__ Do you, yourself, have problems with wanting things your way? Flexibility may be a genetic trait. Adults who can shift gears themselves will have an easier time finding a variety of responses to young people's stubborn behavior. Even rigid adults are generally more flexible than problem children.

__ Do you have a realistic image of your children? Are you expecting them to do things that they currently can not consistently perform?

---

[1] Fully described in *The Explosive Child* by Ross Green, Ph.D. (New York: HarperCollins, 1998)

Prevent problems.

Develop strategies for difficult times: Use deadlines that carry weight. Children are far more likely to pick up their things before they can watch TV than prior to leaving for school. Give ample time to switch gears! Negotiate a starting time and then act—Pick up the telephone extension, turn off the TV, or take away a toy.

Teach skills: Ask yourself, "Why is this hard for my child?" "What is getting in his way?" "How can I help?" Break large tasks into small ones. Assist or monitor task completion—"What do you need to do next?"

Gently point out flaws in beliefs and behaviors—"I know you think I'm always mad but I was really pleased when you . . . ." "When you . . . I feel . . . and don't want to . . . ."

Prioritize struggles.

Nonnegotiable issues include safety, school, and basic responsibilities. Ask your-self, "Is this issue important enough for a power struggle? Is my child capable of performing what I'm asking consistently? Do I have control over the behavior?" Saving your authority for essential issues will actually give you more credibility.

Negotiable issues are not important enough for a major power struggle but are still a high priority. Reaching a compromise is not giving in. It teaches children to see others' views, generate solutions, and think things through. Both the parent and child state, "I want . . . because . . . "; repeat each other's position; and generate mutually satisfying solutions. Differences diminish when people turn resentments into requests.

Unimportant issues are not worth power struggles or negotiation. They include behaviors parents don't like but are not eminently harmful—ice cream for breakfast, appearance, and beliefs. As children learn skills, more items can be negotiated.

Pre-empt explosions.

Empathize: Understand what is upsetting children and show it. Label and rate feelings—"How disappointed, frustrated, or annoyed are you?" Use numerical or color codes. Zero or green means calm and ten or red means boiling mad.

Use descriptive language: Say, "You're having trouble seeing options right now," rather than, "You're being stubborn." Be careful of sarcasm, assuming, mind reading, predicting catastrophes, and getting off track. Model self-control.

Think things through: Instead of trying to convince children to see your point, first consider what they want and the logical extension of their desires—"That might be a good idea. Show me how you would do that. What will happen after you . . . ?"

Distract: Tell a joke or take a break in the early stages of frustration—"Why don't you talk to your friend or shoot some baskets while I think about this." Encouraging children to do something they enjoy breaks the tension and helps them think clearly.

Downshift: Do a little bit of what the child wants and gradually switch over to your agenda—"I'd like my beeper back as soon as you finish pressing that button." "You can find a toy to carry with you in the store, but we'll return it before we check out."

Restore coherence when children lose control.

Stop negotiating when it is deadlocked. People cannot think during angry outbursts. Take a break and don't pursue children who run to their rooms and slam doors.

Do not personalize cursing or back talk. Later, you can ask children to express what they said appropriately before they become involved in a desired activity.

ANGER AND VIOLENCE

Whenever you or a loved one has a problem with anger, the potential for violence always needs to be addressed! Violence is not an expression of anger, but a strategy to maintain power in a relationship. Some people feel entitled to power and maintain this belief through self-pity, denial, rationalization, manipulation, and disregard for their partner's feelings. Underneath this drive for power can be deep feelings of inadequacy, guilt, and fears of abandonment. The potential for violence can be seen in people who:

- Define manhood through competition, maintaining power, and devaluing women.
- Do not take responsibility and constantly blame others for their feelings and behavior.
- Defend against emotional pain with substance abuse, excitement, and anger.
- Are hypersensitive, rigid, and moody and expect partners to meet all their needs.
- Rationalize their need for control as necessary for others' well-being and safety.
- Have a history of past violence.

RECOGNIZING THE CYCLE OF VIOLENCE

Violent tactics are rarely seen early in a relationship. Initially, a person may be intensely romantic and pressure his or her partner to make a commitment. Gradually, a cycle develops of tension building toward abusive action followed by an expression of remorse or romance. Emotional and verbal abuse may appear before actual violence. One out of 6 women reports that her partner hit her at some point in her marriage. Because 70% to 80% of murdered women are killed by their husband, a family member, or close male friend, it is very important to become aware of how violence can progress over the years:

Nonphysical Indicators ⟶	**Violence—No Contact** ⟶	**Violent Contact**
Extreme standards, blaming Intimidating looks, gestures Insults, name-calling Mind games Making all the decisions Controlling the money Isolating from work, family, friends, or school Accusations of infidelity Questioning about activities, stalking, or checking up Threatening divorce, taking the children, suicide, and violence—"I'll beat you."	Punching walls or doors Throwing objects Destroying objects Breaking windows Tearing clothes Driving recklessly to scare Blocking exits or the car Taking keys Taking money or credit cards Unplugging the phone Cruelty to animals or children	Pushing, shoving, grabbing, or twisting arms Holding down, pinning against a wall, or carrying against one's will Slapping, spanking, or punching Kicking, kneeing, or biting Choking, banging head on floor, or hair pulling Forced sex Inflicting pain or burning Use of weapons

THERAPY FOR BATTERERS

Hidden feelings of powerlessness are often expressed in the need to control others. In group therapy, people can recognize vulnerable feelings in others that they have hidden from themselves. It can take 18–24 months to eradicate the misuse of power that feeds abuse. Management of violence can actually be accomplished early in treatment, but control issues require lengthy intervention. Offenders need to:

- Admit that they alone are responsible for violence.

- Experience vulnerable feelings that underlie the need for power.
- Find acceptable channels for relieving pressure: sports or expressing insecurity.
- Recognize the cycle of violence and its triggers—"I can't stand it when . . ."
- Learn to use steps to reduce anger danger: time-out, positive self-talk, and more.
- Learn to mutually share power in a relationship and resolve conflict equitably.
- Rediscover initial interests and pleasure that attracted partners.

THERAPY FOR VICTIMS

To recognize and treat victims of battering, common misconceptions about domestic violence must be challenged:

Domestic Violence	
Fiction	**Fact**
1. Uneducated, poor, or minority people with few job skills are more likely to be battered.	1. Violence occurs in all strata of society. The poor are prosecuted more often.
2. Dependent, masochistic women may seek out violent partners.	2. Mental health problems are the result of, not the cause of, battering.
3. Many people do things (unintentionally) that cause their partner to hit them.	3. Violence is an individual character trait, not a relationship dysfunction.
4. Women return to abusive partners because they are unable to separate.	4. Family, friends, and clergy often urge women to make the relationship work.
5. People who have been battered will tend to get into another violent relationship.	5. Most people who have been battered go on to establish good relationships.
6. People who have been violent can change with a different person or reduced stress.	6. People who batter will continue to have violent relationships until they get help.
7. Violent people are uneducated, unsuccessful, or lacking in conscience.	7. People with a variety of backgrounds, accomplishments, and values can be violent.
8. Once a person leaves a relationship, he or she is safe from violence.	8. People are in greatest danger right after they leave a violent relationship.

Statistics and other ideas come from *Spouse Abuse* by Michele Harway and Marsali Hansen (Professional Resource Exchange, 1994). See also *Getting Free* by Ginny Nicarthy (Seal Press Feminist Publications, 1997), *Abused Men* by Philip Cook (Prager, 1997), 800-799-SAFE, www.domestic-violence.org.

Therapy does not start by pushing people to end abusive relationships. Battered women make an average of seven attempts to leave before doing so permanently. They return due to a lack of financial and emotional support. Individual counseling is needed to create the safety for victims to:

- Recognize and admit that abuse is happening.
- Place blame entirely on the violent partner (unless both are abusive).
- Learn that symptoms of depression, disinterest, low self-esteem, indecisiveness, and anxiety are reactions to battering rather than character flaws.
- Realize that they cannot "save" their partner. Recovery must happen in groups with other batterers who can help offenders recognize abuse and take full responsibility.
- Develop a safety plan with an exit route, a strategically placed safety kit (clothing, medication, money, keys), prearranged shelter, and knowledge of when to leave.
- Build a sense of personal power, support, and the ability to make decisions.

TAKING DANGER OUT OF ANGER

Who is in charge—you or your anger? You may not even be aware that you have become a slave to rage and that it is no longer working for you. If you answer no to any of the following questions, it's time to get a new boss—yourself!

- Does your anger help you feel better about yourself?
- Does it help you achieve your long-term goals?
- Do any good feelings you get from anger last?
- Does your anger keep you safe from danger?

A brief release of anger can be energizing and direct you toward action that will resolve conflicts. However, prolonged agitation creates mental, relationship, and physical problems. Even people who are (biochemically) reactive to their surroundings can learn to reduce the duration of flare-ups to minutes instead of hours or days. To lay the groundwork for taking charge of your temper, identify people and situations that trigger reactions and the early warning signs that your buttons are being pushed.

Anger's Warning Signs			
External Triggers —>	**Sensations**	**Feelings**	**Outer Expression**
People	Tension in:	Used	Grit teeth, grimace
Boss, coworkers	Head	Betrayed	Glare or stare
Spouse or children	Eyes	Jealous	Make a fist
Relatives or friends	Jaw	Envious	Walk fast or pace
Other drivers	Neck	Disrespected	Talk fast or loudly
Salespeople	Chest	Victimized	Gossip
Complaints or criticism	Stomach	Powerless	Curse
Laziness and incompetence	Back	Helpless	Grunt or grumble
Lying, injustice, tardiness	Hands	Unimportant	Tap foot
Arrogance or rudeness	Shoulder	Neglected	Jiggle leg
Politics or prejudice	Sweat	Ashamed	Drum fingers
Disagreements	Feel hot	Defective	Point finger
Boredom or waiting	"See red"	Like a saint	Throw things
Other:	Other:	Other:	Other:

STEPS THAT REDUCE ANGER

Once you are on the alert for anger triggers and recognize your internal reactions, you can rate you distress. Use colors or numbers. Zero or green would mean no distress and 10 or red would be a major explosion. Each person has a different "point of no return." People with some control might deal with a situation until they are in the orange range or over six "units" of anger. If your feelings take over in a flash, start to reduce your anger when you have yellow or three units of frustration.

Distress Units **Distress Units**

0 1 2 3 4 5 6 7 8 9 10

Green (Calm Zone) Yellow Orange Red (Danger Zone)

Taking Danger out of Anger

With practice, you can streamline the following release-reduce-reexamine-request steps into a unique package that will help you wage peace, not war: [1]

1. Physically release anger in private. Remove yourself from the trigger situation or person. Tell significant others that you need a short break so you can think more clearly. Go to the restroom, for a walk, swing your arms, scrub the floor, smash aluminum cans, yell (into a pillow), growl, or hit a punching bag. Beware of exercise that makes you more agitated. You only need five minutes.
2. Reduce anger by noticing where tension "lives" in your body and using the following to detach from it. Learn which technique(s) works best for you:
   - Create a symbol that represents your anger (not the target): a firecracker, a volcano, a barking dog, or boiling water. Focus on the symbol and watch it change. If necessary, add another element to help: see the lava cool, hear the firecracker fizzle, drop ice cubes into the boiling water, or feed the dog a steak.
   - Tap acupressure points that reduce anger "by removing an imbalance in the body's electrical flow."[2] While focusing on anger sensations, tap (about 7 times each) the outside of the little fingernail (lf) and an inch under the collarbone (cb) just to the side of the sternum. After noticing some calming, further reduce anger by moving your eyes in a horizontal figure 8 while tapping the outside points of your eyebrows, humming a few notes, counting to three, and humming again. Then, repeat the lf and cb taps.
   - Pair relaxation with arousal to decondition it. Look down until your lids are almost shut. Slowly roll your eyes up as if you were trying to see your eyebrows. When it is too tiring to look up anymore, allow your lids to flutter closed. Take three deep, full breaths. Count to three as your breathe in and to six as you breathe out. Fully expand your lungs by pushing out your stomach.
   - Temporarily distract yourself. Listen to music, read, watch TV, play with your pet, shoot baskets, or take a warm bath. Let the back part of your mind tackle the problem while you do something that you enjoy.
3. Reexamine the event that triggered your anger after detaching from it. Rule out anything that might have fed your distress by asking yourself:
   - "Did this incident bring up any of my own insecurities?"
   - "If I did not get angry, would I have felt exposed, powerless, rejected, inadequate, unimportant, guilty, ashamed, empty, bored, hungry, or tired?"
   - "Was I trying to control others, make things perfect, look tough, distance, avoid painful feelings, or get an adrenaline rush?"
   - "Were any of my rights taken away?" "How important is this battle?"
4. Turn resentment into specific requests or action that you can take if you were truly violated. When you are ready, state your feelings, requests and solutions calmly—"I feel . . . when you . . . ." "Would you . . . , . . . , or . . . ?" "I will (not) . . . ."

---

[1] Steps adapted from *Mastering Your Moods* by Melvyn Kinder (Simon & Schuster, 1994) and *Letting Go of Anger* by Ron and Pat Potter-Efron (New Harbinger, 1995).

[2] For further information contact Callahan Techniques at 760-345-4737, www.tftrx.com; or fgallo@energypsych.com; or see *Energy Psychology* by Fred P. Gallo (CRC Press, 1998).

PRACTICE MAKES PEACE

People are born with the ability to move but must be taught how to dance. Likewise, we are given the gift of anger but must learn how to use it to our advantage. Think of situations that trigger your temper. In your mind, rehearse the strategies below and use any mad moments as opportunities to practice peaceful power. Your initial awkward responses will become automatic the more you apply the following techniques:

BETRAYAL, JEALOUSY, AND OTHER WOUNDS

- Don't blame or use "should" and "you."
- Express your feelings with a statement that starts with "I"—"I feel . . . when you . . . ."
- Make requests and give choices—"Would you . . . , . . . , or . . . ?"
- Set limits by knowing what action you can take—"I will (not) . . . when you . . . ."

COMPLAINTS

- Don't make excuses or pass the buck.
- Agree—"Yes, you have had to wait way too long."
- Apologize or wish—"I'm sorry we are so busy today. I wish we had more help."
- Appreciate—"I'm glad you're pointing out how frustrating this is."
- Act—"I will definitely bring it to the attention of our management."

ASSUMPTIONS AND GENERALIZATIONS

- Don't attack, defend, or be adversarial.
- Subtly point out incorrect statements by repeating them as a question—"I *never* help?"
- Show concern—"I'm sure you have good reasons for feeling that way."
- Identify specifics—"What do you mean by . . . ?" "Can you give me an example of . . . ?"
- Identify underlying issues—"What is really hurting you most?"

REHASHING OLD ISSUES

- Don't try to make people forget the past.
- Keep a list of resentments to avoid lengthy descriptions of past wrong doings—"Oh yes, you're talking about resentment number . . . ."
- Admit what you did, even if it's for the umpteenth time—"You're right, I did . . . ."
- Find out why the issue is resurfacing—"What's making you think of that now?"
- Turn resentments into requests—"What can I do right now to help?"

CRITICISM AND ADVICE

- Do not attack, defend or withdraw.
- Agree with any actual or possible truth—"I *could* have been better at . . . ."
- Exaggerate wrongdoing to help others back off—"I guess I was totally thoughtless."
- Clarify confusing criticism—"How was what I did difficult for you?"
- End criticism with consideration—"I'll give your ideas full consideration."
- Make your own decisions about what you need to change. (See demands.)

DEMANDS, EXPECTATIONS, AND SOLICITATIONS

- Avoid excuses and "can't" or "but" words.
- Focus on what you can do—"I can do that as soon as I . . . ."
- Use the words "wish" and "and"—"I wish I could . . . and I need to or can . . . ."
- Set limits when necessary—"I know you want me to...and I'd rather . . . ."
- Refuse with sympathy—"I know it's hard on you when I don't . . . ."

CONFLICTS OF INTEREST

- Don't insist on having your way.
- Clearly state the conflict—"I want . . . and you want . . . ."
- Use "and" instead of "but" to be inclusive—"You think . . . and I think . . . ."
- Express confidence and use the word "we"—"I'm sure we can resolve this."
- Suggest solutions and seriously consider others' ideas.
- Point out how both parties will benefit from suggestions.
- Anticipate deadlocks and voice alternatives—"I know you're concerned about . . . and I think we can get around that by . . . ."
- Reevaluate impasses. Make sure you understand the other person's objections.
- Stay focused on the issue—"Let's get back to . . . ."

DIFFERENCES OF OPINION

- Do not try to prove your point or change someone's mind.
- Point out the process—"I disagree." "You would really like me to reach your conclusions."
- After saying you disagree, wait to be asked for your opinion. It is a waste of words to express your ideas when others don't want to listen.
- Appreciate other viewpoints—"Your ideas have helped me clarify my own."

LAZINESS, NEGLIGENCE, AND UNFAIRNESS

- Don't exaggerate, judge or be "one-sided."
- Empathize with others' position. There is a reason for behavior you don't like.
- Put it in perspective. How important will this be a year from now?
- Pick your battles. Decide what issues are worth your energy.
- Generate solutions—"What can we do so this doesn't happen again?" "What can we do to put this behind us?" "Is there anything I can do about this?"
- Maintain a future orientation. "From now on . . . ." "Next time, would you . . . ?"
- Use a positive tone—"I know you meant to . . . .Would you . . . ?"

NOSINESS AND PRYING

- Don't answer, refuse to answer, or focus on others' insensitivity.
- Thank people for their interest—"It's so sweet of you to be concerned about . . . ."
- Answer a question with a (humorous) question —"Is this an official survey?"

HEAD GAMES AND MANIPULATIONS

- Don't focus on content by attacking or defending.
- Point out the process—"Do you want me to break a confidence?"
- Use the word "try" to weaken others' tactics—"Are you trying to put me in the middle?" "Are you trying to pressure me into reaching a decision?"
- Use compliments to change the game—"You're good at putting me on the spot."

RANDOM ACTS OF RUDENESS

- Do not take insults seriously, attack, or withdraw.
- Treat cruelty as kindness—"Why, thank you." "You're just trying to help me . . . ."
- Use humor to distract and confuse—"You say that like it's a bad thing."
- Elicit the cause of meanness—"What's really bothering you?"
- Set limits when you've had enough—"I'll talk to you when you're in a better mood."

For more information about any of these areas, see *Tongue Fu* by Sam Horn (St. Martin's Griffin, 1996, www.samhorn.com; *When I Say No, I Feel Guilty* by Manuel Smith (Bantam Books, 1973); or *How to Handle Bullies, Teasers, and Other Meanies* by Kate Cohen-Posey (Rainbow Books, 1995).

BELIEFS THAT EASE ANGER

When someone takes away your power it is natural to get mad. The justified anger of childhood comes from having to give up primitive wants and desires in favor of socially acceptable behavior. The firm, controlled voice of adult anger can replace the strident outbursts of youth when three things happen:

1. Society's rules become your own.
2. You can trust yourself to find both support and freedom.
3. You acquire enough self-esteem that it cannot be taken away by an off comment or a minor mishap.

Once these developmental tasks are accomplished, people can look through others' eyes to see the whole picture and decide when they need to take action to correct a true loss of power. If you have many mad moments, it may be because beliefs instilled during early life experiences make it difficult to empathize with others and consider your options.

Directions: Mark any of the thoughts below that you've had in your "mad moments." Then, mark the beliefs you would like to have to pick your battles and take constructive action.

Turn Provocative Thoughts into . . .	Beliefs That Ease Anger
Underlying painful thoughts	**Underlying healing beliefs**
__ I'm unimportant if I don't get my way.	__ I still count even when I don't get my way.
__ I'm weak or a loser If I don't defend myself.	__ My power comes from understanding others.
__ I'm stupid or foolish if I'm deceived.	__ Deception is caused by others' dishonesty.
__ I'm defective or guilty if I'm corrected.	__ I have the right to cry and be illogical.
__ I'm a failure if I don't make things go right.	__ I'm responsible only for my part.
Thoughts of entitlement	**Accepting, responsible beliefs**
__ People should accept me as I am.	__ People can love me without liking all of me.
__ I should get what I want.	__ I can ask for what I want and negotiate.
__ I shouldn't have to	__ I can take care of myself, do my part, and say "No."
__ I should be able to release all my anger.	__ I can turn my anger into effective action.
__ Others cause my anger.	__ I'm responsible for how I handle my anger.
__ Others are too sensitive.	__ Understanding others gives me choices.
Generalizations and distortions	**Observant, curious beliefs**
__ People are evil, greedy, out to get me.	__ There are reasons for the worst behavior.
__ All men (women) are	__ I can see differences in people.
__ I cannot trust anyone.	__ I can learn whom and find people to trust.
__ I know what others feel without asking.	__ Assuming without asking is asinine.
__ The worst will happen.	__ Most of my "catastrophes" don't happen.
Perfectionist, rigid thoughts	**Realistic, flexible beliefs**
__ I'm better than others.	__ I'm as good as others and they're as good as I.
__ My way is the best.	__ There are many good ways of doing things.
__ Things are either right or wrong.	__ I can respond when I don't like others' actions.
__ People should be appreciative, courteous. hardworking, fair, good drivers, etc.	__ Others don't have to live by my rules and can experience the consequences of their mistakes.

For more ideas, see *Feeling Good* by David Burns (Avon Books, 1980); and *EMDR: The Breakthrough Therapy* by Francine Shapiro (Basic Books, 1997).

INSTILLING BELIEFS THAT EASE ANGER

When you are not upset, the beliefs that prevent (unnecessary) anger may seem completely true. It will be harder to maintain them during conflicts of interest, when you feel controlled or unsupported or when things aren't going "right." To begin to change thinking patterns, start keeping a journal of your mad moments. Use the questions below and the previous table to identify the provocative thoughts that each incident triggers. Write a calming belief that you would like to have instead and affirm it regularly.

- When others disturb me, what does that mean about me?
- How do others' actions make me feel about myself?
- When did I first have this disturbing thought about myself?

Journal of Mad Moments		
Upsetting Incident	**Provocative Thought**	**Preventive Belief**
Someone cuts you off while you're driving.	I have to do something or I'm weak.	If I can report him, I will. Otherwise, he'll eventually get caught.
Your boss blames you for a mishap you didn't cause.	I must be defective. I have to make her understand.	I can understand her reasoning and then decide what to do.
A sales clerk keeps following you, even though you've said you are just looking.	No one respects my wishes—not even salespeople.	She's just doing her job. I can be kind and firm in my wishes.

BACK UP BELIEFS WITH ACTION

You can bolster beliefs that reduce the frequency of mad moments by acting on them. Don't wait until you feel good enough to change your behavior. Acting as though the beliefs you want are true is the fastest way to make them work for you. You will find yourself going from fury to frustration, anger to annoyance, and ballistic to bothered without even realizing it. Check the strategies you most need to adopt:

__ Practice seeing the whole picture. Look for good intentions in others' behavior and positive possibilities in negative situations.

__ Do not hide from hate. Admit what you are feeling and examine the incident that caused it. Identify the choices you now have. Take action to reclaim any power you lost. It is your responsibility to recover from past hurts.

__ Check out your assumptions and generalizations with at least two people who do not have problems with anger.

__ Burn your bridges. Let significant others know how you use anger for power, to look tough, or to distance.

__ Act as if healing beliefs are true—"I am good (enough), I'm loveable, I belong." Hold your head high, quit apologizing, take praise, and be more open. Don't turn your lack of self-esteem on others.

For more strategies, see *Letting Go of Anger* by Ron and Pat Potter-Efron (New Harbinger, 1995).

CLAIM IT AND AIM IT

Avoiding anger is as self-damaging as constant fuming. People may totally suppress anger, express it in sneaky ways, or disown their hostility and see it in others. If you do not claim your anger, it will "own" you. When you embrace your anger, you can contain it and aim it in a direction that will serve you well. Each means of short-circuiting anger has costly payoffs:[1]

- Suppressed anger causes people to lose themselves. Having a relationship takes priority over having a self. Giving in, going along with, and putting others first causes feelings of confusion and being used. Wants and needs don't get met because they are unknown. In the extreme, people lose enjoyment of and interest in life. Headaches, ulcers, or other physical problems may develop. Some people deny their feelings until they explode or turn anger against themselves.
- Stealth anger invites bad will from others due to constant excuses, procrastination, playing helpless, and ignoring requests. Experts at avoiding what they do not want, have trouble knowing what they do want and reaching goals. They rarely receive appreciation or approval from others and ultimately lose self-respect.
- Disowned anger makes the world look hostile. By seeing their own anger in others, people gain a temporary excuse to retaliate. However, it is necessary to be on guard all the time and easy to feel victimized, envious, and jealous. Others view these people as suspicious, unpredictable, and not believable. Eventually, the anger that is seen in others becomes a self-fulfilling prophecy.

EMBRACE ANGER TO CONTAIN IT

Anger is the least understood and most maligned of all the emotions. Whereas sadness and fear can be private affairs, anger connects us to others. Inappropriate expressions of anger are especially noticeable and the cause of much misinformation in society. This can lead to the internalization of thoughts that disarm us. Learning correct information and identifying beliefs that contradict incapacitating thoughts helps reclaim anger.

Directions: Mark any of the thoughts that you have that suppress anger. Then, mark the beliefs that would help you use your anger wisely.

Turn Thoughts That Avoid Anger into . . .	Beliefs That Embrace Anger
Misinformation	**Correct information**
__ Anger is bad, judgmental, or a weakness.	__ Anger is a natural reaction to a loss of power.
__ Anger is a sin.	__ Anger is neutral. Its use can be good or bad.
__ Ladies do not get angry.	__ Anger is a part of a woman's passion.
__ Anger is dangerous.	__ Actions are dangerous, not anger.
__ Other people are vulnerable.	__ Others can learn from appropriate anger.
Incapacitating thoughts	**Empowering beliefs**
__ If I get angry, I'll lose control.	__ If I release some anger, I'll gain control.
__ If I start feeling angry, I'll never stop.	__ If I release some anger, I'll feel relief.
__ If I show anger, I'll be punished.	__ I choose how I respond to others' reactions.
__ If I show anger, others will leave me.	__ I can resolve differences with others.
__ If I show anger, I'll hurt or damage others.	__ Others are responsible for their reactions.

[1] For further information see *Letting Go of Anger* by Ron and Pat Potter-Efron (New Harbinger, 1995) and *The Dance of Anger* by Harriet Goldhor Learner (HarperCollins, 1997).

DIALOGUE WITH DISPLEASURE

Once you accept your anger, you can hear what it is telling you. Every mad moment is a message that something is wrong. If you are a master conflict-avoider, you may not want to recognize that you are being used or betrayed. However, you can right a wrong with less turmoil in the early stages of mistreatment than when it becomes blatant abuse. Any of the following questions can begin a dialogue with your displeasure:

- If I were angry right now, what would be bothering me?
- What is it about this situation that troubles me? What do I think and feel?
- What do I want to accomplish? What, specifically, do I want to change?
- Who is responsible for what? What am I willing and not willing to do?
- When I make excuses, play helpless, or ignore others, what is really bothering me?
- When I think others are angry, disrespectful, or betraying me, how might I be angry with, disrespectful, or unfaithful to them?
- When I think others are greedy, envious or jealous, what is it that I'm wanting?

THE AIM OF ANGER

Anger needs direction. Without focus, it gets sidetracked into a laundry list of complaints, bitterness, and irritability. Anger avoiders often choose to be victimized, evasive, or guarded and do not take decisive action. They think of anger as a weapon rather than a problem-solving tool. Once you've reclaimed your anger and identified what is bothering you, practice using annoyance to express your feelings, wants, and limits:

- Rehearse expressions of anger with sentences that start with the word "I"—"I feel . . . when you . . . ." "Would you . . . , . . . or . . . ." "I will (not) . . . ."
- Put a new face on anger. Change strident outbursts into firm, controlled expression. Turn resentment into requests. Imagine taking an action when words don't work.
- Allow others to be angry. It's OK for spouses, children, and friends to be upset when you don't do what they want. Be firm and then sympathize with their distress.
- Practice making decisions. When you don't know what you want to do, pretend you know. Every decision helps you learn more about who you are and what you want.
- Say "No" instead of, "I forgot," "Yes, but . . . ," "I'll do it later," or playing helpless, withdrawing, and ignoring. Don't say "Yes" unless you plan to follow through.
- Have a yes/no fight. Say "Yes" and have a support person say "No" with different tones and volumes. Then switch roles. Get the feel of it.
- Make a no-gossiping rule for yourself. If you must talk about someone with whom you are angry, do it with the agenda of planning how to be direct.
- Hang in instead of making excuses. Avoid telling yourself, "Why should I bother?" "I just don't feel like it," or "It's useless." Say things "for the record" rather than to accomplish an outcome.
- Stay angry long enough to make sure something good happens.

EXTRA HELP FOR ANGER

It is entirely the responsibility of explosive people to learn to tame their temper. However, it is an easier task when family and friends are willing to learn responses that do not fuel a flare-up. Mark any strategies below that you would like others to use to help you or that you are willing to use to calm your significant others:

__ Discuss rules for dealing with anger during calm times in public places. Agree that either party can terminate a discussion if he or she fears it is heading toward violence or verbal abuse.
__ Assess any risk of violence during actual disagreements and do your best to leave if there is a remote possibility of abuse.
__ Set limits on verbal abuse—"I will leave the room when you yell or call me names."
__ Give reminders to take a five-minute break for a brief release of emotional energy alone when discussions become too tense.
__ Deal with your own discomfort with others' anger, which often comes from childhood fears of being punished or disappointing. Tell yourself to stop thinking of a rebuttal and listen to understand the other person's point.
__ Nod and make listening noises. Rolling your eyes and looking away intensifies other peoples' tirades and their desperation to make you understand.
__ Help others convert their resentment into a request or statement of feeling—"Would you tell me what is hurting you or what you want?"
__ Rephrase, label feelings, and validate the other person before you make your point—"You're saying I always put others before you. You must feel neglected. It makes sense that my other obligations are hard on you."
__ Ask if the other person wants to hear you position before making any attempt to explain yourself—"You sound convinced that I don't spend more time at home because I don't care about you. Do you want to consider any other ideas?"
__ Ask the other person to rephrase what you've said after making your point—"I'm not sure if I'm making sense, would you tell me what I said?"
__ Overlook minor outbursts and do not take them personally. Remind yourself that people who are reactive to their environment tend to increase volume when they are excited or upset. Accepting occasional irritability may be a part of enjoying a passionate person's temperament. But, take a time-out for yourself when you cannot be calm.
__ Pick your battles with people who tend to be inflexible. Point out when you are going along with something that is not your preference—"That's not my way of doing things, but I don't mind making a change in this situation."
__ Set limits on issues that are important to you—"I'm really not comfortable with what you want. I'm sure we can reach a compromise, and until we do, I thoroughly sympathize with how disappointed you are."
__ Give inflexible, explosive people time to consider new ideas—"I really want . . . . It is important to me because . . . . Please don't give me your reaction until you've had time to think about it."
__ Help others think through "unreasonable" demands by considering the logical extension of what they want instead of totally rejecting their ideas—"That might be a good idea. What would we do if . . . happens?"

FRIENDLY CAUTIONS

Avoid asking for help from friends and relatives who are pushy, disinterested, inept, or rigid. Attempts to involve them in your recovery or make them change will hinder your progress. Be cautious of bad advice. Input that makes you feel even worse about yourself is probably not correct. Do not argue with bad advice or try to make others understand. Thank people for their concern and tell them you'll consider what they are saying.

NATIONAL NETWORKS AND SUPPORT GROUPS

Because there are numerous causes for problems with anger, there are few nationwide organizations or networks devoted to this issue. However, many 12-step groups (Alcoholics Anonymous, Narcotics Anonymous, Alanon for family members, and Adult Children of Alcoholics) often deal with this topic and are essential when substance abuse contributes to difficulties. Most communities have shelters and treatment groups for domestic violence. Mental health centers and courthouses are good sources of information. Websites and books can offer additional assistance:

- Domestic violence hotlines: 800-799-SAFE, www.domestic-violence.org/.
- General Internet sites and links: www.cmhc.com.
- *Anger Kills* by Redford Williams and Virginia Williams (Harper Mass Market, 1998).
- *Anger: Deal with It, Heal with It and Stop It from Killing You* by Bill Defoore (Health Communications, 1991).
- *The Dance of Anger* by Harriet Goldhor Lerner (HarperCollins, 1997).
- *Facing the Fire* by John Lee (Bantam, 1995).

MEDICATION

- Mood stabilizers and hormone treatments can markedly reduce volatility that can happen during episodes of depression, agitation, or PMS.
- Stimulants that help hyperactive people focus can reduce impulsive outbursts of anger.
- Antidepressants that increase levels of serotonin often reduce irritability in people who are highly reactive to their surroundings or compulsively preoccupied with rules, details, order, ethics, and cleanliness.
- The herb Saint-John's-wort can be used by people who are reluctant to take medication (if they are not overly sensitive to sun exposure or at risk for cataracts). However, some people may not find it as effective as prescription medication.

PROFESSIONAL HELP

Counseling is very important when anger interferes with work or personal relationships. When physical abuse has occurred, the treatment of choice is group therapy in a domestic violence program. Couples should not be seen in counseling together until batterers have begun to manage destructive urges.

Chapter 9

Getting Focused

GETTING FOCUSED

OBJECTIVES FOR TREATMENT PLANNING

1. Identify patterns of attention deficits (ADD) and hyperactivity (ADHD).
2. Distinguish ADD and ADHD from other disorders.
3. Understand neurological causes of ADD.
4. Understand how medications that treat ADD are related to possible causes.
5. Understand benefits and limits of medication.
6. Explore alternative treatments (for those reluctant to use traditional psychopharmacology).
7. Make a decision to take medication if it is indicated.
8. Take medication responsibly as prescribed by a physician.
9. Report using tactics that decrease intensity and frequency of ADD/ADHD symptoms.
10. Coordinate use of effective strategies with school personnel.
11. Become involved in support group for ADD/ADHD.

MINI INDEX FOR CHAPTER 9

USING THE HANDOUTS

- Assessment: *Detecting Attention Deficits, ADD Types and Lookalikes.*
- Treating ADD/ADHD: *Attention Deficits Causes and Cures, Limits and Benefits of Medication, Alternative Treatments.*
- Review sheets for behavior strategies: *Limits and Benefits of Medication; Achievement, Productivity, and Behavior; Organization and Transitions.*

- Handouts for family and friends: *ADD at Home and in the Workplace, Extra Help for ADD and ADHD, and Social Skills.*
- *Social Skills* has activities and games that are ideal for presentations and offer an interactive way of introducing difficulities people with ADD face.

CAUTIONS AND RECOMMENDATIONS

- *Detecting Attention Deficits* should be considered a preliminary assessment to determine if standardized rating scales are needed.
- Supplement behavior strategies in *Achievement, Productivity, and Behavior; Organization and Transitions;* and *ADD at Home and in the Workplace* with handouts from *Powerful Parenting* (Chapter 4), *Couple Magic* (Chapter 3), and *Taming Your Temper* (Chapter 8).
- Reinforce above behavior strategies with the *self-monitoring charts* (9.11) in *Limits and Benefits of Medication.*
- Supplement p. 9.11 *Self-Monitoring Charts with School Reports* (4.19) in *School-Related Problems* (Chapter 4).
- Become familiar with laws designed to help people with diagnosed disorders:[1] *Section 504 of the 1973 Rehabilitation Act* (Office of Civil Rights) and the *Americans with Disabilities Act of 1990.*

SOURCES AND ACKNOWLEDGMENTS

- Criteria for ADD and ADHD used in *Detecting Attention Deficits* are adapted from *Diagnostic and Statistical Manual,* 4th edition (American Psychiatric Association, 1994); the Utah Criteria developed by Paul Wender found in *Attention-Deficit Hyperactivity Disorder in Adults* (Oxford University Press, 1995); and the writings of Edward Hallowell and John Rately in *Driven to Distraction* (Simon & Schuster, 1994).
- Various behavioral approaches are found in *Achievement, Productivity, and Behavior; Organization and Transitions;* and *Limits and Benefits of Medication.*
- A family therapy orientation to treatment, which sees problems affecting systems as well as individuals, is addressed in *ADD at Home and in the Workplace.*
- *Driven to Distraction* by Edward Hallowell and John Rately made major contributions to *ADD Types and Lookalikes, Attention Deficits Causes and Cures, Extra Help for ADD,* and *ADD at Home and in the Workplace.*
- *Beyond Ritalin* by Stephen Garber, Marianne Daniels Garber, and Robyn Freedman Spizman (Harper Perennial, 1996) inspired *Limits and Benefits of Medication, Alternative Treatments,* and *Social Skills.*
- *Alternative Treatments* also cites ideas from *Miracle Cures* by Jean Carper (HarperCollins, 1997), inner ear theories developed by Harold N. Levinson in *Total Concentration* (M Evans & Co., 1990), biofeedback developed by EEG Spectrum (www.eegspectrum.com), and therapies that use acupressure originated by Callahan Techniques, Indian Wells, CA 92210, 760-345-4737, www.tftrx.com.

---

[1]Contact the EEOC, 1801 L Street, NW, Washington, DC 20507, 202-663-4900, www.eeoc.gov or Civil Rights Office, PO 65808, Washington, DC 20035-5808, 202-514-2151, www.usdoj.gov/crt.

DETECTING ATTENTION DEFICITS

Attention deficit disorder (ADD) or attention deficit hyperactivity disorder (ADHD) is increasingly being acknowledged as the cause of problems with school, work, and relationships. Although many people speculate that it is overdiagnosed, it can just as easily go unrecognized. ADD is often difficult to detect in a one-on-one, novel situation in which people are motivated. Therefore, rating scales of how people operate in different settings are better indicators of problems than psychological tests. Six or more items marked "O" in the left column suggest ADD; six or more items in the right column suggests ADHD; and six plus items in each column suggest a combination of both.

ADD/ADHD Rating Scale[1]	
Directions: Mark items with an A (always) or O (often) to show rate of occurrence.	
Inattention:	**Hyperactivity:**
__ Difficulty sustaining attention, completing tasks, without monitoring.	__ Fidgets with hands and feet, squirms in seat, grabs or touches excessively.
__ Skips from one activity (or topic) to another.	__ Difficulty sitting still or remaining seated.
__ Easily distracted by extraneous stimuli.	__ Runs or climbs too much (children), or feels restless (adolescents and adults).
__ Does not appear to be listening or following a conversation; daydreams.	__ Louder than others; makes noises.
__ Poor attention to instructions or directions.	__ Always active, "on the go" or seems to be "driven by a motor."
__ Fails to pay attention to details, makes careless mistakes, rushes.	__ Talks excessively, excitable, easily upset.
__ Avoids tasks that require sustained (mental) effort, easily bored, needs reminders.	**Impulsivity**:
__ Difficulty organizing tasks and belongings.	__ Blurts out answer; ignores consequences.
__ Forgetful, loses things, easily frustrated.	__ Difficulty waiting or following a routine.
	__ Interrupts or intrudes on others.

[1] Adapted from criteria for ADHD with permission from the *Diagnostic and Statistical Manual of Mental Disorders,* 4th edition. Copyright 1994, American Psychiatric Association.

HISTORY

In addition to rating scales, it is important to take a careful history. Family, friends, relatives, and school records are good sources of information. Mark all items that apply:

__ Symptoms of inattention or hyperactivity appeared before age seven and have persisted for more than 6 months. (Age of onset of symptoms: _______.)
__ Symptoms are present on a consistent basis, rather than appearing in cycles.
__ Other family members have had problems with __ attention, __ excessive activity, __ impulsivity, or __ underachievement. (Relationship: ______________________.)
__ The person was adopted. (ADD occurs more often among adopted people.)
__ There was use of __ alcohol, __ drugs, or __ nicotine during pregnancy.
__ There are problems __ falling asleep, __ staying asleep, or __ waking in the morning.
__ Symptoms cannot be explained by problems with __ allergies, __ asthma, __ breathing, __ blood sugar, __ anemia, __ seizures, __ thyroid, __ ear infections, or __ lead poisoning.
__ Medication or drugs containing stimulants or excessive caffeine are not being used.
__ Other problems (__ high stress, __ depression, __ anxiety, or __ nervous tics) are not factors.

DETECTING ATTENTION PROBLEMS IN ADULTS

Difficulties with hyperactivity and attention used to be considered a disorder of childhood. It was believed that as young peoples' brains matured, they grew out of it. More current estimates suggest that 30% to 70% of children with ADD will continue to have problems as adults. It may be that high numbers of adults have ADD, but they developed coping strategies to manage symptoms and even use them to their advantage. Researchers at the University of Utah[2] suggest the following standards for adult ADD:

Core Measures (all three must be present)

__ Childhood evidence of ADD or ADHD with school problems, excitability, or temper.
__ Persistent motor activity: restlessness, difficulty settling down, "nervous" energy, pacing, drumming fingers, and feeling edgy or moving from one place to another.
__ Attention deficits: distractibility, difficulty staying on task, or forgetting or losing things.

Additional Measures (two out of five must be present)

__ Moodiness seen in sudden changes from excitement to discouragement, lasting from hours to days and not as extreme as people with mood disorders.
__ Hot temper or short-lived outbursts that may be frightening to self and others.
__ Reacts to stress with anxiety, anger, and depression.
__ Impulsive, hasty, or risky decisions about work and relationships.
__ Disorganization seen in going from one project to the next or leaving things unfinished, especially when school, parents or spouses are not present to provide structure.

Some writers are concerned that the Utah criteria fail to detect ADD without hyperactivity in adults. Although the ADD/ADHD Rating Scale and the Utah measures can identify problems, the following themes paint a clearer picture of the kind of difficulties adults with attention deficits can have:

Core Measures (both items must be present)

__ Other medical or emotional disorders do not explain the problem.
__ Childhood evidence of problems with attention, daydreaming or underachievement.

Additional Measures (nine or more items must be marked)

__ Procrastination due to reluctance to sustain effort on tasks lacking interest or novelty.
__ Difficulty prioritizing projects causing problems completing anything.
__ *Speaking out without considering the timing or appropriateness of the remark.
__ *Thrill seeking and searching for exciting, novel, or stimulating experiences.
__ *Addictive tendencies with alcohol, cocaine, gambling, shopping, eating, overwork.
__ Avoidance of boredom or relaxation by involvement in projects or excitement.
__ High distractibility, "tuning out" while driving or reading, and losing one's place.
__ Hyper focus on activities of interest and completely "tuning out" one's surroundings.
__ High tolerance for chaos or disorder, which may allow for creativity.
__ Low tolerance for frustration in areas of disinterest.
__ Work problems such as relating to bosses, following the chain of command, managing paperwork, meeting deadlines, punctuality, or workaholism.
__ *Impulsiveness with spending money, changing plans, or career decisions.
__ Excessive worry, particularly when not focused on novel or high-interest tasks.
__ Disassociation or difficulty staying with painful emotions unless they are immediate.
__ Low self-esteem, insecurity, and sense of underachievement in spite of accomplishments.

---

[2] See *Attention Deficit Hyperactivity Disorder in Adults* by Paul Wender (Oxford University Press, 1995), pp. 241–243 for full description of criteria. Also see *Driven to Distraction* by Edward Hallowell and John Rately (Simon & Schuster, 1994). Starred items may indicate ADHD rather than ADD.

ADD TYPES AND LOOKALIKES

Attention deficit disorder (ADD) and hyperactivity (ADHD) can be difficult to recognize because they have variations, mimic, or are combined with other conditions. The following descriptions are offered to help make distinctions:[1]

ADD WITHOUT HYPERACTIVITY

Because ADD was first identified in hyperactive children, it was often missed in people who daydream, go off on tangents, procrastinate, appear spacy, lose their place while reading, or forget where they are when driving. This distractibility or preoccupation happens for reasons other than having too many tasks to do or depression. High toleration for chaos, risk taking, and impulsivity can foster creativity and imagination in these people.

ADD AND HIGH STIMULATION

Some people with ADHD constantly seek stimulation. They enjoy a fast-paced life, doing many things at once, debating, fighting, bungee jumping, car racing, gambling, overspending, tight deadlines, intense romance, or heavy exercise. They will do anything to avoid boredom.

ADD AND MANIA

ADHD people are more consistently overactive than people who have periods of mania with high activity, distractibility, impulsively, and risk taking. Hypomanic (mildly manic) people can have long periods of excessive activity, talkativeness, and impulsiveness; however, they are more likely to feel confident and hopeful than people with ADD are. An ADD verbal style is meandering and detailed, whereas a manic one is pressured, propulsive, and long-winded.

In ADD, an underenergized brain cortex may have trouble inhibiting movement, whereas during mania, the brain is overenergized. Drugs for mania reduce brain excitability, and medications for ADD stimulate the brain. When drugs for mania are not helpful, treatment for ADD should be considered, and visa versa.

ADD AND DEPRESSION

Depression can accompany ADD due to a sense of chronic failure and underachievement. People may overlook pleasure, order, and hope. Depressed people can have difficulty pulling thoughts together and focusing, symptoms resembling ADD. However, the exhaustion and low energy found in depression is usually absent in ADD.

Research suggests the left cortex is linked to good feelings, and the right cortex is related to negative emotions.[2] In depression, the left cortex is underenergized. Hyperactive people may have a similar situation, possibly causing moodiness. People with just ADD are more likely to have an underenergized (negative) right brain, possibly giving them protection against depression.

ADD AND WORRY

Worries can result from anxiety about ADD symptoms of forgetting obligations or making intrusive comments. At other times, ADD anxiety is a way of energizing an underactive brain cortex and keeping thoughts focused. When people let go of one worry, they lock onto another in a way that is similar to people who obsess. People with ADD may have difficulty inhibiting movement, impulses, and distractions due to an underenergized brain, or they may be unable to detect false thoughts and stop them from repeating.

---

[1] These descriptions of ADD subtypes were adapted from *Driven to Distractions* by Edward Hallowell and John Rately (Simon & Schuster, 1994).

[2] "Depression: Beyond Serotonin," by Hara Mestroff Marano, in *Psychology Today* (March/April 1999).

ADD AND DISSOCIATION

Dissociation refers to the disconnection of feelings from their cause. While thinking about an upsetting event, people feel cut off from it or numb. Due to distractibility, people with ADD may have difficulty focusing on a feeling for any length of time. They may be more prone to disassociate from trauma and to develop such puzzling disorders as multiple personalities or amnesia in the face of extreme distress. Treatment for ADD can help people focus on feelings during therapy.

ADD AND LEARNING DISABILITIES

A learning disability (LD) is not caused by a lack of intelligence, but results from problems taking in, processing, or expressing information. About 33% of people with ADD have LD, and 40% of people with LD have ADD.[3] Tests can identify LD. Most schools offer such testing, but it may take persistence to have them administer the full battery needed to detect LD.

ADD AND OVERPLACEMENT

Like children with ADD, students who are too young for their grade often show underachievement, poor self-image, restlessness, and reluctance to perform tasks. However, "overplaced" children are more likely to have separation anxieties, shyness, premature births, preferences to play with younger children, and late loss of baby teeth. Whenever a child is younger or more immature than other children in his or her grade are, overplacement should be considered before ADD.

ADD AND SUBSTANCE ABUSE

People may use drugs due to poor impulse control or to escape feelings of low self-esteem that can accompany ADD. Although most people feel a rush of energy when taking cocaine, 15% feel focused rather than "high." They may be "self-medicating" their ADD. Alcohol can quiet the "internal noise" of ADD; however, daily withdrawal and hangovers increase anxiety. Similarly, marijuana stills constant activity but, in the long run, adds to ADD problems with motivation.

ADD AND ERRATIC PERSONALITIES

ADD often appears to mimic problems of people who have unstable relationships, moodiness, impulsiveness, self-destructiveness, and constant conflicts with others. However, people with personality disorders have anger over unmet needs, become disappointed in relationships, and engage in high stimulation to distract from pain, whereas people with ADD have anger due to frustration, become distracted from relationships, and use high stimulation to focus themselves.

ADD AND CONDUCT PROBLEMS

Like their counterparts, people with ADD can have frequent fights, disobey rules, test limits, disrupt others, and break the law. However, their behavior is less motivated by anger, vengeance, "power hunger," and lack of conscience than pure conduct disorders. Likewise, they are less likely to blame others, premeditate destructive actions, or have histories of abuse or neglect.

ADD AND CULTURE

Society bombards us with stimuli and overwhelms us with obligations. Difficulties slowing down and relaxing can resemble ADD. However, people with ADD have symptoms that began in childhood, that are consistent over time, and that interfere with life skills.

---

[3] *Beyond Retalin* by Stephen Garber, Marianne D. Garber, and Robyn F. Spizman (Harper Perennial, 1996).

ATTENTION DEFICITS CAUSES AND CURES

As early as 1937, stimulants were found to have calming effects on disruptive behavior. Although this ultimately led to the widespread use of medications such as Ritalin to treat hyperactivity (ADHD), it did not explain the paradox of stimulants slowing down children who were constantly in motion. The advent of brain imaging technologies in the 1980s began to make sense of the mystery with a surprising discovery.

> The frontal cortex (surface) of brains of people with Attention Deficit Disorder (ADD) and ADHD were found to have more difficulty using glucose (blood sugar) and to have less blood flow than the frontal region of people without ADD.[1]

PHYSICAL CLUES LEAD TO CURES

The above finding gives new meaning to other well-known facts. Thoroughly understanding these helps make sense of treatments for ADD and strategies that minimize it:

1. The prefrontal cortex (a) inhibits impulses, (b) initiates behavior, and (c) controls working memory. Underactivity in the cortex would reduce the ability to:
   - Inhibit movement and screen out irrelevant stimuli, which might be thought of as an ability to attend to everything rather than a "lack of attention."
   - Regulate the motivation system, causing staying on task to be difficult without constant rewards, and explaining why video games that provide rapid and constant feedback are very engaging for people with ADD.
   - Automatically control concentration, causing people to compensate by learning to overconcentrate, which makes it difficult to let go of enjoyable tasks.
2. Dopamine and norepinephrine, the body's natural stimulants, are abundant in the prefrontal area of the brain. An underactive cortex may (a) be less able to use these chemical messengers, or (b) have fewer dopamine neurons that connect the lower brain to prefrontal cortex. It may be a lack of input from the brain stem that decreases energy in the frontal cortex. Therefore:
   - Constant motion and risk taking may be an attempt to energize the brain.
   - Stimulants could be an effective treatment because they increase levels of dopamine and norepinephrine. Antidepressants, which increase the activity of norepinephrine, would give an additional boost to a "sluggish" cortex.
4. Slow brain waves seen in deep sleep (when less energy is being used) dominate the waking states of people with ADD. As children age, low-frequency (slow) brain waves decrease and the cortex becomes better regulated. "Low-energy" brainwaves (measured by EEG) in people with ADD may be further evidence of decreased blood flow and glucose use in the cortex. EEG biofeedback training claims to help people eliminate problems with ADD by increasing higher frequency (alert) brain waves.[2]
5. Decreased blood flow in the right hemisphere is also detected by brain imaging in some people with ADD. This side of the brain manages cause-and-effect relationships, spatial perception, and decision making. An underactive right hemisphere may cause trouble with seeing the whole picture, poor spelling, getting lost or losing things, and difficulty adapting to unexpected situations.

---

[1] Statistics and information on the physiology of ADD from *Driven to Distraction* by Edward Hallowell and John Rately (Simon & Schuster, 1994).

[2] For further information on EEG training, contact EEG Spectrum, 16100 Ventura Boulevard, Suite 10, Encino, CA 91436-2595, www.eegspectrum.com.

6. Heredity appears to account for some of the physiological and maturation differences between people with and without ADD. A particular combination of genes creating the full syndrome is strongly suggested by statistics. At least 30% of parents of ADD children have (or had) the disorder themselves. Only 4% to 6% of the general population has ADD. Fetal exposure to lead, alcohol, cocaine, or nicotine could also be factors.

TREATMENT FOR ADD

In mild cases, people can learn to manage ADD symptoms by learning behavioral strategies. However, failing to consider medication for people who may have an energy shortage in the brain cortex can handicap school or work performance. Stimulants reduce symptoms in 75% to 80% of people with correct diagnoses. Although their effects are immediate, it can take months of trial and error to determine the right dose. Certain antidepressants help approximately 70% of those who do not respond to stimulants. Other drugs also help ADD or increase the effectiveness of medication:

Medication for ADD	Side Effects and Benefits
Stimulants:	
• Ritalin, Dexedrine, and Adderal increase the body's natural stimulants dopamine and norepinephrine. Effects start within 30 minutes and can last 5 hours. Time-released forms may last 8 hours.	• Increase blood pressure and heart rate, decreased appetite, sleeplessness, and aggravation of any tics. Initial headaches and nausea usually pass. Suppression of growth is rare.
• Cylert takes several weeks before benefits are seen but effects are long-lasting.	• Can affect liver functioning and may not be as effective as other stimulants.
Blood pressure medication:	
• Corgard and Inderal are beta blockers.	• Decrease jittery side effects of stimulants.
• Clonidine (Catapres).	• Reduces impulsivity and may help sleep.
Antidepressants:	
• Norpramin and Tofranil increase norepinephrine, which increases brain energy.	• Dry mouth, holding urine, heart arrhythmia in high doses. Low doses often work well.
• Wellbutrin (bupropion) may work by increasing norepinephrine and dopamine.	• Agitation, stomach distress, headaches, or sleep problems rare when dose is correct.

MEDICATION GUIDELINES

- Start with the minimal dose and increase in small increments until benefits are seen. Responses vary greatly. Some people need much more or less than the usual amount.
- A "rebound effect" of irritability is seen in 30% of people taking stimulants as medication wears off. Smaller doses in the afternoon or time-release formulas can reduce this.
- Have a trial of both Ritalin and Dexedrine to see which is the more effective (10 mg of Ritalin = 5 mg of Dexedrine). Once the correct dose is set, time-release forms can be tried.
- Use "drug holidays" for a week every 6 months to find out if medication is still needed. Stopping drugs over the summer gives children time to catch up on any (rare) growth loss.
- Others may notice improvement in behavior before people with ADD do.
- Stop stimulants immediately if tics are noted and try antidepressants. Antidepressants are also helpful when moodiness or poor social skills accompany ADHD.

LIMITS AND BENEFITS OF MEDICATION

A major obstacle to treatment for hyperactivity and attention deficits is the refusal of people or a key figure in their lives (parent, teacher, or spouse) to accept the diagnosis. They may think that labels of ADHD and ADD are excuses for laziness, the wrong values, or not trying hard enough. Even if this hurdle is passed, there may be resistance to the use of drugs. Making the decision to take medication and measuring its effectiveness stands a much better chance with a full understanding of its limits and benefits:

Limits and Benefits	
Medication Can Help	**Medication Does Not Help**
Academic and Job Performance	
• Improve quiz and test scores.	• Improve achievement test scores.*
• Improve visual memory and handwriting.*	• Improve comprehension.*
• Increase accuracy of work.	• Replace core skills missed in the past.
• Increase amount of work completed.	• Change defeatist attitudes.
• Decrease frustration.	• Correct learning disabilities (but may improve attention for special instruction).
• Increase task orientation and attention span.	
Behavior	
• Improve compliance to rules.	• Supply the will to conform or comply.
• Increase delay of gratification.	• Motivate people to attain goals.
• Increase effectiveness of rewards.	• Teach decision-making skills.
• Improve responsiveness to punishment.	• Teach where to place attention.
• Decrease overall activity level.	• Teach how to relax.
• Increase ability to sit still longer.	• Improve sleep.
Organization	
• Increase effective use of time.	• Teach organization and graceful transitions.
• Decrease distractibility.	• Improve short-term memory.*
Social Skills	
• Decreased aggression.	• Teach conversation and relating skills.
• Decrease impulsivity and disruptiveness.	• Improve self-esteem or confidence.
• Decrease negativity and reactivity.	• Teach anger control.
• Improve ability to "fit in."	• Reduce stigma of taking medication.

Adapted from *Beyond Retalin* by Stephen Garber, Marianne D. Garber, and Robyn F. Spizman (Harper Perennial, 1994). Starred items are not true in all cases.

SELF-MONITORING

In mild cases, self-monitoring may eliminate the need for medication; with more difficult problems, it can pick up where medication leaves off. Self-ratings of behavior can be compared with that of a buddy or coach who has good organizational and social skills and is capable of being objective and positive. In turn, people with ADD can rate buddies who serve as models for appropriate behavior. Learning internal dialogues is also important—"I stayed on task"; "I did what I said I'd do." It is best to work on one area at a time. The following charts are suggested for building routines and practicing social skill.

SELF-MONITORING CHARTS

Social Skills			
Name: **Date:**	**Rated by:**		
Points: 2 (mostly) 1 (sometimes) 0 (rarely)	**Self**	**Buddy**	**Parent/Teacher**
I respected others': • Personal space • Mood and needs I interacted with others by: • Making eye contact • Using inviting greetings • Starting conversations • Appearing attentive • Using listening skills and staying on the topic I handled my emotions by: • Showing a positive attitude • Expressing distress without anger • Resolving conflicts of interest • Defusing rejection and rudeness			

Note: self-monitoring social skills often shape behavior without rewards, but bonuses can be given.

Routine Building							
Routines (work on one at a time)	**Number of Days (Minutes) in a Row Routine Was Kept**						
1. Getting up on time 2. Leaving the house on time 3. Taking everything needed to school/work 4. Coming home with everything needed 5. Completing chores or errands 6. Completing assignments 7. Minutes stayed on task (without talking) 8. Turning in assignments 9. Taking medication 10. Putting important items in proper places 11. Closing drawers and cabinet doors 12. Coming home on time 13. Going to bed on time							
Bonus reward for beating each record: ____________.							

Use calendars and stop watches to visually reinforce the number of days or minutes in a row the routine was kept.

ALTERNATIVE TREATMENTS FOR ADD AND ADHD

Home remedies and more unusual alternatives for the treatment of attention deficits (ADD) and hyperactivity (ADHD) are abundant. Before using the stimulants generally recommended for the disorder, people who are leery of medication may want to try other approaches. Although some are deserving of serious consideration, they should not be used to avoid needed medication or counseling that can help manage problems. For general information and statistics on treatment alternatives, see *Beyond Retalin* by Stephen Garber, Marianne D. Garber, and Robyn F. Spizman (Harper Perennial, 1994), pp. 187–197. The pros and cons of various procedures follow:

REDUCING SUGAR

Reducing sugar intake should always be examined. Some people find that excessive use of sugar definitely aggravates symptoms of ADD and aggression, though others find that the amount of sugar consumed makes little difference. There is some research that shows a physical basis for the sugar effect. Eating sugar may cause people with ADHD to increase production of the hormone cortisol, released by the body during stress. Sometimes sugar may prevent proteins from reaching the brain. Sugar may generally be better tolerated when people consume adequate amounts of protein.

FOOD ADDITIVES AND SUPPLEMENTS

Avoiding artificial flavorings, food coloring, and preservatives was thought to be an important treatment of ADHD in the 1970s. Over the years, there has been little evidence to support these claims. Individual cases can vary and it may be important to watch the effect certain food additives have on behavior. Following strict diets can be very challenging for parents and children. For more information, contact The Feingold Association, 127 East Main Street, Suite 106, Riverhead, NY 11901, 516-369-9340, www.feingold.org.

Omega 3 fish oils can be used to reduce deficits in fatty acids. Some people report that this supplement improves attention and folklore has always proposed that fish is "brain food." However, the amount needed to improve ADHD is not clear. There are medical tests for deficits in fatty acids. Excessive thirst, frequent urination, dry skin, strawlike hair, dandruff, and small bumps on arms, thighs, or elbows are also signs of the problem. This complex nutritional approach is further explained in *Miracle Cures* by Jean Carper (HarperCollins, 1997).

Herbs from grape seeds and pine bark (Pycnogenol) have been marketed as a treatment for ADHD. Although more research has been done on Pycnogenol, it is twice as expensive as grape seeds and it has the same active ingredient. Improvements in symptoms of ADHD could be related to the herb's ability to regulate enzymes that control dopamine and norepinephrine levels, which may be unsynchronized in ADD. Like stimulants, reduction in symptoms should be seen in 15 minutes and last about four hours. Therefore, if this approach has any benefits, they should be readily observable. The suggested dose is 20mg of the active ingredient (OPC) per 20 pounds of body weight for children and 40mg/20 pounds for adults. Further information can be found in *Miracle Cures* by Jean Carper (HarperCollins, 1997).

NEUROFEEDBACK

Neurofeedback, a form of biofeedback, uses EEG training to increase the strength of brainwaves common in alert states and suppress the strength of brainwaves that operate during sleep states. Increasing the strength of "alert" brain waves could increase blood flow, strengthening the ability to inhibit impulses and movement and filter distracting stimuli. The use of neurofeedback training was started in the 1970s, and research in the 1990s has shown some promise for this approach. However, it may take 20–40 sessions to produce results, and this can be expensive when not covered by insurance. For more information contact EEG Spectrum, 161 Ventura Blvd., Suite 3, Encino, CA 91436-2505, 800-789-3456, www.eegspectrum.com.

ANTIMOTION MEDICATION

Antimotion medication used to treat ADD is based on the theory that a malfunctioning vestibular system (inner ear and balance center) may cause a shortage of energy in the cerebellum. If misshapen inner ear filters block the flow of neural impulses to the cerebellum, a state of sensory deprivation could be created that causes fidgeting. Vestibular problems might be especially suspect when people have motion sickness, coordination problems, difficulty reading, sloppy writing, poor sense of direction, or sensitivity to sound. Further information can be found in the book *Total Concentration* by Harold N. Levinson (M. Evans and Co, 1990). Although Dr. Levinson cites cases in which antimotion medications such as Antivert, Marezine, and Dramamine and antihistamines such as Benedryl and Dimetapp can help ADD, there has been little research to support this.

EXERCISES

Meditation and relaxation exercises can be very helpful for anxiety disorders and other emotional problems. However, people who need to be moving all the time can find attempts to be still excruciating. Those who have only ADD may respond well to the focusing techniques of meditation. Proponents of kinesiology and therapies that use acupressure points suggest specialized postures, breathing, and tapping that can help ADHD people become more organized and focused. For more information, contact Fred Gallo, 40 Snyder Road, Hermitage, PA 16148, 724-346-3838, www.energypsych.com, or Callahan Techniques, 45350 Santa Rosa, Indian Wells, CA 92210, 760-345-4737, www.tftrx.com.

ADDITIONAL READING

- *Hyperactivity Hoax* by Sidney Walker (St. Martins, 1998) explores how problems ranging from metabolic and genetic disorders to heart conditions, infections, anemia, brain cysts, hearing and vision problems, and toxic exposure can cause ADD symptoms.
- *Ritalin-Free Kids: Safe and Effective Homeopathic Medicine for ADD and Other Behavioral and Learning Problems* by Judyth Reichenberg-Ullman, Robert Ullman, and Edward Chapman (Prima Publishing, 1996) cites success stories and explains the homeopathic approach to ADD and other disorders.

ACHIEVEMENT, PRODUCTIVITY, AND BEHAVIOR

Because the part of the brain that screens out distracting stimuli and inhibits extraneous movement is underactive in people with hyperactivity (ADHD), there can be significant impairment in school, productivity, work, and even family life. In mild cases with adequate structure, disruptive, off-task behavior can be managed without drugs. For others, both medication and behavioral interventions are needed to tame the beast. Mark any of the following strategies that you think would be helpful to you or your loved one:[1]

ACADEMICS

__ Have students repeat instructions or restate the purpose of the task before starting it.

__ Vary type, length, format, and color of worksheets. Intersperse movement with sedentary activities. Use computer programs when possible.

__ Teach how to organize information into outlines and charts. Buy textbooks so key points can be highlighted.

__ Maintain close feedback between home and school. Parents can add extra incentives for on-task behavior. Time allowed for highly valued privileges (telephone, TV, or video games) can be earned according to the percent of time spent on task in school.

__ Obtain tutoring to make up for past deficits in (premedication) learning or to keep up with current skills. ADD people learn best in one-on-one situations.

__ Have testing done to identify learning disabilities and arrange special training.

__ Make specific arrangements for standardized tests such as extended time limits or a quieter setting. A letter from the clinician who made the ADD diagnosis can help.[2]

__ Make distinctions between ADD and intelligence. Even if a car has a powerful engine (intelligence), it may need brake fluid (to stop unnecessary movement) and a tighter steering wheel (to stay on task). Identify positive role models from family or history who have had ADD: Thomas Edison, Mozart, and Einstein.

__ Get counseling to change defeatist attitudes and improve self-image.

PRODUCTIVITY

__ Break large tasks into smaller units. Set deadlines for small parts. Reinforce completion of each unit with points that can earn prized privileges. Using the computer, running errands, or free wandering time can be effective rewards.

__ Make lists and prioritize what needs to be done first, second, and third. Having small parts on lists to mark off gives a great sense of accomplishment.

__ Use white boards with colored markers for list making. They are more fun and attention-getting and less likely to get lost than paper. Have one in every room.

__ Use a stopwatch to self-monitor. Estimate how long it will take to complete (part of) a job and find out if you're right. This increases motivation to stay on task.

__ Use immediate consequences for off-task behavior. Redirect children to the task, sit at a time-out desk away from others, or run laps during recess. Adults can use self-talk—"I'm off task. I won't let myself use the computer until this gets done."

---

[1] Adapted from *Beyond Retalin* by Stephen Garber, Marianne D. Garber, and Robyn F. Spizman (Harper Perennial, 1994) and *Driven to Distraction* by Edward Hallowell and John Rately (Simon & Schuster, 1995).

[2] Section 504 of the 1973 Rehabilitation Act (Office of Civil Rights, P.O. Box 65808, Washington, DC 20035-5808, 202-514-2151, www.usdoj.gov) requires schools to accommodate students with disabilities (psychiatric diagnoses) with suggestions similar to the above.

__ Find the best places for staying focused at school, the office, or home. Avoid facing windows and open doors. Place TVs and other major distracters where they will not interfere with task completion.
__ Identify working conditions that improve productivity. Some people work best doing two or three things at once. Others need a minimum of distractions.

TIME-OUT

__ Think of time-out as interrupting disruptive, off-task behavior rather than as punishment. Time-out is important for both ADD adults and children
__ Identify behaviors ahead of time that require time-outs and make agreements about when these will happen. Focus on actions that threaten safety or other's rights.
__ Pick a location for time-out with few distractions. Often, this may be someplace other than the child's room. The car can be used for time-out when you're away from home.
__ Give a three-count warning for starting time-out if a behavior doesn't stop. If you are an adult, count to yourself, and if you cannot calm down, take a time out. Start time-outs before the point of no return is passed.
__ Hold children on the time-out seat until they can comply for at least one minute. Often, this is needed until children realize they cannot avoid time-out. Gradually increase time but never for more than one minute per year of age. Time-outs that require ADHD children to be still for too long can cause worse behavior later.
__ Use creative time-out. This may include aerobics (running laps or jumping jacks) or very brief time-outs that can build concentration and coordination (standing on one foot while holding the other foot and pointing to the ceiling with the opposite hand, walking on a balance beam, holding a sand timer or glitter wand, balancing a book on the head, or breathing exercises). Find out what helps you or your child focus best.
__ Allow children to choose between (shorter) creative or traditional time-outs that are one minute per year of age. Conventional time-out may have little impact on ADD children because they are daydreamers and can sit still for long periods of time.

BEHAVIOR AND MOODS

__ Recognize needs for high-stimulation behavior. Balance moderately exciting activities with brief periods of "down time." Find diverse sources of excitement to avoid "addictions" to one thing.
__ Develop healthy addictions (crafts, hobbies, or exercise) on which to get hooked. This provides structure for the need to keep busy.
__ Keep small, tactile objects handy for fidgeting: felt, Velcro, Koosh balls
__ Arrange 30 minutes of daily "piddle" time to waste guilt-free and recharge batteries. However, warn children in advance so they can plan for unstructured time.
__ Recognize the "ADD blues": an overreaction to or letdown after an engaging event. Refocus on something enjoyable or take out frustrations on pillows.
__ Praise on-task behaviors—"You didn't need any reminders today to finish . . . ." If you cannot find anything to compliment, break tasks into smaller units and force yourself to notice at least two positive things a day. If you are an adult, find a coach or contract with a family member to praise you when you do things well.
__ Reframe tendencies toward mistakes as expertise on foibles. There are advantages to not being a perfectionist who falls apart whenever a blunder happens.
__ Make a list of successes and refer to it to combat hopelessness. Have a "success (bulletin) board" in a prominent place in the home for both children and adults.

ORGANIZATION AND TRANSITIONS

People with attention deficits (ADD) or hyperactivity (ADHD) are often thought to be willfully avoiding tasks or lazy. However, there are physical reasons for disorganization and poor follow-through. The area of the brain that initiates behavior, anticipates consequences, and controls short-term memory is underenergized, causing poor task completion. In some people, there is also decreased blood flow to the right hemisphere that handles spatial perception and decision making. This can add to problems of losing things or getting lost. Mark any of the following strategies that you think would help you or your loved one with organization, memory, and helpful habits.[1]

ORGANIZATION

__ Place important items for school or work on hooks or racks by the door the night before. Have the most organized family member monitor this until it is a routine.

__ Designate places for important items at home, school, and work. Place items in their proper location as soon as they are not needed: keys, glasses, purses, lunch boxes, uniforms, bookbags, or briefcases.

__ Buy furniture and containers with lots of drawers, shelves, and hooks. Label places for things and keep surfaces uncluttered. Overorganization is important!

__ Create file drawers and folders for important papers and schoolwork. Throw out items that are no longer needed.

__ Put medications in weekly pill keepers. This makes it easier for others to monitor if medications have been taken until it is a routine.

__ Have a weekend box for anything left out of place. Everything in the box must be put away before weekend free time begins. Place a bag of things that need to be put away in front of the TV.

__ Do not let messes pile up. Clean up one activity before starting another. ADD people can create chaos.

__ Avoid "to do" piles. Whenever possible handle paperwork only once. Throw it away, file it, or take whatever action is needed as soon as possible.

FORGETFULNESS

__ Keep a "day list" by the door with everything you or your child might need: keys, glasses, notebook, lunch, snack, medicine, retainer, wallet, or sweater. Make a habit of scanning the list before you leave.

__ Have a What-have-I-forgotten? list in your car or on a key chain, or have it memorized: hat, gloves, glasses, assignment book. Make children repeat their list five times as a consequence for forgetting items not brought home. Build the habit of asking the above question every time you leave a place.

__ Use a "must remember" bag for nonroutine items that need to come home by placing high-priority items (car keys or snacks) in the bag.

__ Call your answering machine and record reminder messages of things you need to do as soon as you think of them. Answering machines with flashing lights by the door are important.

__ Use alarm watches for reminders to take medication, start chores, or leave a friend's house. Set other timers for five-minute warnings before it's time to leave for school or other activities. People with ADD lose track of time!

---

[1] Adapted from *Beyond Retalin* by Stephen Garber, Marianne D. Garber, and Robyn F. Spizman (Harper Perennial, 1994) and *Driven to Distraction* by Edward Hallowell and John Rately (Simon & Schuster, 1995).

___ Use assignment books that list homework, tests, and other important dates. Coordinate with teachers and monitor tasks until children establish a routine.
___ Buy spiral notebooks with pockets in which to place assignments due the next day, or designate a special homework pocket in bookbags.
___ Keep a calendar or planner for all important dates and events.
___ Keep notepads and pens in the car, by the bed, or in your purse to write down ideas and things you need to remember to do. Read with a pen in hand for the same reason.
___ Schedule weekly errands at the same time so they won't be forgotten.

ESTABLISH ROUTINES

___ Wake-up routines may include extra alarm clocks, water sprays, rambunctious pets, ice cubes, or ammonia swabs.
___ Bedtime routines are important for both children and adults: bathing, watching (nonstimulating) TV, reading, calming music, and relaxation exercises.
___ Be dressed and ready for school or work before eating breakfast or watching TV. There are many instant, nutritious foods that can be eaten on the way to work or school. Prized privileges can be withheld until a child is ready on time for school.
___ Set clocks and watches ahead to decrease chances of being late.
___ Make lists for routines and put them on white boards or Post-it Notes placed in strategic locations (refrigerator, TV, video control box): feed pets, have snack, put dishes away, do homework, make bed, put belongings away, free time.
___ Monitor tasks that require a sequence of actions until it is independently mastered: "What do you need to do next? Next? Next?"
___ Use a stopwatch to time how long it takes to complete (part of) a task. Then make a game of gradually decreasing time. Similarly, time how long a person can sit still in the car or at dinner and gradually work on increasing time.
___ Break large tasks into smaller units and provide immediate rewards or breaks after each one is complete. Physical activity and stretching may be especially important.
___ Make eye contact, announce instructions, say them and have them repeated—"I'm going to tell you what still needs to be done. You need to . . . What did I say?" Use many gestures or sign language if it helps focus attention.
___ When something has been left out of place or a step is out of sequence, interrupt what you or your child is doing before returning to the desired activity. This reinforces neural links in the mind.
___ Do not start a new task before completing a current one.
___ Link undesirable tasks with high-priority activities: Domestic chores must be completed before using the computer. Place pill keepers in front of toothbrushes.
___ Train organized family members to remind instead of nag—"I know you meant to . . . Would you do it . . . ?" "How about if the TV goes off after this show until . . . gets done." Keeping expectations realistic will go a long way to increase patience.
___ Reinforce routines with rewards. Pick one routine on which to concentrate and keep track of the number of days in a row it is done. Identify a reward and use it each time a record is broken. Once something is done 14 days in a row, it is a habit.

SOCIAL SKILLS

Very often people who have attention deficits (ADD) or hyperactivity (ADHD) feel isolated from peers. Both disorders affect socialization by causing intrusiveness or lack of attention. In mild cases people can be taught coping skills. Although medication can decrease aggression and disruptiveness and improve focusing, people may need to learn ways to interact that they missed in their premedication days. The following games and activities are designed for use in classrooms and social skills groups. They can also be adapted for family activities, Sunday school, support groups, or scout meetings and can be redesigned as consequences for undesirable behavior.[1]

RESPECTING BOUNDARIES

- Practice respecting personal space by playing Run-&-Stop. One person runs towards another who is the "stopper." The runner must halt before invading the stopper's "comfort zone." Make the game more challenging by having people skip or hop and use a stopwatch to combine the ability to be both fast and respectful of personal space. Feedback can be given on how well the runner did. Use yardsticks to measure each person's personal comfort zone.
- Practice respecting others' moods by playing Approach-Retreat. One person is "it" and nonverbally expresses an emotion she reads on a card—bored, tired, excited, mad, lonely, mischievous, sad, hostile, or friendly. Each person in the group must decide how many steps to walk towards or away from the person who is it, and what words (or silence) would make the best contact. Both observers and the person who is it can give feedback on which approaches or retreats seemed best.

INTERACTING

- Teach eye contact by playing Laser. Several people sit in a circle. Everyone is given a scrap of paper. The person with an "L" on his or her scrap is the "laser." Whoever that person makes eye contact with is "wiped-out" and announces, "I'm down." At any time people who are still in the game can guess who is the laser. If the guess is correct, the round is over, if the guess is wrong, the guessor is out.
- Practice showing interest by playing Bla Bla Bla. Choose a panel of listeners and one speaker. The speaker gives a talk by saying nothing but, "Bla, Bla, Bla . . ." The group votes on which listener appears most interested by making eye contact, leaning forward, or nodding. The group can feed back exactly what each person did to appear interested. The game can be made more challenging by instructing the speaker to be as boring as possible. Use a stopwatch and gradually increase the length of the game.
- Practice conversation starters by playing People Openers. Group members write questions that they would like to know about the person who is "it"—facts, beliefs, opinions, and interests. Encourage people to put their curiosity in charge. Every question is signed but read anonymously. The people who are "it" rate how open or closed each question made them feel on a 0–10 scale. Totally inappropriate questions can be censored. This is a good game for parents who often don't know how to start conversations with their children.

---

[1] Topics for activities were taken from *Beyond Ritalin* by Garber, Garber & Spizman (HarperPerennia, 1996)

- Practice conversation keepers with listening circles. One person expresses a feeling or role-plays a comment that bothered him or her. The next person makes a listening response. Speakers (or the group) give a percentage rating of how well the person was heard. Responses can be scored. To make the game more interesting the speaker can throw a beanbag to the person who will make a listening response that rephrases the thought (1 Pt.), labels the feeling (2 Pts.) or Validate (3 Pts.)—"It sounds like you're saying. . . . Do you feel . . . ? It makes sense that you would feel . . . because. . . ."
- Practice greetings by playing Turn-on/Turn-off. People in the group are given a card with a feeling (perky, bored, superior, inferior, annoyed) or a situation (seeing an old friend, faking it with someone you don't like, or making someone feel special.) They choose a greeting that would express the feeling or situation—Hi, Hello, What's up? How you doing? How are? A spinner is used to choose who will receive the greeting. The recipient and group discuss if the greeting was a turn-on or turn-off without knowing what was on the card. This game can generate humorous, inviting greetings.

HANDLING EMOTIONS

- Practice positive attitudes by asking for a rephrase. Simply say, "I'll need to hear you say that differently before you go to recess, lunch, or get out of your seat." Play Instant Rewind as a group activity. Parents or teachers repeat their comment and who- ever responds in the best tone gets a reward.
- Practice expressing feelings without anger with Assertive Language Circles: Place an empty chair in the center of a circle. Each person makes a statement that starts with "You" to someone they imagine sitting in the chair—"You are . . ." "You make me feel . . ." Go around the circle three more times changing the you-statement into one that starts with the words "I" or makes a request—(1) "I feel . . . when you. . . ." (2) "Would you . . ., . . ., or. . . ." (3) "I will (not) . . . if you. . . ."
- Practice handling conflicts by playing Resolution. Have the group write down examples of conflicts they've experienced. Partners role-play resolving the conflict by stating it clearly, considering the other person's ideas, staying focused on the issue and generating at least 3 solutions—"I want . . . and you want. . . ." "I know you're concerned about . . . and I think we can get around that by. . . ." "Let's get back to. . . ." The group rates how well each pair resolved the conflict. Extra points can be given for expressing confidence and using the words "and" and "we"—"You think . . . <u>and</u> I think. . . ." "I'm sure <u>we</u> can resolve this."
- Practice dealing with rejections and rudeness by playing Bully Bust. People write an insult, criticism or comment that has or would bother them. Comments are signed but read anonymously. Whoever is "it" makes a "bully bust" that defuses the put-down. Points are taken away if the retort is an attack, defense or withdrawal and points are given if the response makes a bully bust by:[2]
    1. Treating cruelty as kindness—"Why, thank you. Are you trying to help me. . . ?"
    2. Using humor to distract and confuse—"You say that like it's a bad thing."
    3. Asking questions to find the cause of meanness—"What's really bothering you?"
    4. Setting limits—"I'll talk to you when you're in a better mood."

---

[2] See *How to Handle Bullies, Teasers and other Meanies,* a parent-child resource, by Kate Cohen-Posey (Lakeland, Fl: Rainbow Books, 1995)

ADD AT HOME AND IN THE WORKPLACE

Attention deficits (ADD) and hyperactivity (ADHD) can create havoc in the modern home and workplace with tight schedules, easy access to highly stimulating activities, and decreased opportunities for physical exertion. Until proper diagnosis is obtained, problems are often attributed to stupidity, poor motivation, and immorality. Once the disorder is recognized, many options for modifying difficulties become available. The first step is to recognize the part ADD plays in relationship and group situations. Further insights on ADD and families can be found in Driven to Distraction by Edward Hallowell and John Ratey (Simon & Schuster, 1995).

PARENT-CHILD RELATIONSHIPS

A vicious cycle happens when ADD children chronically fail to do chores, complete schoolwork, get up on time, and come home late. As punishments become more severe, children grow increasingly defiant, less cooperative, and more alienated. Over time, the youngster with ADD becomes the "problem child" and other family members feel ignored. When diagnoses or treatment is received after years of struggling, family members may have difficulty overcoming guilt or resentment. Several steps can help:

- The diagnosis of ADD needs to be made and understood. Even when the concept of ADD is accepted, family members may resist looking at it as a neurological condition that cannot be controlled at will.
- Hidden issues need to be addressed. There may be "payoffs" from having a problem child. Focusing all the attention on one person may help parents avoid their conflicts or siblings escape scrutiny.
- Family members need to adopt realistic expectations of anyone with ADD and accept the need for more task monitoring and gentle reminders. It is best to designate one or two people for this job so those with ADD do not feel like they have too many bosses. Often, it is best for people to choose who is to act as the coach or monitor and have other family members work through that person.
- Negotiate and clearly define deadlines for tasks and limits for intrusive behavior. Consequences need to be spelled out and contracts signed if necessary.
- Develop routines to manage especially difficult times: doing homework, getting ready in the morning, dinnertime, bedtime, choosing TV shows, and spending family time together. Brainstorm solutions when the problem is not occurring.
- Make special efforts to mention positive qualities and tiny improvements. If positives cannot be found, tasks are not being broken down into doable parts.
- Set aside specific time for everyone in the family. Non-ADD children need to have one-on-one time with parents and parents need to go on "dates." Everyone needs to have private time alone and time away from the family.
- Develop outside sources of support in the extended family, with professionals, or with support groups.

COUPLES AND OTHER RELATIONSHIPS

Similar vicious cycles happen when one person in a relationship has ADD. Symptoms of forgetfulness, disorganization, distractibility, and impulsiveness annoy the other person. That person becomes increasingly critical, and the partner with ADD withdraws; criticism mounts, and the added stress increases ADD symptoms. Often, spontaneous, creative ADD people and organized perfectionists are drawn to each other because they seek what they lack in themselves.

This greatly compounds problems. However, there are solutions. The above steps can be adapted to couples with a few additional pointers:

- Take time to understand the impact the disorder has on relationships. People with ADD need to realize their partner's frustrations and partners need to recognize the constant devaluing people with ADD experience.
- Overcome relationship extremes. People with ADD must make a commitment to learn strategies that manage symptoms. Partners need to value positive qualities, develop realistic expectations, focus on one change at a time, notice improvements, and use a sense of humor. Avoid master-slave patterns in which one person does all the work, or parent-child relationships in which one person is overbearing and critical.
- Make specific requests and brainstorm solutions. Use lists, bulletin boards, and note pads. Designate specific places for must-find items and overorganize!
- Delegate tasks according to ability. Structured people can handle jobs that demand organization, and ADD partners can take over those that require creativity and energy.
- Blame the condition, not the person. Recognize ADD tendencies of inattention, preoccupation, busyness, or flash anger. Plan time to spend together for leisure, romance, and communication. Agree on strategies to manage temper and impulsivity.
- Recognize the impact of the disorder on sexuality. People with ADHD may use sex as a form of intense stimulation to help them focus. Due to impulsiveness, infidelity can occur. Understanding the source of the problem, medication that aids self-control, and planning ways to manage temptation can help. People with ADD may have problems with arousal and orgasm due to difficulties focusing on bodily sensations. Discussing the problem and providing additional erotic stimuli (talking, fantasy, or music) can suppress nonsexual preoccupations.

THE WORKPLACE

Due to inexhaustible energy, the need to keep busy, and creativity, people with ADHD can be ideal workers in some jobs. Other people have difficulty keeping jobs due to lack of punctuality, disorganization, and outspokenness. ADD is a disability protected by the *Americans with Disabilities Act of 1990.*[1] Diagnosis and treatment by qualified professionals is a prerequisite to use of the law. Employers may be required to make "reasonable accommodations" (structure, reminders, reduction of distractions, and flexibility on deadlines), but employees need to demonstrate that they are making every effort to cooperate with treatment and learn strategies that manage symptoms.

[1] Contact the Equal Employment Opportunity Commission, 1801 L Street NW, Washington, DC 20507, 202-663-4900, www.eeoc.gov for information about this law.

EXTRA HELP FOR ADD AND ADHD

It is especially important for people with attention deficits (ADD) and hyperactivity (ADHD) to have help from family and friends. Often, people with these disorders are the last to realize they are "out of sync" with others and need feedback. Until they build internal controls by learning routines and habits, they will need external structure from those who care about them. Mark any strategies below that you would like others to use, or that would help you help your loved one.

__ Find sources of support. Having an ADHD person in the family can be exhausting. Join groups that understand this condition and offer useful tips.

__ Read everything you can to help you understand ADD. The more you understand, the less responsible you will feel for causing or controlling problems, and the better you will be able to manage them.

__ Know your limits. Make a "Do Not Disturb" sign for moments when you must regain your strength. If you catch exhaustion soon enough, you will revive faster.

__ Make agreements ahead of time on behaviors that go overboard. Make sure that ADHD people understand their impact on others. Plan brief time-outs when energy gets overcharged. If necessary, put time-out contracts in writing.

__ Ask people with ADD what best helps them stay on task or calm down. Personal insight is often overlooked.

__ Expect to give reminders about chores and errands. This can be done in apatient and loving way once the problem is understood. Make lists and keep calendars of the family schedule and give advanced warnings about any changes.

__ Don't make excuses or do things for people with ADD because it is easier. With proper incentives, reminders, monitoring, and breakdown of tasks, responsible habits can be learned.

__ During conversations or when giving directions, ask for feedback—"Did that make sense? What did I just say?" Use a timer. Do not let one person speak for too long. Let ADD people know when you are losing their point.

__ Ask questions that encourage self-awareness—"Do you know what you just did?"

__ Encourage understanding of ADD of everyone who has contact with people with the disorder: family, friends, and, most important, the people themselves. Make it clear that some of the greatest geniuses of our time have had ADD. The intelligent part of the mind can be very strong, but the part of the brain that blocks unneeded movement and distractions may be underenergized.

FRIENDLY CAUTIONS

Find people who appreciate and understand you and make an effort to stay in touch with them. Don't stay too long where you're not wanted. Avoid people who give advice that makes you feel uncomfortable or who refuse to believe in ADD. Find a coach who will help you get organized, stay on task, offer encouragement, signal you if you're talking too much, or interrupt if you are in hyperfocus. Choose someone who is objective and positive for home, school, or work.

Keep others informed in subtle ways—"I get distracted easily so let me know if I'm getting off the topic," "I can move around a lot, so tell me if it bothers you." Learn to joke about yourself without putting yourself down—"I'm one of those clueless geniuses." If others demean you, handle it lightly—"They'll never let you in the ADD support group if you talk like that." "I'm trying out for the Albert Einstein award this year."

NATIONAL NETWORKS, SUPPORT GROUPS, AND OTHER RESOURCES

As more is learned about ADD, the number of support groups, newsletters, and books for individuals and families grows. Many organizations and books offer important advice on how to advocate for yourself or your child at school or in the workplace:

- Children and Adults with Attention Deficit Disorder (CHADD): Suite 201, 8181 Professional Place, Landover, MD 20785, 800-233-4050, 301-306-7070, www.chadd.org.
- National Attention Deficit Disorder Association (NADDA): PO Box 1303, Northbrook, IL 60065-1303, www.add.org.
- ADDvance Resource Site for Women & Girls with ADD: www.addvance.com.
- One ADD Place (an excellent internet site): www.oneaddplace.com.
- Books for Adults: *You Mean I'm Not Lazy, Crazy, Stupid or Dumb* by Kelly and Ramundo, 1995; *Driven to Distraction* by Hallowell & Ratey (Simon & Schuster, 1994).
- Books for Parents: *Maybe You Know My Kid* by Fowler, *Beyond Ritalin,* by Garber, Garber, and Spizman (Harper Perennial, 1996); *Attention Deficit Disorder and the Law* by Latham and Latham, 1992; *Taking Charge of ADHD* by Barkley (Guilford Press, 1995.)
- Books for Children: *Shelly the Hyperactive Turtle* (Ages 3-7) by Moss, 1989; *Putting on the Brakes* Ages 8-12) by Quinn, 1992: *Learning to Slow Down and Pay Attention* (Ages 6-12); *Help4ADD@Highschool* by Nadeau, 1998.

MEDICATION

Sometimes, an accurate diagnosis of ADD and education is all that is needed to manage problems. When behavior strategies or alternative treatments (herbs, diet, or biofeedback) are not helpful, it may be essential to try medication. Stimulants are the drug of choice, they are not addicting for people with ADD and will not remain in a person's system after being discontinued. Some people can stop using medication as their organizational skills improve; others will continue to need them in adulthood. For the 20% to 25% of people who are not helped by stimulants, certain antidepressants will be effective and are especially important if moodiness is a part of the problem.

PROFESSIONAL HELP

Education and coaching to learn behavior strategies and social skills may be more important than counseling for the actual neurological disorder of ADD. However, until it is diagnosed, there may be much damage caused by family and relationship problems, not to mention academic or other trauma. Often, medication will be needed to provide sufficient focus to work through past difficulties. Counselors may need to be directive, as people with ADD can lose track of their therapeutic agenda.

Chapter 10

In Search of Self

IN SEARCH OF SELF

OBJECTIVES FOR TREATMENT PLANNING

1. Recognize self-defeating behavior patterns and report making adaptive changes.
2. Recognize self-defeating behavior in loved ones and make decisions on how to reduce impact on one's self.
3. Understand how temperament and environment contribute to problems.
4. Identify early wounds and soothe the hurt "inner child."
5. Describe thoughts and tactics that help change undesirable traits.
6. Demonstrate compliance in the use of any prescribed medication.
7. Become involved in appropriate support groups.

MINI INDEX TO CHAPTER 10

USING THE HANDOUTS

- Assessment of personality disorders: *Disorders of the Self, Starting the Search.*
- Identifying and changing dysfunctional behavior: *Caring Less about Abandonment, Valuing Your "Ordinary," Prizing Imperfections, Conquering the Divide, Finding Strength in Surrender, Self Discovery, Better Living through Chemistry.*
- Dealing with resistance: *Starting the Search* can be used to give paradoxical suggestions with a technique described by Peggy Papp in *The Process of Change* (Guilford Press, 1983). The clinician and client form a therapeutic alliance against the handout—*"According to the handout, the frail legs on your person mean you are too afraid to become independent, but I think you want to be your own person."* Some of the behavior experiments in *Conquering the Divide* also make use of paradox.

- Handouts for family and friends: *Extra Help for Disorders of the Self* and specific handouts that identify characteristics for family members or friends.
- Workshops, presentations, and group therapy: Many of the behavior experiments in personality subtypes are ideal for group therapy and workshops. The person drawing in *Starting the Search* is a good way to introduce types of personalities.

CAUTIONS AND RECOMMENDATIONS

- *Personal Styles in Disorders of the Self* and *Person Drawing in Starting the Search* should be considered preliminary assessments and can be verified by standardized tests. They can be used to identify which other handouts would be most helpful to clients or their families.
- *Starting the Search* is not diagnostic for thought disorders, sexual orientation, or children's pictures and is based on general literature for interpreting drawings.
- Offer *Self Discovery* to contrast with dysfunctional styles.
- Offer all pertinent handouts if criteria are met for more than one personality type.
- Delay use of handouts with clients in the narcissistic or schizoid clusters until a therapeutic alliance has been made. Surprisingly, borderlines can tolerate feedback about behavior; narcissists and schizoids may need extensive mirroring.
- Supplement *Disorders of the Self* with *Types of Temperament* (7.4) to help identify biochemical contributors to personality disorders.
- Supplement *Caring Less about Abandonment* with assertive exercises in *Effective Expression* (1.6).
- Supplement *Valuing Your "Ordinary"* with exercises on listening skills in *The Art of Understanding* (1.4).
- Supplement *Conquering the Divide* with the *Erasing Embarrassment* (5.16).
- Reinforce various behavior strategies with those from *Mending Marriages* (3.10–3.22).

SOURCES AND ACKNOWLEDGMENTS

- Criteria for disorders are adapted from the *Diagnostic and Statistical Manual of Mental Disorders,* 4th edition (American Association Press, 1994) and reworded to avoid denial by fragile egos. Likewise, some diagnostic labels are replaced with more descriptive or positive terms.
- Object relations theory as explained in *Split Self/Split Object* by Phillip Manfield (Jason Aronson, 1992) was used to suggest clustering of disorders.
- *The Search for the Real Self* by James F. Masterson (The Free Press, 1988) was used to develop criteria for the "adaptive personality" in *Self Discovery.*
- Psychodynamic, biosocial, cognitive-behavioral, interpersonal, and integrative formulations found in the *Handbook of Diagnosis and Treatment of the DSM-IV Personality Disorders* by Len Sperry (Brunner/Mazel, 1995) and *Reinventing Your Life* by Jeffrey Young and Janet Klosko (Penguin Books, 1994) contributed to information on the origin of disorders, defenses, cognitions, and behavior experiments.
- Psychopharmacological treatment of personality disorders found in *Better Living through Chemistry* is based on the work of Sonny Joseph, M.D. in *Personality Disorders, New Symptom-Focused Drug Therapy* (Haworth Medical Press, 1997).
- EMDR formulations for negative and positive cognitions explained in *Eye Movement Desensitization and Reprocessing* by Francine Shapiro (Guilford Press, 1995) are found in *The Challenge of Change* in various handouts.

DISORDERS OF THE SELF

From time to time, everyone needs others for reassurance, gratification, and support. However, some people are almost entirely unable to control, affirm, comfort, understand, or soothe themselves. They focus on others to feel protected, cared about, powerful, or important. In the process, they lose themselves and develop personality traits that impair relationships and employment. This sad state of affairs solidifies by late adolescence or early adulthood, as seen in the following:

- Others are seen as the source of problems. When relationship issues arise, the concern is "Why is my partner doing this and how can I change her?" rather than, "How am I contributing to this problem and why do I tolerate it?"
- Others' standards are wholeheartedly endorsed or rejected outright without developing a personal set of values, interests, and goals. This makes people vulnerable to criticism, easily influenced, or unable to amend the beliefs with which they were raised.
- Feelings are managed by splitting positive and negative emotions. Loving images of others are protected from periods of rage by flipping perceptions from loving to cold, on-the-pedestal to in-the-gutter, or protective to attacking.
- Self-perception is also split—"When I'm good, I'm very good (superior, obedient, powerful), and when I'm bad, I'm awful (unlovable, worthless, nothing)." Feelings change from euphoric to hateful, grandiose to ashamed, or safe to alienated without warning.
- A "false self" is created by rejecting parts of oneself. There is a push to always be compliant, perfect, superior, charming, in control, or self-reliant instead of being a multifaceted human with imperfections, needs, and strengths.
- The "pleasure principle" is used to avoid painful emotions instead of struggling to control, think about, or express them. This is accomplished by evading disturbing topics, denying difficulties (even to oneself), or acting them out. Insecurity can be acted out by clinging or not allowing others to express differences.
- When feelings are noticed, they are hard to identify. There may be a vague sense of uneasiness, physical concerns, or lethargy. Anger and resentment may mask other emotions. Any depression may be experienced as detachment, and love is confused with feeling dependant on, admired by, or safe with others.
- Expression of feelings is tailored to expectations and demands of others. Instead of having internal dialogues about the pros and cons of an issue, time is consumed ruminating with monologues explaining, justifying, or complaining to others.

CAUSES OF DISORDERS OF SELF

Problems can range from personal styles to true disconnection from the self, in which people are at the mercy of others for satisfaction and fulfillment. Any disorder is due to a combination of:

- Temperament based on physical tendencies to overreact to stimuli and back away or strike out, or to underreact and turn inward for interest or outward for excitement.
- Character that results from adjustments to caretakers who can be nurturing, firm, overprotective, demanding, critical, withholding, indulgent, or negligent. People acquire varying abilities to be self-directed, cooperative, open, and to transcend difficulties.

IDENTIFYING PERSONAL STYLES AND PROBLEMS

In 1994, the American Psychiatric Association (*DSM-IV*) identified 10 disorders that create problems with relationships and careers. They can be simplified into five patterns.

Personal Styles

Directions: Circle the letter for each item that best depicts your feelings, behavior, and history and underline words that are especially descriptive. Force yourself to make a choice and if none of the options seems accurate, have others rate you.

1. I feel best when I am:
   - A. Loved or cared for.
   - B. Noticed or valued.
   - C. Achieving, asserting myself, or special.
   - D. Safe from rejection/attack or alone.
   - E. Getting what I want.
2. It is easy for me to feel:
   - A. Resentful, helpless, abandoned, moody.
   - B. Confident, special, sensitive, or slighted.
   - C. Critical, criticized, or betrayed.
   - D. Awkward, private, rejected, or indifferent.
   - E. Powerful, carefree, or little remorse.
3. I often act:
   - A. Too nice, clingy, gullible, or like a martyr.
   - B. Proud, boastful, or emotional.
   - C. Controlling, rigid, skeptical, or demanding.
   - D. Shy, aloof, or like a dreamer or drifter.
   - E. Devious, aggressive, or competitive.
4. At my best I am:
   - A. Tactful, nice, passionate, or caring.
   - B. Lively, affectionate, confident, assertive.
   - C. Dependable, cautious, or perceptive.
   - D. Discreet, loyal, objective, or curious.
   - E. Bold, courageous, or charming.
5. I tend to think others are:
   - A. Special, awful, unfair, or strong-willed.
   - B. Obligated to me, inattentive, or impolite.
   - C. Disorganized, not trying, or attacking.
   - D. Judgmental, dangerous, or unusual.
   - E. Weak, challenging, or in my way.
6. As a child I was:
   - A. Too nice, sneaky, or argumentative.
   - B. Noticed for my talents, abilities, or looks.
   - C. Responsible, dependable, but shamed.
   - D. Shy, a misfit, or rejected by peers.
   - E. A troublemaker or rebellious.
7. My parents:
   - A. Were too helpful, overprotective, undependable, or controlling.
   - B. Pushed my abilities, were self-involved.
   - C. Expected a lot or were attacking.
   - D. Were rejecting, ridiculing, uncaring, cold, distant, or gone a lot.
   - E. Hostile, abusive, weak, or absent.

Discover Your Personality Type:

Notice which letter-choices you picked most often. The more your answers favor one letter, the greater the chance that you have a distinct style:

Choice A indicates dependent or erratic personalities who attach to others to avoid feeling helpless or abandoned but may distance if closeness becomes suffocating. They often choose strong or overbearing partners or people who need "fixing."

Choice B indicates dramatic, inflated personalities who seek attention or exaggerate their self-worth to keep from feeling unloved or unimportant. They often seek partners with superior traits or who will adore and admire them.

Choice C indicates compulsive or guarded personalities who strive for perfection or watch for criticism and betrayal to prevent uncertainty. They may choose free-spirited partners who represent their suppressed side or people they can control.

Choice D indicates avoiding, isolated, or eccentric personalities who withdraw rather than risk rejection or harm even though they (unconsciously) crave connection. If they have relationships, it is with very accepting or nondemanding people.

Choice E indicates defiant personalities who try to rule everyone around them (including their partners) because they never learned to soothe or govern themselves.

STARTING THE SEARCH

Person drawings can reveal personality traits and lead you to lost parts of the self. Draw a picture of *any* person of your choosing on a blank sheet of paper with a pencil. Artistic quality is unimportant, but do your best. Draw before reading further!

Person Drawing

Directions: Mark any of the following characteristics that you see in your drawing. Examine the proportion of one part to the rest of the person to determine if it is large or small.

Placement
__ Central: normal, self-directed
__ Side edge: feeling suppressed
__ Left side: impulsive, extrovert, past oriented
__ Right: controlled, inhibited, future oriented
__ High: ambitious, optimistic, fanaticizes, aloof
__ Low: insecure, inept, depressed; but can be calm, down-to-earth, thoughtful thinking, stable
__ Bottom edge: needs support, fears independence, depressed

Size
__ Normal: about 3/4 of the paper height
__ Very large: aggressive, egotistical, overreactive, manic
__ Very small: inadequate, inhibited, withdrawn, anxious, shy, depressed

Line Quality
__ Firm or curving: secure, flexible
__ Jagged: hostile, impulsive
__ Sketchy: insecure, timid, compulsive
__ Long strokes: controlled, reserved
__ Short strokes: excitable
__ Scribbling: excitable, hyperactive
__ Vertical: assertive, determined, hyperactive
__ Horizontal: weak, fearful
__ Very straight: compulsive, aggressive
__ Shading: anxious, submissive
__ Heavy shading: agitated depression
__ Light pressure: timid, inept, low energy
__ Heavy pressure: tense, high energy, ambitious, aggressive, suspicious
__ Excessive erasing: uncertain, restless, dissatisfied, anxious

Style
__ Ground line drawn: need for security
__ Extreme symmetry: compulsive
__ Asymmetrical: attention deficit, excitable
__ Transparencies: poor judgment, flashy
__ Lack of detail: withdrawn, empty
__ Excessive detail: compulsive, hypersensitive, manic

Head (intellect and fantasy)
__ Large: intellectual, aggressive, fantasizes
__ Small: feels inept, helpless, weak
__ Hair emphasis: sexuality, self-absorbed
__ Hair lack: sexual inadequacy, low energy

Face (communication, reality contact)

Eyes
__ Large or emphasized: suspicious, anxious, hypersensitive, proper
__ Small or closed: introverted, hostile
__ Pupil omitted: guilt, introverted, isolated
__ Button or circle eyes: immature
__ Eyebrows arched or raised: critical, refined
__ Bushy eyebrows: gruff, uninhibited

Ears
__ Large: poor hearing, sensitive, suspicious
__ Omitted: normal or avoidant
__ Question marks: suspicious

Nose (sexuality, power, stereotypes)
__ Button or triangle: immature
__ Pointed: aggressive
__ Omitted: shy, depressed
__ Underemphasized: guilt, envy, hostility
__ Overemphasized: sexual inadequacy, depression, aggression

Mouth
__ Emphasized: dependent, critical, immature
__ Full lips or cupid bow: sexual, flashy
__ Open: passive, dependent
__ Wide, upturned line: compliant, congenial
__ Omitted: guilt, depression, isolated
__ Tiny: independent, compulsive, arrogant
__ Frown: passive, dependent, depression
__ Teeth showing: aggression
__ Objects in mouth: sexual needs/aggression
__ Slash or short, heavy line: (cautious) aggression, critical

Neck (separates intellect and emotion)
__ Short, thick: gruff, stubborn, rigid, impulsive
__ Long: cut-off emotions, rigid, formal, moral
__ Single line: poor impulse control
__ Omitted: impulsive, immature

Torso (drives and emotions)
__ Large: unsatisfied drives or goals
__ Long or narrow: isolated
__ Rounded: passive, feminine, immature
__ Shading: anxiety about impulses
__ Small: denial of feelings, inferiority

Shoulders (power)
__ Neatly rounded: normal
__ Large: feeling strength, power
__ Pointed/square: pushy, hostile, defensive
__ Tiny: feeling inferior or inept

Waist (separates strength from sexuality)
__ Emphasized, high or low: (sexual) conflicts
__ Broken line: tension about impulses
__ Tiny: poor impulse control

Breasts (normal on females)
__ Large: dependence, flashy
__ Small/omitted: normal, stingy, immature

Anterior Limbs (contact, relationships)

Arms
__ Normal: relaxed, flexible appearing
__ Outstretched: desire for contact or help
__ Broad: strength, striving
__ Long: ambitious, aggressive
__ Reinforced: desire for power, assaultive
__ Short: lack ambition, dependent
__ Frail/limp: weak, inadequate, ineffective
__ Omitted: guilt, depression, withdrawal
__ Behind: evasive, controlled hostility, guilt
__ Right angle: immature, unemotional
__ Akimbo (on hips): bossy, self-involved
__ Folded: suspicious, hostile, rigid, passive
__ Winglike: eccentric

Hands
__ Small: insecure, helpless, not confident
__ Large: hidden inadequacy, inept, impulsive
__ Mittenlike (no fingers): hidden aggression
__ Omitted: normal, but can show conflicts, guilt
__ In pockets: guilt, evasive, suspicious
__ Behind back: evasive, guilt

Fingers
__ Fists: aggression, rebelliousness
__ Detailed with nails: compulsive, aggressive
__ Without hands: aggression, assaultive
__ Large: aggression, assaultive
__ Long: unemotional, flat
__ Petal or grapelike: dependent, immature
__ Shaded: guilt about stealing, sex
__ Straight lines/spiked: hostile, suspicious
__ Extra fingers: ambitious, aggressive
__ Missing fingers: inadequate, self-punitive, guilt, poor social skills

Locomotor Limbs (mobility, support)

Legs
__ Short or omitted: immobile, constricted
__ Long: striving for self-reliance
__ Cut off by bottom edge: lack of autonomy
__ Crossed: defensive
__ Unequal size: conflicts about independence
__ Reinforced: aggressive, assaultive
__ Frail: lack of autonomy and independence
__ Pressed together: rigid, suspicious
__ Wide stance: aggressive, defiance

Feet
__ Long: insecure, sexual needs
__ Pointed: hostile
__ Opposite directions: autonomy conflicts
__ Toes: aggression
__ Omitted or small: helpless, depressed

Clothing
__ Belt: normal in males
__ Excessive: flashy, egocentric, repressed, extroverted, sociable, approval seeking
__ Underclothed: showy, isolated, art student
__ Transparent: poor judgment, flashy
__ Stripes: compulsiveness
__ Buttons: dependent, inept, immature
__ Pockets: dependent, deprived
__ Ties: sexual concerns, aggression
__ Earrings emphasized: flashy, suspicious
__ Trouser fly: sexual concerns
__ Weapons: hostility

Figures and views
__ Standing, walking, playing: normal
__ Profile: avoidance, reserved, suspicious
__ Back view: suspicious, isolated
__ Leaning/seated: insecure, dependent
__ Straight down arms and legs: rigid
__ Clowns, soldiers, witches: hostile
__ Cowboys: immature, macho
__ Snowman/woman: avoidance, poor body image
__ Cartoons: avoidance, distancing
__ Stick figures: avoidance, uncooperative, hostile, poor body image
__ Seductive: dramatic, excitable

As you study the size, style, and representation of body parts in your drawing, you can discover clues about your need to attach, inflate self-worth, draw attention, control uncertainty, avoid contact, and overpower others to compensate for early unmet needs.

CARING LESS ABOUT ABANDONMENT

The natural direction of psychological growth is toward discovery of uniqueness and self-rule. When this process threatens families, people must abandon desires for self-definition and independence to avoid abandonment by caretakers at too early an age. This rejection of self-sufficiency becomes a vicious cycle of transferring power to others (that had to be given to caretakers), and trying to gain strength from others that is imagined to be lacking in oneself. By losing all sense of self-support, people seek attachment and believe that their problems can be resolved only if others change. Six or more items marked in either column below suggest that the self has become a clinging vine instead of the freestanding individual it was meant to be.

Personality Types	
Dependent Personalities[1]	**Erratic Personalities**[2]
__ Need advice and reassurance about everyday decisions and can be gullible.	__ Avoid real or imagined abandonment but can switch from clinging to distancing.
__ *Feel helpless and inadequate when alone.	__ *Easily feel empty or bored (when alone).
__ Need others to take responsibility for major areas of their lives.	__ Have unstable and intense relationships with extreme changes in perceptions: others are wonderful or terrible.
__ Lack confidence. May be underemployed. *Often think relationship problems are due to their inadequacies.	__ Are uncertain about themselves—their goals, values, or even sexual orientation. Often fail when on the verge of success.
__ *Try to fix others to be able to lean on them or to avoid abandonment.	__ Are impulsive in two or more ways that could be self-damaging: spending, sex, recklessness, drug use, or binge eating.
__ *Avoid disagreements due to fear of losing support. Will take the blame and cover up for others to avoid conflict.	__ Repeat suicide attempts, gestures, or threats, or self-mutilating behavior.
__ *Are too tolerant of abuse or neglect. May constantly give or do things they don't like in hope of being cared for in return.	__ Have rapid mood cycles (excitement, despair, anxiety) lasting hours or days.
__ *Urgently seek another relationship when one ends to gain care and support.	__ *Have intense (inappropriate) anger, constant irritability, or repeated arguments.
__ *Are preoccupied with fears of disapproval or being left to care for themselves.	__ Can be violent, feel unreal, or believe people are against them under stress.
__ Can appear docile, *controlling, or nice.	__ Can appear oppositional or passionate.

Starred items suggest the well-publicized problem of co-dependency. At the time of this publication, the American Psychiatric Association had not listed separate criteria for this pattern of behavior.

[1] Adapted from criteria on pp. 672–673 with permission from the *Diagnostic and Statistical Manual of Mental Disorders,* 4th edition. Copyright 1994, American Psychiatric Association.

[2] Ibid. p. 654.

ORIGIN OF PROBLEMS

People with the above characteristics may have had overinvolved, intrusive parents who imply "You can't do it by yourself" or "If you grow up, bad things will happen (to me)." Dependent personalities may have had good parenting in the dependent phases of their lives but felt squelched when it was time to pull away as 2-year-olds and teens. Erratic people often had inconsistent support when they needed it and too much control when they tried to explore their environment or the world. There may have been actual abandonment (due to death, divorce, or desertion) or abusive intrusiveness, including incest.

People can be predisposed toward dependency by sickly constitutions, low energy, timid temperaments, and difficulties handling peer taunting that elicits parental (over)protection. Erratic personalities may have physical deficits in emotional regulation or may have been irritable, difficult-to-soothe infants who taxed caretakers' abilities to nurture.

THE CHALLENGE OF CHANGE

Disagreeing with or letting go of others can be frightening. You may literally feel you will die on your own. For some people, the only way to become freestanding is to live alone and discover the universe of friends and organizations that are ready to offer support. One's (true) self can only be found through a variety of experiences. The goal is interdependence in which time is spent apart to discover interests and values that can later be shared with others. Dependent or erratic people often feel powerless, frustrated, or resentful. Use these reactions to identify the thoughts that actually cause your distress and limit you.

Directions: Mark any thoughts you get about yourself or others in your worst moments. Then, identify beliefs you would like to have and affirm these new ideas regularly.

Turn Defeating Thoughts into . . .	Beliefs That Promote Change
__ I can't . . . , shouldn't have to	__ I can take care of and speak up for myself.
__ I'm not able to . . .	__ I can succeed step by step.
__ I'm helpless, powerless or trapped.	__ I have choices now. I can recover.
__ I can't stand it or handle it.	__ I can stand it, handle it, and trust myself.
__ I cannot show emotions.	__ I can show emotion, ask, and set limits.
__ I don't matter. Others come first.	__ I can decide what's right for the situation.
__ If others leave me, I'm flawed.	__ I can start over when relationships end.
__ I can't find love, caring, or a purpose.	__ I can find love, caring, and a purpose.
__ People are all good or all bad.	__ Each person has both good and bad qualities.
__ I am empty, alone, or abandoned.	__ I'm fulfilled, connected. I belong.

BEHAVIOR EXPERIMENTS

It will be easier to identify your defeating thoughts by intentionally creating situations that bring them to the surface. Pick any of the following exercises that sound hard or distasteful. Find a family member or friend to be your coach.

- Spend time alone and log any feelings of inadequacy or emptiness you have. Ask yourself "What would I like to do by myself?" Include things you avoid doing alone but enjoy. Gradually increase the amount of time and things you can do on your own.
- Notice every time you ask for advice or help. Encourage others to give you feedback. Make an agreement that they will not give input until you have expressed your own ideas or made an attempt to tackle a task yourself.
- Purposely disagree or make requests every day. Use the phrase, "I would like to . . . ," "I believe . . . ," or, "Would you . . . ? Make a contract with others to say your opinion first.
- Designate a posture to sit in when you feel helpless or alone. Exaggerate feelings of inadequacy and desertion. Designate a posture for the independent you and act as if you were competent. Switch postures and have a dialogue between your two parts.
- Draw a picture of the independent you and spend increasing amounts of time acting as if you were that person. Log any discomfort you have. Have the clingy you tell the independent you, "I won't let you succeed because . . ." and listen to the response.
- Make good-bad lists. Include wonderful and awful qualities about significant others. Make additions to the lists any time your feelings change. When you are idolizing a person, study his or her "awful list" and vice versa. Start with a list about your coach.

VALUING YOUR "ORDINARY"

Everyone is both special and ordinary. People who have buried feelings of being worthless and unlovable run from being average by inflating their abilities or seeking attention. Both types easily feel slighted, but inflated personalities often become enraged because their whole self-concept is threatened by undesired responses, whereas dramatic personalities only risk losing support. Inflated people may openly or subtly belittle others to bolster their fragile egos. Dramatic people are far too charming for this and rely on their manipulative skills. Both find it useful to busy themselves with big productions or exciting activities to avoid emotional pain. Six or more items marked in either column below can suggest that the ordinary self has been pushed aside by the performer.

Personality Types	
Inflated Personalities[1]	**Dramatic Personalities**[2]
__ Feel important, special, and unique and prefer to associate with "equals" who (supposedly) can best understand them. __ Often mention successes and can monopolize conversations. __ Like admiration and attention and hope others will notice (unproven) abilities. __ Have fantasies of success, fame, fortune, brilliance, beauty, or ideal love. __ Feel entitled to special treatment or automatic compliance with their desires. __ Can take advantage of others when their needs "must" be met. __ Have difficulty empathizing with others' feelings and understanding their needs. __ Can feel wounded, humiliated, or rageful when others are unresponsive or critical. __ Often feel envious of others or believe that others are envious of them. __ Can appear arrogant, boastful, haughty, or overly sensitive to others.	__ Exaggerate emotional expressions and can seem dramatic or superficial. __ Change emotions rapidly, which can be "at the surface." __ Are uncomfortable when not noticed and like being the center of attention and creating excitement. __ Give special attention to appearance to attract attention (rather than to avoid criticism). May be ultra macho or feminine. __ Use stylized speech to create an impression, but may be unable to supply details. __ Use seduction, flirtation, and being shocking as ways to attract attention. __ Act more intimate than is warranted. __ Constantly seek reassurance, approval, praise, or special consideration. __ Are suggestible and easily influenced by others or circumstances. __ Can appear charming, manipulative, or superficial to others.

[1] Adapted from criteria on p. 661 with permission from the *Diagnostic and Statistical Manual of Mental Disorders,* 4th edition. Copyright 1994, American Psychiatric Association.
[2] Ibid. p. 657.

ORIGIN OF PROBLEMS

People with the above characteristics may have been attractive, talented, or advanced as children and indulged by their parents. However, high praise and attention may have been contingent on displays of ability, and young ones may have felt devastated when they did not meet expectations of being special. Their parents may have modeled similar inflated or dramatic characteristics and viewed their children as extensions of themselves—"Be wonderful for me. Do my bidding." Like their parents, they learned to feel entitled to special treatment. Seductive qualities can develop when the opposite-sex parent is more available and nurturing and the same-sex parent is not affectionate or supportive.

Unusual abilities and attractiveness suggests that nature plays a role in the development of these problems. In addition, inflated personalities may be prone to overrespond to their environment and handle stress with nonstop talking or striking out. Dramatic people may be less reactive and seek excitement for energy and to fill an internal void. Difficulty turning inward to pause and reflect and caretakers who pushed performance with little understanding of vulnerability may create problems with compassion and empathy.

THE CHALLENGE OF CHANGE

Giving up exaggerating, belittling, seeking attention, manipulating, playing on sympathy, and busyness can be painful. Without such defenses, you may fear you have no value; however, these patterns can drive others away and make it impossible to gain the very things you want most. Recognizing what you are doing is a giant step forward. No matter how good your ability to feel accomplished and gain attention, you will have moments of deep hurt. These are opportunities for growth. Keep a journal of upsetting incidents and use them to turn inward and identify what others' behavior means about you.

Directions: Mark any thoughts you get in your worst moments. Then, identify beliefs you would like to have about yourself and affirm these new ideas regularly.

Turn Defeating Thoughts into ...	Beliefs That Promote Change
__ I'm defective if I'm corrected.	__ I have value even when others disapprove.
__ I'm unimportant when I'm not "respected."	__ I still matter when others don't "respect" me.
__ I'm better than others are.	__ I'm as good as others and visa versa.
__ People should accept me as I am.	__ People can love me without liking all of me.
__ Releasing my anger helps me feel better.	__ Understanding others helps me feel better.
__ Others are uncaring and disrespectful.	__ Others have needs and struggles of their own.
__ Everyone must love me.	__ I am worthy even when others aren't loving.
__ I have to be the most attractive person.	__ I'm still loveable when others are attractive.
__ I cannot survive rejections.	__ I've survived before and I'll survive again.
__ It's awful when things don't go my way.	__ I can handle it when things don't go my way.

BEHAVIOR EXPERIMENTS

It will be easier to identify your defeating thoughts by intentionally creating situations that bring them to the surface. Pick any of the following exercises that sound hard or distasteful. Find a family member or friend to be your coach.

- Have dialogues instead of monologues. Use a timer and give yourself no more than three minutes to talk about yourself or make your point with your coach. This will help you pace yourself with others.
- Pretend you are a TV interviewer and challenge yourself to have a conversation in which you don't mention anything about yourself. Log your discomfort later; however, pat yourself on the back when you help someone else open up.
- Ask questions to find out if you understand the other person's point or experience—"Are you saying (feeling) . . . ?" This ensures that you are attending and defeats boredom. Pick specific times to practice this basic listening skill, for example, in your carpool or at dinner.
- Play the "Blah Blah" game. Have a conversation in which your coach says nothing but, "Blah, Blah." Your job is to look interested and encourage him or her to keep blabbing. Your coach can rate how well you did. Discuss what the experience was like for each of you.
- Pretend you are reserved. Tone down your makeup or dress. Seek only one person's attention at a time and make sure it is reciprocal. Be aware of any flirtations. Practice this on specific occasions and log your feelings.
- Rate "catastrophes" on a scale of 0–100. One hundred might be your child dying or your house burning down. Think "How important will this be in five years?"

PRIZING IMPERFECTIONS

Denying flaws in oneself requires psychological gymnastics of striving for perfection at all costs or displacing imperfection (hostility, disapproval) onto others. In both cases, feelings of defectiveness and vulnerability have been buried. Although compulsive personalities can be demanding, they expect the same or more of themselves and feel responsible to prevent minor mistakes and major disasters. The anxiety of this enormous task is avoided by intellectualizing and taking pride in strict standards. Guarded people are less demanding of themselves because they displace (project) their flaws and self-loathing onto others. Resulting tension is handled by lashing out, and the loss of relationships is replaced with pride in independence and decisiveness. Five or more items marked below suggests that the self has been disenfranchised of its right to err.

Personality Types	
Compulsive Personalities[1]	**Guarded Personalities**[2]
__ Have concern with details, rules, or schedules that interferes with happiness.	__ Have unfounded concerns that others want to hurt or take advantage of them.
__ Are devoted to work and productivity to the exclusion of leisure activities.	__ Worry about and doubt the loyalty or trustworthiness of friends and associates.
__ Have overly strict standards that can prolong task completion and cause indecision.	__ Are often suspicious about faithfulness of partners without proof of wrongdoing.
__ Feel responsible for everything and need to prevent chaos, disorder, and mistakes.	__ Read criticism or threats into harmless comments or events.
__ Want others to do everything "right" and may do things themselves to avoid errors.	__ React angrily when they imagine their character, space, or reputation has been attacked.
__ Dominate peers and subordinates but are very respectful of authority.	__ Carry grudges and do not forgive insults, injuries, or slights.
__ Are overly conscientious and strict about morals, ethics, or values.	__ Are reluctant to confide in others due to concerns of betrayal; are secretive.
__ Are unable to discard worthless objects even when they have no sentimental value.	__ Believe they know what others are thinking without asking and discard facts that don't fit their preconceptions.
__ Have difficulty spending money so it can be saved for catastrophes.	__ Can appear suspicious, tense, cold, humorless, aggressive, and observant.
__ Can appear rigid, possessive, intellectual, conventional, or dependable to others.	

[1] Adapted from criteria on pp. 672–673 with permission from the *Diagnostic and Statistical Manual of Mental Disorders,* 4th edition. Copyright 1994, American Psychiatric Association.
[2] Ibid. pp. 637–638.

ORIGIN OF PROBLEMS

People with these characteristics had controlling parents with high or unrealistic standards—"You must do better to be worthwhile" or "You must be special, different, and loyal, but you are inherently flawed." Both types may take on characteristics of their cruel or controlling parent(s) to keep the "defective" parts of themselves in check. Guarded people may find that being a good, lovable person is so far out of reach that, as adults, they avoid intimacy unless they can control partners or they choose sadistic partners who recreate their childhood drama. Compulsive people generally had consistent discipline and could escape punishment by meeting demands. They may choose free-spirited, loving partners who represent the side of themselves that they suppress.

Compulsive personalities are often first-born and even as infants can have difficulty experiencing pleasure. Guarded people may be predisposed to overrespond to their environment and have difficulty inhibiting impulses (to strike out) under stress.

THE CHALLENGE OF CHANGE

Modifying high standards, allowing emotions, and being more accepting and less attacking can be threatening. Such changes can make you feel defective and vulnerable. However, staying the same creates self-fulfilling prophecies that your significant others will not succeed or betray you. Recognizing what you are doing is a giant step forward. No matter how good you are at meeting your standards or scrutinizing others, you will have moments of great tension. These are opportunities for growth. Keep a journal of upsetting incidents and use them to turn inward and identify what others' behavior means about you.

Directions: Mark any of the thoughts that you get in your worst moments. Then, identify beliefs you would like to have and affirm these new ideas regularly.

Turn Defeating Thoughts into . . .	Beliefs That Promote Change
__ I'm defective if I make a mistake,	__ I have value even if I make mistakes.
__ if my loved ones make mistakes, or	__ Others can make mistakes and learn from them.
__ if I don't fix problems the "right" way.	__ I'm responsible only for my part.
__ I can be certain of the future by taking the right course of action or saving things.	__ There are many ways to do and fix things. __ I can handle mishaps in the future.
__ If people are friendly, they are using me.	__ Most people have genuine, worthy qualities.
__ If people are distant, they don't like me.	__ Others have needs and struggles of their own.
__ People are deceptive and untrustworthy.	__ I can find good intentions and ask questions.
__ I feel worthless if people reject, deceive, or criticize me, and I'm entitled to retaliate.	__ I'm worthy despite others' comments and actions. __ I can defuse criticism and find out its cause.

BEHAVIOR EXPERIMENTS

It will be easier to identify your defeating thoughts by intentionally creating situations that bring them to the surface. Pick any of the following exercises that sound hard or distasteful and find a family member or friend to be your coach.

- Challenge your beliefs. Seek feedback about reasonable standards for and perceptions of people. Ask teachers, therapists, or others who have enjoyable, satisfying lives.
- Notice tension that occurs when others don't behave as you want. Learn to catch these reactions and take a moment to count to three while you inhale and to six while you exhale. Remind yourself, "I'm still worthy when others act in ways I don't like."
- Create a catastrophic fantasy of the failure or deception you fear. Focus on any tension and use the breathing described above to help it pass. Make your fantasy so extreme that it's ridiculous. As your stress lessens, practice healing thoughts—"I can handle future mishaps. I can understand the emotional pain that causes others' undesirable actions."
- Identify changes that would lower your standards by 25%. Put them into action little by little. Intentionally make minor mistakes, be silly, or reveal a truth about yourself. Go on a (blindfold) trust walk or fall into your coach's arms.
- Role-play handling upsetting comments. Agree with any (possible) truth in criticism and ask questions to understand how your behavior is difficult for others. Log attacks you make on others and find ways to reword them.
- Identify early abuse or pressure from caretakers that made you feel flawed. Use fantasy to help your young self understand what he or she could not comprehend as a child.

CONQUERING THE DIVIDE

All humans begin their lives connected to another. Healthy symbiosis between parent(s) and infant continues this link after the umbilical cord is cut. When contact with caretakers is absent or too painful, people must find ways to avoid their need for nurture:

- Avoidant people evade contact and rationalize their behavior. Intense mental activity becomes a refuge from people. They fantasize about relationships they secretly desire, talk about (intellectualize) their problems, or avoid painful subjects.
- Isolated people deny that they have wants. They split off internal neediness, which can surface under stress. They can be successful because achievement equals independence and safety from unmet needs. In relationships, they take a servile role to avoid attack. They may withdraw and shut down when others get too close.
- Eccentric people transfer the painful contact of their early years into the present and perceive a world filled with power and danger. To counter this, they endow themselves with unusual abilities (ESP, clairvoyance, mind reading) and develop rituals to undo "evil" forces.

Five or more items marked in any category below suggests that the self has cut its tether and has been set adrift from humankind.

Personality Types		
Avoidant Personalities[1]	**Isolated Personalities**[2]	**Eccentric Personalities**[3]
__ Avoid occupational activities that involve contact with others due to fear of rejection or disapproval (and become drifters).	__ Lack close relationships and neither fear nor desire contact, even with family or partners.	__ Share characteristics of isolated and avoidant personalities and are rarely at ease.
__ Avoid involvement with people unless they are certain of being liked.	__ *First-degree relatives may be their only friends or confidants.	__ Think comments refer to them when they don't. Can be suspicious.
__ *Are restrained with people close to them due to fear of ridicule.	__ Choose solitary activities almost always.	__ Have unusual beliefs: mind reading, superstitions, ESP, or magical ideas.
__ Are awkward in new situations because of feelings of inadequacy (and of being misfits).	__ Enjoy few activities or none at all.	__ Have unusual perceptual experiences: body illusions, feeling spirits, sixth sense.
__ In social situations, fear being criticized, rejected (or that people are against them).	__ Have little interest in sex with others.	__ Have flat or inappropriate emotions.
__ See themselves as inept or unappealing.	__ Can be indifferent to praise or criticism.	__ Talk in vague, symbolic, or elaborate ways.
__ Avoid new activities or personal risks due to fears of embarrassment.	__ Talk in a loose, tangential, or forgetful way.	__ Appear odd, peculiar, unusual, or curious.
__ Appear shy, withdrawn, or loyal.	__ Appear cold, flat, aloof, or self-reliant.	

[1] Adapted from criteria on p. 645 with permission from the *Diagnostic and Statistical Manual of Mental Disorders,* 4th edition. Copyright 1994, American Psychiatric Association.
[2] Ibid. p. 641.
[3] Ibid. pp. 664-665.

ORIGIN OF PROBLEMS

Avoidant people may have had good early nurturing, possibly reinforced by a reactive temperament that elicited caretaking. Later, they were humiliated in matters of being proper ("Who would want you?") and ridiculed by siblings and peers. Thus, they have a taste of bonding but seek it only if acceptance is assured. Isolated individuals may have been underreactive, "easy" babies that required or were offered little from withdrawn, formal caretakers. The message is "What do you want?" The experience of eccentrics is even more extreme. The greater the underreaction to environmental stimuli, the more mental activity is needed to fill the void. Abusive, controlling caretakers ("I know what you're up to!") may foster distorted thinking styles that defend against intrusions.

THE CHALLENGE OF CHANGE

Decreasing avoidance, withdrawal, fantasy, intellectualizing, magical thinking, and rituals can seem like punching holes in a coat of armor. Even if your isolated existence feels comfortable, it leaves you trapped on the inside and unable to access life support at times when hurt cannot be pushed away. Awareness of distancing patterns is the first step. Use any difficult moments to identify what the situation means about you. If you often feel numb and empty, search your past for times when you were alive enough to feel pain.

Directions: Mark any of the thoughts you get in your worst moments. Then, identify beliefs you would like to have and affirm these new ideas regularly.

Turn Defeating Thoughts into . . .	Beliefs That Promote Change
__ I'm different, deficient, or unlikable, and . . .	__ I (can learn to) belong, fit in, make contact.
__ I'll be rejected, criticized, or embarrassed.	__ Disapproval does not equal rejection.
__ It's foolish to risk devastating rejection.	__ I can (learn to) handle rejection or criticism.
__ I'm basically alone (and prefer it that way).	__ I can (learn to) enjoy contact with others.
__ I don't want the burden of a relationship.	__ I can find freedom in relationships.
__ People are needy and controlling.	__ People have good, appealing attributes.
__ I know what others think (about me).	__ I must ask questions to understand others.
__ I am the cause of bad things that happen.	__ I'm responsible only for my part (if at all).
__ If I cause my bad luck, I can control it.	__ I can (learn to) handle what I can't control.
__ Discomfort is caused by outside forces.	__ Discomfort is usually caused by my thoughts.

BEHAVIOR EXPERIMENTS

It will be easier to identify your defeating thoughts by intentionally creating situations that bring them to the surface. Pick any of the following exercises that sound hard or distasteful and, if possible, find a family member or friend to be your coach.

- Seek feedback from others about how your distancing affects them: children, spouses, or extended family. Log thoughts you have while hearing this input.
- List advantages and disadvantages of your relationship style. If you cannot think of disadvantages, seek ideas from people with satisfying, enjoyable lives.
- Pick a situation outside your "comfort zone" and imagine taking part in it. Notice any tension and count to three while inhaling and to six while exhaling until it passes. Claim your right to be accepted and participate in social situations until you're at ease.
- Find positive aspects of any "flaws" you think you have. If you have a gap between your teeth, imagine using it to squirt water at people you don't like. If your skin is pitted think of how you help people with one or two pimples feel better about themselves.
- Take a survey of people's most embarrassing or humiliating moments. If necessary, write them down and review them when you fear public censure.
- Intentionally invite embarrassment or rejection. Ask where the lettuce is in a hardware store. Start a conversation or ask people for dates until you've had two rejections.
- Require yourself to make eye contact and say "Hello" once a day. Log any discomfort and gradually increase frequency of interaction. Practice with your coach.
- Test your "ESP": Imagine what your coach is thinking and ask if you're right. Take note of magical thoughts and say, "There I go trying to know (control) the unknown."

FINDING STRENGTH IN SURRENDER

Babies are dependent on their primary caretakers for strength. Through repeated experiences of having infantile frustrations met, they bond with parents when they are between 2 and 36 weeks old. If this bond does not happen because needs were not met or anticipated before any frustration could happen, young ones never internalize a caregiver or authority figure. They cannot soothe or govern themselves. Instead, they act out rage from unmet needs by trying to rule everyone around them. They become masters at minimizing their behavior and denying risks.

Four or more items marked below suggests that the self has become deprived of nurture causing a willfulness that runs over everything in its path. For a defiant personality to be fully present, serious conduct problems are generally evident before the age of 15 and solidified into a consistent pattern (not just when high) after 18.

Defiant Personalities[1]
__ Act unlawfully by repeatedly performing acts that are grounds for arrest.
__ Are deceitful and repeatedly lie, use false names, con others, or act unfaithfully.
__ Act impulsively by failing to plan ahead, abusing drugs or alcohol, and moving a lot.
__ Are irritable and aggressive with repeated physical fights or assaults.
__ Are reckless and disregard the safety of self or others.
__ Are consistently irresponsible with financial obligations, children, or steady employment.
__ Lack remorse and show indifference or make excuses for hurting, mistreating, or stealing.
__ Can appear competitive but are poor losers, distrustful, shallow, stubborn, and charming.

[1] Adapted from criteria on pp. 649–650 with permission from the *Diagnostic and Statistical Manual of Mental Disorders,* 4th edition. Copyright 1994, American Psychiatric Association.

These characteristics cannot be explained wholly by care given in the first 9 months of life. These personalities may be predisposed to overeact to stimuli and handle that stress by striking out. Inhibitory centers of the nervous system may be underenergized. Difficulties in infancy may have interfered with normal attachment and increased the likelihood of abuse or neglect. Some people may have attached as infants but later lost a bond with a primary trust figure and then rejected authority.

THE CHALLENGE OF CHANGE

Because people who defy society rarely feel depressed, anxious, or guilty, they have little desire to change until their rampage of self-will is (externally) stopped. Even then, they will have difficulty "surrendering" to another without a hidden agenda. This bond of trust is needed to (1) accept feedback about exploitive behavior, (2) explore advantages of self-control and delay of gratification, (3) identify excuses for willful behavior, (4) learn to understand others and negotiate, and (5) manage self-discipline and anger. If impulses can be controlled and consequences anticipated, defiant people can focus on changing beliefs that trigger many of their behaviors.

Directions: Mark any of the thoughts you get in your worst moments. Then Identify beliefs you would like to have and affirm these new ideas regularly.

Turn Defeating Thoughts into	. . . **Beliefs That Promote Change**
__ I'm weak/a loser if I don't defend myself.	__ My power comes from understanding others.
__ My needs come before rules or others.	__ I can ask for what I want and negotiate.
__ Others help me get power, money, or sex.	__ Others provide support for growth and change.
__ I can only rely on or trust myself.	__ I can rely on others and learn to trust them.
__ Success means power, control, and survival.	__ Success comes from achieving and learning.

SELF-DISCOVERY

Where and how do we find ourselves? There are seven directions to look: front, back, left, right, up, down, and inward:

- When we identify others as the source of our problems and wholeheartedly adopt (or reject) their standards, we have not learned to turn inward.
- When emotions are experienced as a vague sense of uneasiness, lethargy, or physical complaints instead of the full range of feelings that accompany life's joys and hardships, we have not learned to turn inward.
- When we avoid or dramatize anxiety instead of contemplating and internally transforming it into some constructive purpose, we have not learned to turn inward.

Mastering the seventh (inner) direction happens little by little through the formation of the self—the container of our separate, unique identity that can adapt to changing situations by expressing and realizing authentic wishes. Six or more items marked below suggests that an exquisite gyroscope lies within that can negotiate the terrain of life.

Adaptive Personalities[1]
__ Can experience a wide range of feelings with depth, vigor, and spontaneity.
__ Have confidence to achieve goals, experience pleasure, and overcome obstacles.
__ Can take initiative to achieve goals and assert desires while tolerating related anxiety.
__ Can maintain commitments to relationships and goals in spite of setbacks.
__ Have the self-esteem to recognize their skills, abilities, and limits.
__ Have a continuous sense of their value that is unchanged by successes or failures.
__ Can flexibly change usual ways of thinking or acting to solve problems.
__ Can soothe themselves when rejection, criticism, or failure occurs.
__ Can manage their lives alone (for extended periods) when others aren't available.
__ Have intimate relationships without fear of abandonment or suffocation.

[1] Criteria and descriptions of the "adaptive self" were adapted from information in *The Search for the Real Self* by James F. Masterson (The Free Press, 1988).

THE ORIGINS OF THE SELF

When needs for support, independence, self-expression, and limits are met according to a person's inner timetable, he or she is able to manage the journey from total fusion with caretakers in infancy to the adaptive self of adulthood. This happens in stages:

- Toddlers begin the dance of balancing conflicting needs for independence and support. "Drunk" with their own power to move, taste, and explore, they still need to know there is someone bigger and stronger who can contain and support them.
- Preschoolers have internalized many contradictory images, are beginning to fuse them, and are starting to realize that the mother who scolds and the mother who hugs are one, and the self who cooperates and the self who disobeys are the same. As this consistency develops, young ones can identify with caretakers and control their own impulses.
- Later years are spent acquiring skills, discovering interests and talents, and exploring people and values that validate the true self. A pattern emerges from repeated refinement of goals that allows self-expression and achievement of meaning and purpose.

BETTER LIVING THROUGH CHEMISTRY

Medications that help emotional problems were discovered in the 1950s. For many years, they were only used to help symptoms of disturbed mood, anxiety and thought. In the 1990s, some doctors started using them to help dysfunctional personality traits. To understand this change, it helps to know how these drugs affect the major players in biopsychology—secretions of glands (hormones) and neurons (neurotransmitters):

- Adrenaline—prepares for action by increasing blood flow and muscle tension.
- Gamma-aminobutyric acid (GABA)—inhibits the action of adrenaline.
- Norepinephrine—enables the nervous system to respond to incoming stimuli.
- Serotonin—balances the action of Dopamine and Norepinephrine.
- MAO (monoamine oxidase) is an enzyme that breaks down adrenaline and serotonin.
- Endorphins—bind to opiate receptors in the brain and cause suppression of pain.
- Dopamine—enhances pleasure and stimulation. Too much produces racing (distorted) thoughts. Too little causes problems focusing and inhibiting movement.

Psychotropic Medications	Effects
DB—Dopamine blockers (some also block serotonin): Thorazine, Stelazine, Prolixin, Haldol, Clozaril, Risperdal, Zyprexa, Serlect	Reduce racing thoughts and distorted thinking and perceptions. Improve thought organization.
MS—Mood Stabilizers and Anticonvulsants reduce brain excitability: Lithium, Depakote, Depakene, Tegretol, Neurontin	Reduce racing thoughts, impulsivity, agitation, and anger. Lithium can boost serotonin and enhance mood while preventing mania.
Stm.— Stimulants boost activity of dopamine and norepinephrine: Ritalin, Dexedrin, Adderal, Cylert.	Increase activity in the brain cortex improving the ability to inhibit movement, screen out irrelevant stimuli, and stay on task.
BZ— Benzodiazepines stimulate the activity of GABA which counter-acts adrenaline reactions: Xanax, Klonopin, Tranxene, Valium, Ativan	Reduce anxiety. It is best to use them briefly or as needed as they can be addicting or lose effectiveness over time.
OB—Opioid Blockers inhibit the effects of opioids: Revia. Kudzu, an herb, may affect the breakdown of alcohol and boost endorphins.	Reduce pleasure from alcohol use and craving and may also reduce self-mutilation, which can stimulate release of endorphins.
(MAOIs)— MAO inhibitors increase levels of adrenaline and serotonin by stopping their breakdown by MAO: Nardil, Parnate	Help atypical depression with low energy, anxiety, over eating, and poor sleep without low mood. They were first used for TB
TCAs—Tricyclic antidepressants increase the flow of norepinephrine and serotonin: Elavil, Sinequan, Tofranil, Anafranil, Pamelor and more	Enhance mood, interest, and motivation. Many can safely treat insomnia.
SSRIs—Selective Serotonin Re-uptake Inhibitors increase serotonin flow: Prozac, Paxil,* Zoloft, Luvox, Celexia	Enhance mood, interest, and motivation and decrease obsessions, compulsions, anger, irritability, bingeing and anxiety.
DM—Designer medications target specific neurotransmitters: Desyrel, Asendin, Serzone* Effexor, Wellbutrin, Remeron*	Enhance mood. Wellbutrin may reduce hyperactivity and smoking and improve attention. Desyrel helps sleep more than mood.

* Items also help anxiety

TREATMENT FOR TRAITS

The use of medication to modify personality makes sense if traits are thought of as symptoms of reduced intensity that become habits over time. Characteristics of various personalities are reworded below to suggest underlying symptoms or biochemistry. Often doses to modify traits are less than amounts needed to relieve symptoms. Drugs won't cure self-defeating habits, but they can alter temperament in a way that gives change a chance. See the previous chart to identify classes of medication used to treat symptoms:

Personality Types and Traits	Symptoms Treated
Dependent and Erratic Personalities	
Fear of rejection or helplessness	Anxiety (BZ)
Obsessions or depression about perceived rejection	Depression (SSRI, TCA)
Depressed self-confidence	Depression (SSRI)
Mood swings and difficulty regulating mood	Mood cycling (MS)
Anger, irritability, hostility	Irritability (SSRI)
Impulsivity, hyper-reactivity	Impulsivity (MS, Stm.)
Compulsions to self mutilate, substance abuse	Cravings (OB and SSRIs)
Suspicions, thought disorganization, irrational thinking	Disturbed thoughts (DB)
Dramatic and Inflated Personalities	
Rejection sensitivity	Improved mood (SSRI)
Obsessive attention to physical appearance	Obsessions (SSRI)
Hyper type reactivity	Impulsivity (DM, Stm.).
Sexually seductive/provocative, inappropriately intimate	Impulse control (MS)
Emotional reactivity, mood swings	Excitability (MS)
Exaggerated self-importance, fantasies of success	Excitability (MS)
Pressured, unusual speech	Excitability (MS)
Distorted perceptions of envy	Disturbed thoughts (DB)
Compulsive and Guarded Personalities	
Obsessed with details, rules, morality, saving, loyalty, trust	Obsessions (SSRI)
Excessive obsessions with above	Excitability (MS)
Compulsive striving for perfection, devotion to work	Compulsions (SSRI)
Insomnia	Sleep (TCA, BZ)
Excessive suspicion, jealously	Disturbed thoughts (DB)
Irritability, anger	Irritability (SSRI)
Difficulty experiencing pleasure	Depression (SSRI, TCA)
Anxiety, vigilance	Anxiety (BZ) as needed
Avoidant, Isolated, Eccentric Personalities	
Social avoidance and obsessive rejection sensitivity	Motivation (SSRI, MAOIs)
Performance anxiety	Anxiety (BZ, beta blockers)
Difficulty experiencing pleasure or interest in sex	Motivation (DM—Wellbutrin)
Suspicions and personalizing comments	Disturbed thoughts (DB)
Distorted, vague, symbolic, elaborate speech	Disorganized thoughts (DB)
Superstitious type obsessions	Obsessions (SSRI)
Defiant Personalities	
Hyper type impulsivity	Impulsivity–Cylert, Wellbutrin
Irresponsibility due to difficulty staying on task	Inattention—Cylert, Wellbutrin
Irritability, aggressiveness, anger	Irritability (MS, SSRI)
Substance abuse	Cravings—Opioid blockers

EXTRA HELP FOR DISORDERS OF THE SELF

People who depend on others to feel important or cared about may focus on controlling their loved ones rather than changing themselves. The methods they use to avoid painful feelings (substance abuse, lashing out, or clinging) create considerable distress for people in their lives. Friends and relatives may need to be the first ones to change before people with self-defeating behavior can begin to alter well-entrenched patterns. Mark any strategies below that you would be willing to make to plant seeds for new growth.

__ Read everything you can to help you understand difficult people. The more you know, the less responsible you will feel and the more options you will have.

__ Return helplessness with helplessness. If you are asked to do all of the problem solving, act as if you don't know the answers. Establish a habit of giving your opinion after others have said theirs. Set limits on what you will and will not do.

__ Model the middle-ground response to excessive reactions. Silent withdrawal or efforts to control extreme behavior are replicas of the circumstances that created it. Instead, show support, identify feelings, and state the truth—"I really care about you. I know you spoke the way you did because you were so frustrated with me. However, I will wait until you can discuss this issue without calling me names."

__ Make an agreement to use a timer during conversations so both people have equal time to express themselves. Repeatedly ask for feedback to make sure the other person is listening—"Did you get my point? Could you tell me what it was?"

__ Set a limit for how long each person can spend talking about himself or herself. Put questions on file cards that the other person can ask to show an interest in you.

__ Determine your own standards for cleanliness, spending money, morals, or dress. Get outside input. Sympathize with your partner's distress when you are not willing to live up to his or her standard, but stay firm about meeting (only) your own expectations.

__ Do not give up your power and blame your partner for "controlling" you. Make your own sensible decisions and sympathize with your partner's reaction—"I know it's hard for you to believe I love you when I don't do what you want me to do."

__ Do not reassure, explain, or attack. Consistently empathize with difficulties rigid people have enduring change—"It must feel awful when I don't do what you want."

__ Do not accommodate to your partner's avoiding or isolation. Make plans to do what you want to do and give your partner the choice to accompany you or stay home.

__ Express any complaints you have as requests for change—"Would you . . . , . . . , or . . . ?" Find out if your partner is willing to work on making improvements.

__ Identify actions you can take if you do not see any cooperation. Implement them one at a time until you notice a difference. Be firm while understanding distress.

__ Determine how far you are willing to go for change. Do not wait until all love dies before taking action. Keep a bag packed as a symbol that you can leave.

__ Do not return home after leaving until the person takes concrete action: attending a certain number of 12-step meetings or talking with a therapist and allowing you to attend a session to gain a professional opinion on the possibilities for improvement.

__ Get help for yourself if you tolerate unacceptable behavior or try to fix people with problems. Support groups and therapy can be helpful.

FRIENDLY CAUTIONS

If you have come to a point in your life where you've decided you need to change self-defeating habits, bravo! Choose family members and friends as coaches who can be honest, firm, and sympathetic with you. Don't look for people who will give you the answers you want to hear. Feedback that makes you feel bad may be accurate. Learn to stay with those emotions long enough to comfort the wounded child within you who has difficulty being self-supporting, admitting mistakes, or connecting with others. Give others' ideas full consideration before you reject them. As you identify your patterns, let others know how they can help—"Give me a signal if I talk too long."

NATIONAL NETWORKS, SUPPORT GROUPS, AND OTHER RESOURCES

There are few nationwide organizations or networks devoted to specific personality disorders. However, many12-step groups deal with self-defeating behaviors people with these problems have. Listings of local meetings can be found in your community newspaper. Web sites and books can offer additional assistance, for example:

- 12-step groups: Alcoholics Anonymous (AA), Narcotics Anonymous (NA), ALANON Family Groups (ALANON), Adult Children of Alcoholics and Dysfunctional Families (ACOA), and Co-Dependents Anonymous (CoDA).
- General Internet sites offer online diagnosis, research articles and information on treatment: www.mentalhealth.com, www.healthguide.com, www.cmhc.com, www.bpdcentral.com for erratic or borderline personalities (BPD).
- *The Angry Heart* by Joseph Santoro and Ronald Cohen for BPD (New Harbinger, 1997).
- *Codependent No More* by Melody Beattie (Hazelden, 1992).
- *I Hate You, Don't Leave Me* by Jerald Kreisman and Hal Straus for BPD (Avon Books, 1989).
- *Lost in the Mirror* by Richard Moskovitz for BPD (Taylor Publications, 1996).
- *New View of Self* by Larry Siever on biochemistry of disorders (Macmillan, 1997).
- *Reinventing Your Life* by Jeffrey Young and Janet Klosko (Penguin Books, 1993).
- *The Search for the Real Self* by James Masterson (The Free Press, 1988).
- *Personality Disorders, New Symptom-Focused Drug Therapy* by Sonny Joseph (Haworth Medical Press, 1997).

PROFESSIONAL HELP

Counseling is very important when personality traits interfere with work or relationships. Often, family members will seek help for people with disorders. Until the late 1990s, the prevailing belief was that treatment of personality disorders took years. When different theoretical orientations and treatment modalities (individual, family, group therapy, and support groups) are combined, significant improvement may be seen in less than a year. Psychopharmacology is the newest addition to the treatment mix. Drugs can moderate underlying temperaments to help people make gains from other forms of treatment. However, the reality needs to be faced that low-functioning personality disorders and defiant, guarded, and inflated people in particular may not be able to benefit from any form of help.

INDEX

ABOUT THE DISK

DISK CONTENTS

Page	File	Title
4.12	0405	Limiting Power
4.14	0406	Attitudes and Back-Talk
4.16	0407	Daily Routines and Habits
4.18	0408	School-Related Problems
4.20	0409	Extreme Measures for Extreme Behavior
4.22	0410	Moral Matters
4.23	0411	Dependent Adult Children
4.24	0412	Disagreeable Distant Adult Children
4.26	0415	Beliefs That Empower Parents
4.28	0414	Child-Rearing Beliefs
4.29	0413	Child-Rearing Skills
4.30	0416	Behavior Contract
4.31	0417	The Be-Kind-to-Others Worksheet
5.04	0501	Relabeling Symptoms of Panic
5.06	0502	Reattributing Causes of Panic
5.08	0503	Retraining Reactions
5.10	0504	Exposure to Difficult Situations
5.12	0505	Revaluing Problems
5.14	0506	Breaking the Vicious Cycle of Panic
5.16	0507	Erasing Embarrassment
5.18	0508	Extra Help for Panic Disorder
5.20	0509	Desired Beliefs
5.21	0510	Anatomy of a Panic Attack
6.4	0601	Relabeling Worries and Habits
6.6	0602	OCD Checklist
6.8	0603	Reattributing the Cause of OCD
6.10	0604	Refocusing and Modifying Techniques
6.12	0605	Practicing with Imagery
6.13	0606	Imagery Practice Chart
6.14	0607	Practicing Exposure
6.15	0608	Avoidance Identification Chart
6.16	0609	Preventing Rituals
6.17	0610	Ritual Identification Chart
6.18	0611	Planning for Recovery
6.20	0612	Extra Help for OCD
6.22	0613	Trichotillomania (TTM)
6.24	0614	Weekly Progress Record for TTM
6.25	0615	Beliefs That Help OCD and TTM
7.4	0701	Types of Temperament
7.6	0702	Sadness and Depression
7.8	0703	Mood Roller Coasters
7.10	0704	Women and Depression
7.12	0705	Banishing the Darkness of Depression
7.14	0706	Getting Down When You're Too High
7.16	0707	Good Grief
7.18	0708	Getting a Grip on Guilt
7.20	0709	Extra Help for Mood Disorders
8.4	0801	Profiles of Anger

Page	File	Title
8.6	0802	Inflexible-Explosive Children
8.8	0803	Anger and Violence
8.10	0804	Taking Danger out of Anger
8.12	0805	Practice Makes Peace
8.14	0806	Beliefs That Ease Anger
8.16	0807	Claim It and Aim It
8.18	0808	Extra Help for Anger
9.4	0901	Detecting Attention Deficits
9.6	0902	ADD Types and Lookalikes
9.8	0903	Attention Deficits Causes and Cures
9.10	0904	Limits and Benefits of Medication
9.12	0905	Alternative Treatments for ADD and ADHD
9.14	0906	Achievement, Productivity, and Behavior
9.16	0907	Organization and Transitions
9.18	0908	Social Skills
9.20	0909	ADD at Home and in the Workplace
9.22	0910	Extra Help for ADD and ADHD
10.4	1001	Disorders of the Self
10.6	1002	Starting the Search
10.8	1003	Caring Less about Abandonment
10.10	1004	Valuing Your "Ordinary"
10.12	1005	Prizing Imperfections
10.14	1006	Conquering the Divide
10.16	1007	Finding Strength in Surrender
10.17	1008	Self-Discovery
10.18	1009	Better Living through Chemistry
10.20	1010	Extra Help for Disorders of the Self

INTRODUCTION

The forms on the enclosed disk are saved in Microsoft Word for Windows version 7.0. In order to use the forms, you will need to have word processing software capable of reading Microsoft Word for Windows version 7.0 files.

SYSTEM REQUIREMENTS

- IBM PC or compatible computer
- 3.5″ floppy disk drive
- Windows 95 or later
- Microsoft Word for Windows version 7.0 (including the Microsoft converter*) or later or other word processing software capable of reading Microsoft Word for Windows 7.0 files.

---

*Word 7.0 needs the Microsoft converter file installed in order to view and edit all enclosed files. If you have trouble viewing the files, download the free converter from the Microsoft web site. The URL for the converter is:
http://officeupdate.microsoft.com/downloadDetails/wd97cnv.htm
Microsoft also has a viewer that can be downloaded, which allows you to view, but not edit documents. This viewer can be downloaded at:
http://officeupdate.microsoft.com/downloadDetails/wd97vwr32.htm

NOTE: Many popular word processing programs are capable of reading Microsoft Word for Windows 7.0 files. However, users should be aware that a slight amount of formatting might be lost when using a program other than Microsoft Word. If your word processor cannot read Microsoft Word for Windows 7.0 files, unformatted text files have been provided in the TXT directory on the floppy disk.

HOW TO INSTALL THE FILES ONTO YOUR COMPUTER

To install the files, follow these instructions:

1. Insert the enclosed disk into the floppy disk drive of your computer.
2. From the Start Menu, choose **Run.**
3. Type **A:\SETUP** and press **OK.**
4. The opening screen of the installation program will appear. Press **OK** to continue.
5. The default destination directory is C:\COHEN. If you wish to change the default destination, you may do so now.
6. Press **OK** to continue. The installation program will copy all files to your hard drive in the C:\COHEN or user-designated directory.

USING THE FILES

Loading Files

To use the word processing files, launch your word processing program. Select **File, Open** from the pull-down menu. Select the appropriate drive and directory. If you installed the files to the default directory, the files will be located in the C:\COHEN directory. A list of files should appear. If you do not see a list of files in the directory, you need to select **WORD DOCUMENT (*.DOC)** under **Files of Type.** Double click on the file you want to open. Edit the file according to your needs.

Printing Files

If you want to print the files, select **File, Print** from the pull-down menu.

Saving Files

When you have finished editing a file, you should save it under a new file name by selecting **File, Save As** from the pull-down menu.

USER ASSISTANCE

If you need assistance with installation or if you have a damaged disk, please contact Wiley Technical Support at:

Phone: (212) 850-6753
Fax: (212) 850-6800 (Attention: Wiley Technical Support)
E-mail: techhelp@wiley.com

To place additional orders or to request information about other Wiley products, please call (800) 225-5945.

For information about the disk see the **About the Disk** section on page D.1.